D1155979

"*Bridgebuilders* should be on the reading list of every public official, CEO, and civic leader. It distills wisdom and best practices from decades of the global transformation from vertical to horizontal structures, offers a host of fresh insights, and explores valuable case studies. It's a manual for all of us who seek to make democracy work for the people it's intended to serve, nationally and globally."

    —ANNE-MARIE SLAUGHTER, CEO, New America;
    author, *The Chessboard and the Web*

"Once in a generation, a book comes along that not only redefines an entire field of study and practice but revolutionizes it. For public management and government reform, Eggers and Kettl's *Bridgebuilders* is that book! Meticulously researched, powerfully illustrated, and compellingly argued, here (finally) is the brilliant blueprint for a new, problem-solving, trust-building, and boundary-spanning approach to public leadership—exactly what's needed in today's free, diverse, and democratic society."

    —JOHN J. DIIULIO, JR., Frederic Fox Leadership Professor
    of Politics, Religion, and Civil Society, University of Pennsylvania;
    coauthor, *American Government: Institutions & Policies*

"Answering the big question of 'how do we govern?' means critically adapting government to societal needs with every generation. Eggers and Kettl take on this formidable challenge, offering a sure-footed and accessible guide to anyone interested in connecting long-standing public values with a changing world."

    —DONALD MOYNIHAN, McCourt Chair, McCourt School of
    Public Policy, Georgetown University; coauthor, *Administrative*
    Burden: Policymaking by Other Means

"Eggers and Kettl offer an innovative, thoughtful, and compelling road map for the federal government to successfully meet America's growing and complex challenges, rebuild democracy's promise, and restore public trust in our nation's most important institution."

    —MAX STIER, founding President and CEO,
    Partnership for Public Service

"Today's problems have become ever more complex: witness climate change, immigration, and the COVID-19 pandemic. The public wants such problems solved, but no government can do so alone. Public leaders must become catalysts for action, partnering with businesses, nonprofits, and other levels of government. In this highly readable book, Eggers and Kettl give public and private leaders a road map—a series of strategies to make what they call 'blended government' work."

—**DAVID OSBORNE,** author, *Reinventing America's Schools*;
coauthor, *Reinventing Government, Banishing Bureaucracy,*
and *The Reinventor's Fieldbook*

"There are dozens of political books that diagnose hyperpartisanship. Eggers and Kettl demonstrate that real solutions are possible when leaders work across parties and across sectors. At the Bipartisan Policy Center, we understand the hard work of governing a divided country. *Bridgebuilders* provides an indispensable playbook for everyone committed to this critical task."

—**JASON GRUMET,** President, Bipartisan Policy Center

"Too many governments continue to be trapped in silo structures that made sense a century ago but no longer do. Thinking, leading, and acting in cross-cutting ways that fit the shape of the problems we face will be one of the great challenges of the years ahead. William Eggers and Don Kettl are authors with the ideal mix of clarity, creativity, and experience to show us how that can be done."

—**SIR GEOFF MULGAN,** Professor of Collective Intelligence,
Public Policy, and Social Innovation, University College London;
author, *Another World is Possible*

"As mayor of Philadelphia, I saw every day how addressing the biggest challenges facing cities today, from homelessness to crime, from traffic congestion to economic development, requires leaders to effectively work across sectors and levels of government. *Bridgebuilders* provides the essential playbook for how to do this."

—**MICHAEL NUTTER,** former Mayor of Philadelphia; David N. Dinkins
Professor of Professional Practice in Urban and Public Affairs,
Columbia University School of International and Public Affairs

BRIDGEBUILDERS

BRIDGEBUILDERS

HOW GOVERNMENT CAN TRANSCEND BOUNDARIES TO SOLVE BIG PROBLEMS

WILLIAM D. EGGERS

DONALD F. KETTL

Harvard Business Review Press

Boston, Massachusetts

HBR Press Quantity Sales Discounts

Harvard Business Review Press titles are available at significant quantity discounts when purchased in bulk for client gifts, sales promotions, and premiums. Special editions, including books with corporate logos, customized covers, and letters from the company or CEO printed in the front matter, as well as excerpts of existing books, can also be created in large quantities for special needs.

For details and discount information for both print and ebook formats, contact booksales@harvardbusiness.org, tel. 800-988-0886, or www.hbr.org/bulksales.

Copyright 2023 Deloitte Services LP and Donald F. Kettl

All rights reserved

Printed in the United States of America

10 9 8 7 6 5 4 3 2 1

No part of this publication may be reproduced, stored in or introduced into a retrieval system, or transmitted, in any form, or by any means (electronic, mechanical, photocopying, recording, or otherwise), without the prior permission of the publisher. Requests for permission should be directed to permissions@harvardbusiness.org, or mailed to Permissions, Harvard Business School Publishing, 60 Harvard Way, Boston, Massachusetts 02163.

The web addresses referenced in this book were live and correct at the time of the book's publication but may be subject to change.

Library of Congress Cataloging-in-Publication data is forthcoming.

ISBN: 978-1-64782-511-9
eISBN: 978-1-64782-512-6

The paper used in this publication meets the requirements of the American National Standard for Permanence of Paper for Publications and Documents in Libraries and Archives Z39.48-1992.

To the bridgebuilders, in and out of government, on all sides of public policy, who are doing the hard work of bringing their organizations together to solve society's biggest problems, both in big crises and in day-to-day operations

Contents

BRIDGEBUILDERS

A New Approach to Help Government Solve Our Biggest Problems

T he thesis of this book is simple: governments at all levels can more effectively tackle society's toughest challenges by collaborating with *bridgebuilders* who bring together different parts of government and tap into other sectors of society.

With every election, a new administration promises big policy ideas and a management revolution to implement them. Many voters, however, come away profoundly disappointed in the results. We think we know why. Historically, many of the management fixes have been based on what Kettl has termed a vending-machine model of government: You have a problem, you build an organization to deal with it, you put money in the slot, and you expect it to yield results (figure I-1).

This vending-machine model *used* to work. Faced with a problem such as, "Buildings are burning down," policymakers would create a fire department, staff it, equip it, and fund it. They could measure the department's value by the number of fires put out, lives saved, and property preserved. Citizens' trust in government grew every time they saw the fire department respond to calls.

Governments were able to improve service: horse-drawn tankers replaced bucket brigades, motorized engines replaced horse-drawn

FIGURE I-1

The vending-machine model

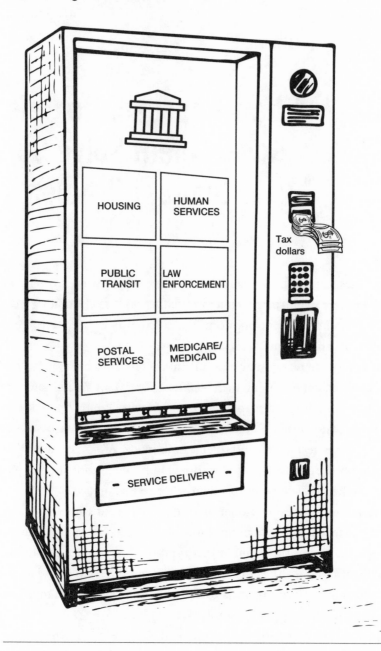

tankers, radios replaced yelling over the crackling of flames, and tall ladders raised from trucks replaced portable ladders that were often too short. New technologies and better communication between departments increased effectiveness and responsiveness. Again, you perceive a problem, you build an organization to deal with it, you put money in the slot, and you wait for results.

But the vending-machine model is dated. It no longer reflects how governments tackle big problems today. Acting alone, agencies can't change quickly enough to match increasingly complex problems that cross boundaries and demand new approaches. Municipal firehouses still hold trucks loaded with ladders and hoses, but in 2020, fewer than 4 percent of all fire calls were for (increasingly rare) fires; the vast majority were for medical assistance. As with much local law enforcement, fire departments have become all-purpose aid organizations that must respond to shifting needs.[1] What used to be a straightforward strategy—staff and fund an organization to fight fires—has become a far more complex, interdisciplinary, interconnected mission to deal with a vast, interconnected collection of problems, only some of which are fires.

Indeed, most societal problems today extend far beyond the legislatively defined boundaries of the agencies or programs lawmakers initially mandated to deal with them. There's no low-hanging fruit or issues with obvious solutions. Consider homelessness: Is it an economic problem? A jobs problem? A mental health problem? A drug problem? A family problem? A criminal justice problem? Is it a problem for government? For nonprofit organizations? For individuals? For local governments—or for states or the federal government? Do private companies help? The answer to each of these questions is *yes*.

And that's why the vending-machine model no longer works. Without a new model of government, we can spend a lot of money on problems, but the problems may not get solved. We're seeing homeless encampments spring up across America, despite the myriad efforts of nonprofit and elected leaders at the federal, state, and local levels to address housing instability. In the West, an outbreak of fires—with no regard for governmental boundaries—requires a concerted response from federal, state, and local teams.

To further complicate matters, public expectations of government action have risen even as cynicism has grown. When problems arise, from floods to baby-formula shortages, people look to government to step up and offer quick fixes. The most important problems, however, require multiple actors in a host of organizations, in both the public and private sectors, offering a wide range of input and resources, all rowing in the same direction. Most agencies weren't organized for the reality of this new world of *blended government*.

The Costs of Falling Short of the New Realities

The two of us have been in the business of improving government—both monitoring reform strategies and trying to nudge policymakers in the right direction—for longer than we're comfortable admitting. Between us, we have more than seventy-five years of experience in the world of public management, with more than thirty published books. We've witnessed a cascade of reforms that have sought to grow, shrink, devolve, privatize, and rewire government, all aimed at making the public sector more effective and efficient.

But things feel worse off. Despite real improvements over the decades, many administrative systems are still antiquated, siloed, and opaque. The public has even less faith in government's abilities and responsiveness.[2]

It certainly isn't for a lack of trying, or for a lack of good intentions. Every one of the last half-century's reforms made a good deal of sense. *Every* administration has succeeded in fixing some problems:

- The Nixon administration's *new federalism* agenda pressed for a substantial devolution of federal power—and money—to state and local governments. Its general revenue-sharing program distributed discretionary cash to local governments, while block grant programs gave lower-level policymakers flexibility in spending on programs ranging from job training to community development. The block grants gradually became encrusted with more regulations during the 1980s, until general revenue sharing finally ended in 1986.[3]

- During the 1980s, the Reagan administration made a major push to transfer government functions to the private sector, either by devolving responsibility or contracting for programs. Business leader J. Peter Grace led a presidential commission to propose programs for elimination or *privatization*, and the administration privatized and contracted out a wide range of functions, from building security to cafeteria services.[4] But no subsequent administration picked up the mantle.

- In 1992, David Osborne and Ted Gaebler wrote *Reinventing Government*, which laid out a ten-point strategy for creating a "government that works better and costs less."[5] Arguing that bad systems stymie the work of good people, the authors suggested ways to streamline systems and free managers to use their judgment and experience. Vice President Al Gore used the book to map out the Clinton administration's reform plan, which recommended eliminating 16,000 pages of regulations and cutting $28 billion a year in regulatory burden.[6]

  Gore aimed to boost trust in government by raising the National Performance Review's profile. He went so far as to smash an ashtray on *Late Night with David Letterman* as an example of well-meaning but onerous regulations—in this case, rules mandating that government-purchased ashtrays be nearly indestructible.[7] The effort achieved significant improvements, especially by strengthening innovation in federal agencies, but the next administration did not vigorously pursue it.

- Beginning with the George W. Bush administration, each White House has announced an agenda to set its *priorities* for management reforms. The Bush administration's prime focus was on setting strategic goals and measuring results. The Obama administration created cross-agency priority goals and pressed federal agencies to set the targets by which they would be assessed. In the

Trump administration, officials focused on IT modernization, data accountability and transparency, and human capital improvement. The Biden team turned to strengthening the federal workforce, improving customer experience, and bolstering processes.[8]

Presidents, of course, set their own agendas. Hence the regular shift in focus. Framing a clear message and motivating career employees to pursue each new program is a major challenge.

In 2016, the Obama administration created the Evidence-Based Policymaking Commission, whose report the following year made a powerful case for improving the use of *analysis and evidence* in policy decisions.[9] In 2018, Congress followed up by legislating many of the commission's recommendations in the Foundations for Evidence-Based Policymaking Act.[10]

Management reforms constantly promise better government, but over time, deficits in trust and performance have grown. These management reforms have contained good ideas, but something important was missing: a strategy for governance in the twenty-first century.

Unlocking Solutions for a Complex World

We wrote this book to help people expand their vision of how government can solve today's problems and, importantly, how it can bridge gaps between agencies; between levels of government; between social service agencies and police departments; between public and private and nonprofit organizations; and even between nations.

The key, we believe, is to create new strategies, with *bridgebuilders* at the helm who can transform governance from hierarchy to networks, from authority to collaboration, from process to mission, and from fuzzy responsibility to accountability for results. Most important, we bring genuine hope and optimism for a new public-sector approach to strengthen the very foundation of democratic governance by improving government's outcomes and restoring public trust.

We've identified ten keys to unlock the solutions:

1. *Knock down barriers,* because siloed thinking hinders success

2. *Seek mutual advantage,* because shared governance builds on mutual pursuit of shared strategies

3. *Nurture private partners,* because effective accountability requires instilling a *public* spirit into *private* operations

4. *Build trustworthy networks,* because improving trust in government depends on excellence in cross-sector collaboration

5. *Grow catalytic government,* because government often doesn't so much manage or deliver solutions as it shapes and integrates them

6. *Focus on outcomes,* because internal procedures can't dominate the search for multisector success

7. *Make data the language,* because data creates not only information but the shared grammar for acting on it

8. *Redefine accountability,* because we need new systems to replace traditional top-down authority

9. *Cultivate cross-boundary leaders,* because all partners in the governance process have a responsibility to lead—jointly

10. *Make the exceptional routine,* because the new era of public management requires scaling bridgebuilding across government

In the chapters that follow, we'll explore these bridgebuilding steps, beginning with how to break down rigid silos, a step that's essential to making blended government a reality. Government's challenges, we've noted, are large—and growing. But we are optimistic that these ten steps can make government far more effective, both in improving government's performance and restoring citizens' trust.

We wrote this book with a range of readers in mind. For government managers who face the challenge of leading collaborative partnerships, the chapters contain tips for making bridgebuilding work. For government's private and nonprofit partners, the book lays out the context of their work and how it connects with the quest for the public interest. Scholars, we believe, will find the book's fresh approach useful in expanding the role of existing public management theory. That, in turn, will make the book useful for students who seek to learn that theory—and who want to become successful leaders in public service. Finally, citizens who want to understand how government really works, and how policymakers can best improve it, will surely be intrigued by the stories of effective government in action.

Indeed, that is this book's true theme. Some existing models of management may be out of date, but a future based on a fresh approach to bridgebuilding is positive and hopeful. Each chapter builds on the successful efforts of agile, energetic leaders who focus squarely on the problem they're trying to solve and who demonstrate how to get the job done. Each of the steps has been tried and proven by skilled leaders somewhere. We propose a plan for bringing these proven steps together into a concerted strategy for the century's biggest problems—and for its routine operations as well.

That takes us to the first step: knocking down the barriers that too often get in the way of effective and responsive governance—and replacing those boundaries with the leadership steps that bring results.

Chapter 1

Knock Down Barriers

A Siloed Perspective Guarantees Failure

As the government's response to Hurricane Katrina's 2005 battering of the Louisiana coast struggled to get rolling, it quickly became clear that the effort needed stronger leadership. CNN's Anderson Cooper walked New Orleans' flooded streets in hip waders. Viewers knew that he was there—but the government *was not*. Images burned into the public consciousness: families stuck on the roofs of their flooded homes, others trying to escape the city only to be met by police determined to stop them—and thousands trapped inside the Superdome while water cascaded from the ceiling.

On Labor Day, a week after Katrina hit New Orleans, Homeland Security Secretary Michael Chertoff called the chief of staff of the Coast Guard, Admiral Thad Allen, and asked him to go to New Orleans to take over the struggling federal effort as the principal federal official in charge of the response.[1]

Learning to Solve the Right Problems

Allen sized up the situation and quickly concluded that "we—everyone—had been trying to solve the wrong problem for a week." Early federal, state, and local responses in Louisiana were clearly chaotic, uncoordinated, and inadequate. The challenge, Allen said, was to create structures "that supported local leaders without assuming their authorities." Allen needed a coalition of the willing, or at least one without opponents.

Allen might have been in charge of the federal response, but he had no legal authority over state and local resources. He recognized immediately that the lack of coordination would cripple the ongoing response. Instead of seeking to give orders, he focused instead on building credibility and trust. In particular, Allen listened to local officials as they explained their struggles and their needs. He saw his job simply: "to collectively create an art of the possible where none previously existed."[2]

The important lesson from Katrina, he said later, "is that no complex problem—be it a natural or manmade disaster, pandemic, or cyberattack—can be addressed by a single entity, individual, agency or company. Effective outcomes are co-produced based on trust, a clear objective and unity of effort."

Thad Allen, the Bridgebuilder

In a crisis, Allen said, "You have to lead from everywhere." Leaders have to understand the problem and define it for everyone. They have to clearly communicate the outcomes everyone seeks and establish the values that will guide their work. And that's what Allen did in the first hours after he arrived in Louisiana. He asked his military aide to locate a place where thousands of responders could meet. She found a Dillard's department store warehouse in Baton Rouge where two thousand people could squeeze in. Allen continued:

> I got up on a desk, with a loudspeaker, and told everybody that I was giving one order: They were to treat anybody they came into contact with who had been affected by the storm like a member of their own family. Their mother, father, brother, sister, whatever. And I said, "If you do that, two things are going to happen. Number one, if you make a mistake, you're going to err on the side of doing too much, and that's okay. Number two, if somebody has a problem with what you've done, their problem's not with you; their problem's with me."

When he said that, the team erupted in a cheer. For days, they had been pilloried for poor performance despite their best efforts. With Allen as bridgebuilder, they turned the corner. "Just a simple set of core values—a North Star to steer by—was, I think, what they were looking for."[3] And this was the moment when the struggling cleanup effort made a dramatic turn toward solving the problems at hand.

Allen found a way to lead in a system with lots of players but no one fully in charge. Finding those who had the resources to solve a particular problem, regardless of what kind of organization they might be in, and then weaving them together in a seamless, coordinated response—that was the core of bridgebuilding. And, as we'll see in this book, that is the key to leaping over the silos that too often handcuff leaders in solving society's biggest problems.

Dealing with Katrina and its aftermath was one of the toughest emergency response efforts in the nation's history. It required pulling together a collection of state agencies across the Gulf, local governments, nonprofit agencies like the Red Cross, and private organizations ranging from Walmart to banks and gas stations. Allen's leadership was truly remarkable. Instead of viewing the cleanup effort as a problem of how to *manage a particular agency*, he worked very hard to *manage the problem* and to pull in the resources needed from all the agencies and organizations involved, wherever they were located. Managing the problem and leading a whole-of-society response was what made Allen a bridgebuilder success.

FEMA's Reforms: "It Takes a Whole Team"

In the years after Katrina, the Federal Emergency Management Agency (FEMA) undertook sweeping reforms. In 2009, Craig Fugate became the FEMA administrator and focused the agency's strategy on a horizontal "whole community" approach, with FEMA seeking to assemble a broad coalition of resources—including federal, state, and local as well as non-profit (like the Red Cross) and for-profit (like big-box stores)—into a coordinated response to disasters.[4]

From his background as both a firefighter and director of emergency management in Florida, Fugate developed new partnerships with state and local governments. He famously developed the "Waffle House index," to gauge the severity of local conditions after a storm. FEMA often found it difficult to size up the impact of a disaster. Throughout the South, the Waffle House chain of restaurants prided itself on remaining open twenty-four hours a day. If a restaurant closed, it was the sign of serious damage in the area. Fugate tracked which Waffle Houses were open, and that provided a quick and clear picture of local conditions following a storm.

Fugate also nurtured the agency's budding relationships with private companies, building on the lessons learned from Katrina. In the first days after the hurricane struck, Walmart managed to get more than half of its damaged stores open again. For parents who needed diapers, families desperate for water, and everyone looking for ice to preserve food, Walmart provided help. The key to Walmart's success was its expertise in supply chain management—and its decision in the aftermath of the storm to give frontline managers support to do what they thought was best. In one store that had suffered severe damage, the assistant manager drove a bulldozer through the store, scooped up what could be salvaged, and distributed it to residents in the parking lot. She broke into the pharmacy in her own store to find the drugs that a nearby hospital desperately needed.[5] FEMA turned to Walmart for important lessons on how to get essential supplies to people following disasters.

Home Depot also learned from the storm. When a major storm threatens, the company pre-positions supplies and preloads trucks to get additional items quickly to hard-hit places. Home Depot created its own emergency operations center to coordinate its response—and to work closely with FEMA.[6]

Emergency Response as Bridgebuilding

The first days after Katrina sent searing images into Americans' homes. But the storm taught an important lesson: success in responding to disasters means moving from a command-and-control approach to a network-building approach. FEMA reorganized its operations and developed a far more effective response system, with a big push to leverage the networks of responders with the capacity to help communities respond to crises. It paid off when the nation broke its previous record of eighty-one disasters in 2010—only to set a new record with eighty-seven disasters the next year.

An essential part of FEMA's new approach was building closer partnerships with its emergency management colleagues in state and local governments, as well as with key private-sector partners. The big-box stores, which had mastered supply-chain logistics, not only taught the federal government how to respond better to disasters—they themselves became a crucial element in the emergency response team.

Fugate proved the value of the new strategy in 2012, when Hurricane Sandy dealt a devastating blow to the shores of New Jersey and New York. It was a new FEMA that responded. Fugate called himself "the most impatient . . . person in the world" and launched a far more agile response, much better coordinated with state and local governments as well as with the private sector. Part of the strategy was pre-positioning supplies so the agency could respond better. Some experts criticized that effort as wasteful, but Fugate responded, "Better to be fast than to be late."[7]

The new partnerships with the private retailers paid off as well. From experience with past storms, Walmart knew to stock up on the staples people would most need—Pop-Tarts (especially strawberry), muffins, and pizza. Sam's Club shipped seven thousand generators to its stores in the Northeast, and employees came from as far away as Pittsburgh to make sure the stores could serve the customers. Home Depot and Lowe's stocked up on chain saws and sump pumps.[8]

Fugate had invested a great deal of effort in building strong partnerships with the big-box stores: to help them provide the aid citizens needed; to focus FEMA's efforts where the stores weren't available; and to learn from the best logistics experts they could find. Within FEMA, Fugate created "lightning bolt" drills, where he would create an artificial disaster and have the agency's employees respond. It all paid off in the aftermath of Sandy.

Speaking of Fugate's instincts, a FEMA official said, "He is very down to earth, and that always helped him out a lot." He "had this 'O.K., that's a problem, let's address it and move on forward' way about him. He doesn't get caught up in the weeds."[9]

It turned out that disaster victims didn't really care where the help came from, as long as it came. That was the core of Fugate's approach as a bridgebuilder. "There's no way government can solve the challenges of a disaster with a government centric approach. It takes the whole team."[10]

The Bridgebuilding Imperative

Understanding the critical role of bridgebuilding begins with the singular proposition that Thad Allen and Craig Fugate demonstrated: no problem that matters can be managed within a single organization.

And the strategy of developing collaborative solutions is doubly true for public policy. The fundamental reality is this: every government agency, no matter how small or sprawling, needs to work across boundaries. Consider the case of resettling refugees from Afghanistan.

In 2021, 1.6 million migrants came to the United States seeking resettlement—but the main US federal agency charged with resettling refugees, the Office of Refugee Resettlement (ORR), had only a mere 150 employees.

When America evacuated Afghanistan in 2021, a massive refugee crisis developed as Afghans who had helped the United States tried to escape the country. In a matter of weeks, more than thirty-seven thousand Afghans came to the United States, a number that had climbed to over eighty thousand by late summer 2022. How would this tiny agency at the core of the American effort manage the billions of federal dollars to supply aid, while also helping the thousands of refugees coming from other countries? It was a very large job for a very tiny agency.

To attack the problem, ORR, an agency within the US Department of Health and Human Services, worked with the State Department to cut red tape in helping evacuees that reached the country settle in the United States.[11] ORR then helped to build a multi-organizational, cross-sector coalition involving 290 local US resettlement agencies and any number of nonprofits and corporations.[12] For instance:

- Airbnb's nonprofit arm partnered with international organizations, the nine US nonprofit resettlement agencies, and a network of thirty-four resettlement agencies across Canada to match more than ten thousand Afghan refugees with temporary housing.[13]

- Walmart and the Walmart Foundation supported new Afghan arrivals directly, with medical items, and prepared "our associates and communities to welcome our new neighbors"—including connecting nonprofits with customers wishing to donate needed items.[14]

- Thirty-two major companies became members of the Tent Coalition for Afghan Refugees, founded by Chobani CEO Hamdi Ulukaya, which joined some 150 others already committed to creating job opportunities and providing training to help Afghans integrate into the US economy.[15]

If there is any lesson that comes from this story of resettlement, it is that the federal government plays a crucially important role—but it cannot fulfill its mission on its own. It works with state and local governments, and all the government agencies partner with networks of nonprofit organizations and for-profit companies, many of which work across national borders. The federal government performs a central, indispensable role in tackling big issues like refugee resettlement, but the White House can't make it happen without tapping the resources, expertise, and personnel far outside the Beltway.

Other nations follow similar patterns of partnership and collaboration. Canada, with only a ninth of the US population, resettled more refugees than any other nation in 2018.[16] To do so, its government leaned heavily on a venerable private refugee sponsorship program that, with community-based support from citizens, business, and nonprofits, works with two-thirds of Canada's resettled refugees—and integrates refugees more smoothly into communities than many government-sponsored programs.[17] In addition, the personal connections forged by sponsorships have improved attitudes toward immigrants and immigration in Canada, with little of the backlash seen in some European countries that accepted large numbers of refugees.[18]

Across government, at every level, the same lesson is surfacing. In implementing public policy, government is essential at every stage to steer the effort, but ultimately, multiple organizations—private, nonprofit, and public sector—must collaborate across boundaries to get things done (figure 1-1). But that collaboration is far from being the standard operating procedure.

Blended Government: The New Reality

Consider a stunning fact. The US federal government charges a single agency, the Centers for Medicare and Medicaid Services (CMS), with managing both Medicare and Medicaid. With only 4,800 employees—0.26 percent of the federal workforce—CMS is responsible for one-third of all federal spending.[19] How does such an enormous program work with so few government employees? The federal government, through CMS, shapes the programs' overall focus and keeps their direction on track, but private medical teams and facilities actually provide medical care and a collection of mega-companies manage the finances.

FIGURE 1-1

The bridgebuilder imperative

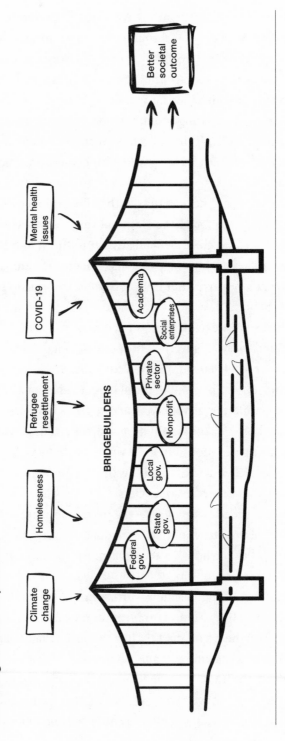

That's how much of government works today, leveraging a framework—whether formal or ad hoc—through which a wide range of organizations convene. When COVID-19 hit the world, the federal government brought together a host of federal agencies, along with state and local governments and nonprofit organizations, to work with private companies developing vaccines and creating immunization centers.[20] The basic data used to track the pandemic and develop vaccines happened through complex networks, which in turn worked together to reduce the disease's death toll.

No agency could have managed the effort on its own. Dr. Anthony Fauci, former director of the National Institute of Allergy and Infectious Diseases and chief medical adviser to the White House over two administrations during the pandemic, called the campaign an "all-of-government approach." But it went beyond that, bringing together the elements of both the government and the private sector needed to tackle the problem and weaving them into an effective team.[21]

Countless everyday government operations take this blended approach. Air traffic control depends on the Federal Aviation Administration's air traffic controllers (for guiding the planes), the National Weather Service (for weather alerts), private contractors (who build and supply the IT equipment on which the system depends), the airlines (especially in developing a next-generation system in which airliners will be programmed to find the quickest route to their destination), and the pilots themselves (who work as partners to controllers).

Indeed, *blended government*—the partnership between government and a host of private, nonprofit, and global organizations—has become the new reality for how government must operate if it wants success addressing major problems.

The traditional approach to government was straightforward: top officials drew neat lines around problems and assigned specific agencies to solve them. In the twenty-first century, however, that is like arming a preschooler with a drawing and a box of crayons: they find it impossible to color within the lines. Everyone understands organizations' classic pyramid structure. Not everyone understands that the hierarchical pyramid that was once the foundation for agencies to function is obsolete.

That was the lesson that the 9/11 Commission drew from its investigation of the 2001 terrorist attacks. Members faced a nagging, inescapable question: *Why didn't the world's best intelligence services see this coming?*

They drew two major conclusions. One was that the intelligence community was plagued by a "failure of imagination," as Deputy Secretary of Defense Paul Wolfowitz put it, in anticipating that suicide pilots might stage an attack on the United States.[22] The nation was vulnerable to attack because it had not anticipated the hijackers' skill exploiting cracks in the nation's defenses.

The other was the failure to connect the dots among the various streams of intelligence collected by different parts of the intelligence community. "No one component holds all the relevant information," the commission concluded. Organizing intelligence around the "collection disciplines of the home agencies, not the joint mission" crippled the nation's ability to see what was coming.[23] On paper, government had become blended. In practice, its approach to understanding these intelligence challenges had not.

Connecting the Dots by Creating New Structures

In the wake of 9/11, reformers looked to overhaul the structure of the nation's homeland security and intelligence operations. Congress responded to this structural diagnosis with a structural solution: the Department of Homeland Security. The new department brought under one umbrella twenty-two different federal agencies aimed at preventing future crises and responding more effectively when they occurred. A separate piece of legislation established a director of national intelligence to harmonize the work of fifteen different federal intelligence agencies and a new National Counterterrorism Center aimed at "connecting the dots" and anticipating potential attacks.

These reforms grew from the instinct that government's core problems were rooted in the government's structure, and that reorganization was the best way to solve them. That, in fact, has been the government's reflex for generations: when problems pop up, reorganize! When the

Brownlow Committee took a careful look at Franklin D. Roosevelt's White House staff, it concluded, "the president needs help," and the help it recommended was the creation of a new structure, the Executive Office of the President.[24] Following World War II, former president Herbert Hoover headed two commissions to look at strengthening federal management, and his commissions produced more recommendations to transform the structure of the federal government.[25]

The recurring pattern, stretching especially across the twentieth century, was clear: identify a problem; understand its roots; prescribe an organizational restructuring to solve it. That instinct was scarcely surprising. Organizations have long been the basic building blocks of government.[26] If there was trouble with government, the solution was crafting new building blocks.

Of course, government agencies regularly need evaluation and, yes, sometimes reorganization. But redrawing org-chart boxes invariably can create new problems as it solves old ones, and the solid lines often leave little room for the kind of external collaboration that's increasingly essential to problem-solving. Government officials should largely consider reorganization a last resort.

The first resort: developing a connect-the-dots culture by nurturing bridgebuilders.

Structures as Silos and Symbols

Structure has long been the building block of government organizations. Restructuring has been the standard solution to new problems. Since the late nineteenth and early twentieth centuries, when rising public challenges spurred the creation of departments to deal with agriculture, commerce and labor, and the safety of food and pharmaceuticals, government looked to new agencies to deal with new functions. As administrative orthodoxy flourished—with a focus on getting authority, structure, the span of control, hierarchy, and accountability just right—the basic instincts of modern American government took shape.

These instincts, in turn, led to the creation of new departments for functions such as health, education, welfare, housing, transportation, veterans' services, energy—and, of course, homeland security. New functions, new problems, new challenges—all fed off the instinct to attack problems by organizing and reorganizing. Adding boxes, combining boxes, renaming boxes. Sometimes, like elevating the Office of Education to departmental status, this had symbolic value. But restructuring rarely solved the big problems in American society. Structure is usually part of every problem. It is rarely the full answer.[27]

The core problem is this: officials routinely try to force new problems into old structures—or to create new structures that often badly fit nascent missions. It's no longer possible for governments to control the myriad tools that produce public outcomes or to put them inside the box of a traditional agency.

In a world that's ever more global and driven by technology and climate change, today's problems and crises are increasingly expansive and complex, spilling over the boundaries we created to manage them, demanding input from a full range of public- and private-sector resources. Government's traditional restructuring strategies are a poor fit for the problems that increasingly define its agenda.

What we need is a strategy of blended governance—with connections across the public and private sectors—to deal with an environment where no one, not even agency heads, assumes that government can control everything for which it's responsible. To govern through blended governance in a boundaryless world, we need bridgebuilders. Fortunately, over the course of time, visionary leaders have shown how to expertly bridge the gaps between sectors.

The Art of Bridgebuilding

The singular point about these leaders is that individuals, not structures, are the essential building blocks in making the connections across organizational boundaries. As organizational structures became holding companies of expertise, and because the solution to complex problems requires drawing on multiple organizations' resources, the key is to grow leaders—develop bridgebuilders—who can forge the needed collaboration. As the stories of Clara Barton, Leslie Groves, James Webb, and Swanee Hunt illustrate, these leaders can create real, effective change.

Four Different Bridgebuilders

Seven years into Clara Barton's tenure as a recording clerk in the US Patent Office, the Civil War began. Barton left her government job to help distribute supplies to wounded soldiers and to launch a new career filling gaps in government service provision. Barton began by aiding a Massachusetts battalion housed in the unfinished Capitol building and soon expanded her volunteer efforts, securing US Senator Henry Wilson's approval to create a private distribution center for medical supplies and to allow her official access to field hospitals.[28] She brought wagonloads of supplies to Union troops at a series of skirmishes—sometimes ahead of military medical units—and grateful soldiers dubbed her the "Angel of the Battlefield."[29]

But Barton's institution-building—a throwback to her young, pre-Washington days in which she founded a series of free schools in New Jersey—remains her real legacy. Making personal contact with soldiers led her to establish the Office of Correspondence with Friends of the Missing Men of the US Army.[30] After four years running the office, she visited Europe and learned of the global Red Cross network and its aim to bring together national, nonpartisan health organizations committed to ministering to people where government capabilities fell short. Barton helped found the American Red Cross, served as its first president for more than two decades, and successfully campaigned for its official US recognition as a quasi-governmental agency. It's through her efforts that the Red Cross is the first place many people—and governments—turn to when disasters happen, especially because of its important role in bridging the work of multiple organizations.

Then there's the case of Lieutenant General Leslie Groves. During World War II, the United States and Germany were engaged in a struggle to be the first to build a nuclear weapon. Groves, having overseen the construction of the Pentagon for the War Department, was tasked with running the US Army Corps of Engineers' Manhattan Project, with a total of some 130,000 people and a budget of about $40 billion (in today's dollars) to develop, manufacture, and deploy the nation's first nuclear weapons.[31]

To accomplish that goal under life-or-death time pressures, Groves built an extraordinarily complex network that brought together more than a dozen colleges and universities, two dozen corporate partners, and thousands of scientists at the federal Los Alamos laboratory. Balancing collaborative assignments with strictly compartmentalized work, he achieved the key goals while somehow keeping the project's aim a secret from not only the press and public but most of the people who contributed to the result. His prime role was bridging the many organizations involved in a project that many experts were not sure would ever work.

Two decades later, James Webb, the first NASA administrator, answered John F. Kennedy's seemingly impossible call to put a man on the moon by the end of the 1960s. Webb may have been the most indispensable contributor to perhaps the greatest public-sector achievement in American history, leading the NASA space program through the political, administrative, and technical challenge of successfully landing a manned moon mission.

Before assuming leadership of Project Apollo, Webb had headed President Truman's Bureau of the Budget and served as a senior executive at Kerr-McGee Corporation. With deep experience in the public and private sectors, Webb was the quintessential bridgebuilder: he understood that large-scale initiatives can't succeed without engaging internal and external stakeholders and rallying them to the cause. Managing the Apollo program—which involved twenty thousand industrial firms, two hundred university labs, and four hundred thousand public and private workers—required Webb to interact with politicians, the press, NASA employees, private-sector contractors, and the public. America put a man on the moon because of Webb's bridgebuilding leadership.[32]

More recently, philanthropist Swanee Hunt has carried on the tradition of building public-private bridges—and taken it to new places by putting powerful women in conversation to discuss big issues and tackle big problems. Hunt's lightbulb moment came when President Clinton gave her, as US ambassador to Austria, a seat at the table at the Serbia-Bosnia Dayton Accords peace process. She soon observed that not a single woman was part of the process, despite Yugoslavia having had the most female doctorates in Europe.[33]

After serving four years as ambassador, Hunt founded the Women and Public Policy Program at Harvard's Kennedy School and, in 1999, broadened her scope to launch the Institute for Inclusive Security, based on a framework treating social and economic concerns as equally important as military and political issues. After decades—centuries!—of women's voices being left out of national security conversations, Hunt aimed to tap women's expertise and experience to prevent and stop deadly international conflicts.[34] Her argument was simple and compelling: sustainable peace in conflict zones is unsustainable when the peace process excludes half the population.

The key to the strategy was creating partnerships with governments, international NGOs, and civil society. The organization has thus far connected more than five thousand officials and two thousand other women from nearly seventy countries, training thousands of "peace builders" and parliamentarians to further peace processes in conflict regions along with helping to create and strengthen national policies on women's inclusion around the world.[35] Thanks in part to her efforts, Afghanistan's post-Taliban parliament at one time had more women legislators than the US Congress, while Rwanda had the world's highest percentage of female parliamentarians.[36] Her peacebuilding was bridgebuilding.

These superstars made an enormous difference in the programs they were managing. We need more of them. But, just as important, we need new systems that can make it far easier for normal people to cross over these falls and get the job done.

Toward a New Generation of Bridgebuilders

The classic theory of bureaucracy relies on a top-down connection down the hierarchy to frontline officials.[37] The rise of blended government and horizontal systems has confounded the traditional approach to accountability—a big reason why people looking to make changes so often face real resistance.

The vending-machine model doesn't dispense the programs and services that citizens want and need. It's no wonder that the candy so often seems to get stuck in the machine, because government—indeed, all public problem-solving—no longer works in a vertical, top-to-bottom mechanical fashion. What does work is bridgebuilding, the challenge of connecting the players involved in producing public policies. It is essential for addressing the performance, trust, and accountability challenges facing governments today.

That, indeed, is the lesson of remarkable bridgebuilding on the morning of September 11, 2001. US Coast Guard Lieutenant Michael Day went to work as usual, with his Staten Island office offering a stunning view of lower Manhattan. Just a bit before 9:00 a.m., he noticed smoke coming from one of the World Trade Center towers. The early reports suggested a small plane, or perhaps a helicopter, had crashed—an emergency, for sure, but not a Coast Guard emergency.

That changed immediately when the second plane crashed into the other tower, fueling an enormous fire. Within a short time, both towers had collapsed. Most of the media attention focused on the sheer enormity of the disaster. It did not show, however, the terror of hundreds of thousands of people trapped between the fires and the Hudson River.

Day got on the radio and broadcast a message: "All available boats, this is the United States Coast Guard aboard the pilot boat, New York. Anyone available to help with the evacuation of lower Manhattan, report to Governors Island," a small spot of land between the Statue of Liberty, Brooklyn, and the lower tip of Manhattan.[38]

People were desperate. Some were injured, while others panicked about the risk of more building collapses and jumped into the water. A few boats, on their own, had started to take people off Manhattan, but that wasn't nearly enough to get the people away from the smoke-covered part of lower Manhattan.

So, Day organized a massive flotilla. His call for help brought in tour boats and dinner cruise boats. There were tugboats and rescue boats from the city's fire and police departments, as well as boats from the Coast Guard. To find a place to dock all the boats, tugs pulled yachts worth millions of dollars away from their moorings. The famed Staten Island ferries came into action, some loaded to far more than their regular capacity. Since electronic communications were virtually impossible because of the crisis, Day resorted to hand signals to organize the flotilla.[39]

Day's operation evacuated five hundred thousand people from Manhattan. It was far larger than the much better-known evacuation of British troops from Dunkirk, France, after advancing German troops had trapped them against the sea. A ragtag British armada evacuated the troops over ten days. Day and his flotilla did its job in just a day. In reflecting later, Day said, "I broke more rules that day than probably I've enforced in my whole Coast Guard career."[40] He might have broken rules, but far more important was building an ad hoc network to evacuate thousands of people from lower Manhattan.

Day's remarkable leadership that day was the product of a fundamental change in the Coast Guard's training that happened after the massive oil spill of the *Exxon Valdez* in 1989. When the tanker ran aground in an Alaskan harbor, the Coast Guard struggled to mobilize help in the area and to build an effective network in response to the spill, which made it even more difficult to clean it up. The Coast Guard's commanders determined to react far more nimbly to the next disaster and shifted the training it gave its personnel. That's why Day was ready—the next *Exxon Valdez*-scale disaster turned out to be not an oil spill but a terrorist attack, but the strategy was the same: break down barriers to create a network focused squarely on the mission.

Day was a bridgebuilder, along with leaders like Thad Allen, Craig Fugate, Clara Barton, Leslie Groves, James Webb, and Swanee Hunt. They all forged the connections in networks that were singularly focused on accomplishing a mission that lay beyond any single organization. This is the key strategy for solving society's most complex problems.

We often have been lucky that superstar bridgebuilders have risen to lead the response to mega-crises like September 11, Katrina, and the COVID-19 pandemic. But we shouldn't have to depend on crises to generate superstar leaders, and government's managers shouldn't have to depend on superstar leaders to chart the way forward. We need fundamental changes in government's strategy to make the lessons of crisis leadership part of everyday leadership, and for that leadership to work through all of government. This means creating an environment where, when bridgebuilders see an opportunity to do good like Day did on 9/11, they will take the initiative—an environment where they don't have to ask for permission, they just do it. That is what we need to make blended government work.

This is the most important lesson of the book—it's a strategy that can be learned, just as Day learned the lessons of the *Exxon Valdez*. The Coast Guard learned the lessons of September 11, which equipped Thad Allen to respond to the next crisis—not a terrorist attack but a massive storm. An oil spill, a terrorist attack, a hurricane—vastly different problems, but all required the same solution: knocking down barriers and building networks, focused squarely on mission.

Ten Ways Bridgebuilders Can Knock Down Barriers

Inside the Organization

- **Avoid the temptation to create a new agency for every new problem and program.** Problems and new initiatives to address them are developing at an accelerating rate. Creating new, permanent organizations to deal with every new issue is unsustainable in a world of rapidly changing demands fueled by equally rapidly evolving technology. Government needs agile, adaptable organizations, driven by fast and flexible decision-making that weaves together the policy networks required to get the job done.

- **Overturn orthodoxy.** Bridgebuilders create an environment where managers can question orthodoxy and explore outside-the-box ideas. "The visionaries that excel at this are both totally in love with their organization and its mission, and proud of it but also very realistic about its flaws," says former DoD official Joshua Marcuse, now head of strategy and innovation at Google. "I was passionate about DoD's mission but spent five years criticizing the organization that I loved, always looking for outside ideas to improve it."

- **Change the definition of what constitutes a public workforce.** Bridgebuilders expand their talent networks to include *partnership talent* (employees who are part of joint ventures), *borrowed talent* (employees of contractors), *freelance talent* (independent, individual contractors), and *open-source talent* (people who don't work for government at all but who are part of a value chain of services). This shift from a closed model to an open, more inclusive one redefines what the "public workforce" actually means.

- **Focus the workforce on accomplishing outcomes.** Most government personnel systems constrain workers by isolating them in separate agencies, behind high walls with little incentive to collaborate. Far more effective can be cross-agency, project-based workforce models that pull together specialists to knock down the barriers to effective action.

- **Break down barriers to improve outcomes.** A focused effort on breaking down barriers can improve results—and vice versa. In 2017, to combat increasingly disparate health outcomes in different regions in the country and rising obesity nationwide, the UK National Health Service created integrated care systems, a new form of partnership among administrative organizations, health-care providers, government agencies, and other local partners, intended to integrate all aspects of client care.[42]

Across the Network

- **Make boundaries flexible.** Bridgebuilders think beyond the walls of the agency and even of government. That is, they are not hamstrung by existing organizational boundaries. Disruption of boundaries often requires a coordinated response across an ecosystem, which is possible only when leaders transform the culture of rules, systems, and processes before the crisis occurs.

- **Expand and open organizational functionality.** Bridgebuilders look beyond their organizations' walls, forging innovative methods to collaborate with partners in different organizations to serve the needs of their mission. The ability to build ecosystems that continuously seek solutions, both internally and externally, tops government managers' emerging essential competency. The COVID-19 pandemic, for example, demonstrated the need for governments, citizens, the scientific community, and the private sector to come together in agile ecosystems to find innovative solutions. Ecosystem thinking helped governments circumvent traditional supply chains— and their inherent problems—to quickly develop and distribute health products.

- **Build cross-cultural competence.** Bridgebuilding requires cross-cultural competence, which reaches not just across race and ethnicities but across organizations and their cultures. "Cross-cultural competence is just as important when you talk about sectors" as it is across groups of people, says New America president Anne-Marie Slaughter.[43]

- **Forge unity from diversity.** Bridgebuilders aggregate diverse stakeholders' capabilities, competencies, and capacities to focus them on a single purpose. COVID-19 forced leaders to quickly break down information silos, coordinate with companies, nonprofits, and universities, and expand existing capabilities to work toward one universal goal.

- **Create new platforms for better engagement.** Bridgebuilders bring together citizens, private organizations, and the nongovernmental sector to discuss, debate, and contribute to solutions for complex issues. In 2015, Ethiopia set itself the bold goal of ending childhood malnutrition by 2030. The multisector initiative aims to increase investments in nutrition infrastructure and empower communities to create and test innovative solutions. Community Labs, a multisector group, assembles health-care workers, school principals, religious leaders, and other stakeholders to find innovative solutions. The program has contributed to a steady reduction in child malnutrition.[44]

Chapter 2

Seek Mutual Advantage

Shared Governance Builds on the Mutual Pursuit of Shared Strategies

Throughout history, malaria has been one of the world's most deadly diseases. In 2020 alone, it killed 627,000 people.[1] The disease is especially dangerous for youngsters. Not too long ago, a child died from it every thirty seconds. Almost half the world's population lives in regions where malaria spreads easily, particularly in Africa, home to 95 percent of the world's cases and 96 percent of malaria deaths.[2]

Malaria is especially hard to combat because the mosquitoes that spread it breed readily in standing water, and the disease itself is carried by highly adaptable parasites that can sidestep preventive measures. Scores of organizations are embroiled in the fight against malaria, sometimes pursuing conflicting priorities and always competing for scarce resources.

The challenges presented by this dreaded disease are enormous. But Bill Gates, whose foundation has spent more than $2 billion in attacking the problem, calls the situation "one of the greatest opportunities the global health world has ever had."[3]

Opportunity? It's a surprising word, even for an optimistic megaphilanthropist, to describe a scourge that people have been trying to eliminate for centuries. But it's also a fair statement about what's possible in the twenty-first century. Indeed, Gates believes the disease can and should be eradicated in a single generation.

His confidence comes partly from the stunning success of recent antimalaria efforts. Thanks to concerted global action, malaria mortality fell by 60 percent between 2000 and 2019.[4] The strategy prevented fully 1.5 billion cases and saved 7.6 million lives.[5] There's been "a huge scale-up in the resources and brainpower focused on this disease," Gates says.[6]

But it *also* comes from new strategies organizations around the world are using to attack many kinds of "wicked problems"—complicated, dynamic, and seemingly intractable social challenges—with renewed vigor. Unprecedented networks of governments, NGOs, social entrepreneurs, health professionals, and international development institutions (and yes, big businesses) are coalescing around them and recasting them as *wicked opportunities.*

The War against Malaria as a "Wicked Opportunity"

The Gates Foundation has been at the forefront of a multifaceted strategy to strengthen the fight against malaria and to use data to drive results. The strategy has employed "next-generation" surveillance systems to reduce mosquito breeding grounds. New treatment pipelines have been developed. Genetic engineering of mosquitoes has been used to make the insects less likely to spread the malaria parasite. Perhaps most importantly, the foundation helped assemble a diverse group of twenty partners, ranging from the Civil Society for Malaria Elimination to the African Leaders Malaria Alliance, to battle the disease.

The Gates Foundation certainly isn't alone in linking coalitions to fight malaria. In 1998, the World Health Organization (WHO), UNICEF, the United Nations Development Programme, and the World Bank formed the RBM Partnership to End Malaria to coordinate global efforts against the disease. The organization fosters global and national partnerships that collaborate to scale up national malaria control efforts. This coordination allows partners to avoid duplicated and fragmented efforts and use their available resources effectively.[7]

These joint efforts have proven remarkably effective, to the point where the idea of *ending* malaria seems within reach. New scientific advances and a lot of money have helped fuel the effort. But the *big* breakthrough is a concerted strategy of blended governance, in which disparate organizations work together toward a common goal. The malaria fight highlights the need for central organizers capable of holding the ecosystem together and creating the space for action that complex problems require.

Such efforts don't need a single solution for all players. Instead of a "moon shot," this is about *buckshot*—a broad portfolio of strategic interventions, with each organization playing to its own strengths.

In the fight against malaria, a broad array of strategies and interventions have been deployed simultaneously (figure 2-1). Vouchers give even the poorest of the poor in Africa access to lifesaving mosquito nets and medicine. Partnerships with the informal retail sector help deliver medicines to rural villages, while social marketing campaigns boost the uptake of these lifesaving products.[8]

Corporations also have played a key role in the fight against malaria. It's good business, not to mention ethically appropriate, for companies to protect their workers and the communities in which their operations reside.[9] ExxonMobil runs a workplace malaria control program in Africa and the Pacific Rim. Since 2000, the program has averted thousands of

FIGURE 2-1

Malaria eradication ecosystem

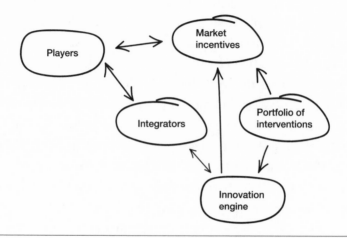

cases of malaria. ExxonMobil also invests in anti-malaria programs run by organizations such as ADDP Angola, PanAfricare, Harvard's T. H. Chan School of Public Health, and the Special Olympics.[10]

Similarly, the private sector plays a major role in the Global Fund to Fight AIDS, Tuberculosis and Malaria, the world's largest source of financing for programs combating these diseases.[11] Under a funding model the organization adopted in 2013, companies can contribute directly to the fund or to programs in individual nations, lend expertise to anti-malaria programs, or provide guidance to grant applicants.[12]

Markets can provide a powerful impetus in scaling solutions to attack big global problems. We've seen this with malaria. Creating huge markets for mosquito nets, malaria medicines, and low-cost rapid diagnostic devices through governmental and philanthropic funding helped drive costs low enough to improve the public health of millions of poor people and encouraged companies to develop new solutions.

And here's another part of the wicked opportunity to end malaria: a low-cost rapid diagnostic test. It allows health workers to detect the disease in a patient within minutes, with 99 percent accuracy and for just fifty cents per test.

The biggest breakthrough, however, is a new malaria vaccine endorsed by WHO for children in sub-Saharan Africa in 2021. "Using this vaccine on top of existing tools to prevent malaria could save tens of thousands of young lives each year," says WHO Director-General Dr. Tedros Adhanom Ghebreyesus. The endorsement followed the success of a pilot program, begun in 2019, that provided the vaccine to more than 800,000 children in Ghana, Kenya, and Malawi.[13]

While the vaccine alone can't eradicate the disease, it holds great promise for dramatically shrinking its impact. A 2020 modeling study indicated that, if rolled out in the nations where malaria takes its greatest toll, the vaccine could prevent 5.4 million cases in children younger than five years of age and prevent 23,000 deaths in that group annually.[14]

The fight against malaria displays many of the key ingredients needed to address the toughest societal problems—a large, diverse group of players from many sectors; the coordination of government and nongovernmental institutions to provide leadership and direction; a portfolio of interventions and technological advances that drive innovative solutions; and market incentives to scale them. Most importantly, it involves a vast array of different groups in a concerted effort to pursue mutual advantage.

The Daunting Challenge of "Coordination"

A senior official in the US Office of Management and Budget (OMB) once was challenged on a tough problem. The answer, the critic said, was simple: "coordinate!" The official replied with a sarcastic head slap: "Why didn't *I* think of that?"

Wicked problems have left no alternative but to assemble collections of organizations making common cause to solve them. Coordination long has been touted as the "philosopher's stone" of management, one that can turn everyday efforts into the gold of effective results and full accountability. But, as our friend from OMB knows, would-be reformers often recommend it without saying *who* should do the coordinating, and *how*.

Solutions to the complex problems that dominate our policy landscape will require coordination among disparate players. As Roger Schwarz pointed out in the *Harvard Business Review,* the key to effective coordination is "the degree to which team members are interdependent—where they need to rely on each other to accomplish the task."[15] And, as a study published by the National Academy of Sciences concluded, "People often coordinate for mutual gain."[16] Effective solutions to difficult issues must build on the ways in which participants see mutual advantage, helping them achieve a joint goal while advancing their own objectives.

So, while coordination might be a philosopher's stone, *mutual advantage* is the magic elixir.

The Hickenlooper Way

The malaria eradication effort shows how solutions to wicked problems require disparate actors working toward a common agenda. The puzzle is how to coordinate organizations with diverse capabilities and often *very* disparate incentives, and align their interests for collective impact. Achieving this alignment is further complicated because it requires coordinating financial, intellectual, and human resources across levels of government and sectors of society.

Solving this puzzle was at the core of John Hickenlooper's governing philosophy, first as mayor of Denver and then as governor of Colorado. "Government is very different than the private sector but, in both cases, generally people start with a narrow self-interest, starting with what they think they really need to get out of each negotiation," Hickenlooper says. "But when you get different voices at the table, it's generally not that difficult to show people that they can benefit from a broader variety of outcomes. Once you get alignment of this self-interest you start to overlap—this is where transactions happen in the private sector and where you create real change and progress in the public sector."[17]

Hickenlooper says the partnerships he cobbled together since his 2003 election as Denver mayor raised more than $295 million for efforts ranging from homelessness prevention to workforce development.

The Hickenlooper approach—an unwavering determination to work across the sectors and find points of mutual advantage for all his major policy initiatives—is at the core of the emerging new model of shared governance.

Hickenlooper's efforts point to five strategies for creating mutual advantage:

1. *Define the problem.* "A broader definition of a problem can change the lens that people use to look at that problem," says Hickenlooper. "You need to get people to look at a different set of outcomes that still favor their self-interest. Yes, it's about making the pie bigger. But it's also coming up with different ingredients and shapes to the pie. When groups of people start to look at the world differently, the chances go up that their self-interests will overlap, and align."[18]

2. *Create an unambiguous shared goal or public purpose.* One key to Hickenlooper's "Road Home," his initiative to eliminate homelessness, was assembling a heterogeneous group of stakeholders to focus on common principles. "We could have spent six months on all we disagreed on," says Jamie Van Leeuwen, who oversaw the program's operations from 2006 to 2010. "But instead, we wanted to focus on what we could agree on." Above all, he says, everyone—companies, developers, homeless shelter providers, nonprofits, city employees—agreed that no one wanted anyone to be homeless.

3. *Keep it local.* From the start, "Road Home" looked to people close to the problem for solutions. "A key strategy was to keep it local," says Van Leeuwen. "Let communities be part of the strategy."[19] So, for instance, the program asked religious congregations to sponsor and mentor qualified homeless individuals, providing $1,200 for a security deposit and first month's rent plus ongoing advice and moral support. Denver's four professional sports teams agreed to donate money or provide stadium boxes for donor events. Mile High United Way lent its fundraising

muscle and provided shelter space for homeless individuals in its headquarters.[20]

4. *Think sideways.* Hickenlooper converted a shuttered minimum-security prison into a treatment center for the chronically homeless population. "Think sideways," he says. "What resources can be put to what new uses? It has to do with using your peripheral vision, metaphorically speaking, and seeing opportunities off there to the side—ones that might seem less real if you looked right at them."[21]

5. *Look for interdependencies.* Chris Conner, director of "Road Home," has explained how program leaders developed deep collaborative arrangements with organizations such as the Denver Rescue Mission. Together, they created the Lawrence Street Community Shelter and worked to provide bus rides for seven hundred guests to and from the shelter every day. The mission then developed programs at a city-owned facility that became the city's largest shelter for those experiencing overnight homelessness. The result was a deep and enduring partnership between the city government and the nonprofit.

Conner says the mission has "responded strongly to deeper coordinated strategies to assist people away from the streets, has cultivated relationships with other providers, and most importantly, those experiencing homelessness, to build successful resolutions." City officials deepened their own knowledge by staying in the shelters overnight. That experience, Conner says, reinforced his sense of "the incredible value of the humanity of all the other guests in the room."[22]

Houston followed these strategies in its own campaign to reduce homelessness, through its Coalition for the Homeless. Since 2011, the city's "Way Home" program reduced the number of people experiencing homelessness in the Houston area by an astonishing 63 percent, moving more than twenty-five thousand homeless people into housing.[23]

The key to Houston's effort is the remarkable weaving together of more than one hundred partners across many sectors. The coalition sees itself as "the 'conductor' of the local homeless response system 'orchestra.'" It convenes the partners for action, collects data, and performs long-range planning. Most of all, it helps the partners in "working together and sharing ideas and information, as well as untangling and realigning multiple, complex funding streams to ensure that we end homelessness for individuals and families as quickly as possible."[24] As in Denver, the key to success was aligning the players so that they could pursue individual goals while collaborating to achieve the goals they jointly share.

Aligning Incentives: The Case of Broadband

For years, many states have struggled to expand broadband access for their citizens. The results often have been disappointing. The Federal Communications Commission (FCC) estimates that about 14.5 million Americans still lacked broadband at the end of 2019; others put the number at almost three times that.[25] Most people think of broadband access as a problem of rural America, and it *is* a major issue there. A 2021 Pew Research Center analysis concluded that 28 percent of those in rural areas don't have a high-speed internet connection. But the access problem hits urban areas as well, where 23 percent of residents lack home broadband.[26] Even in New York City, with its high concentration of people, capital, and technology, roughly 18 percent of residents lack broadband access, according to the Mayor's Office of Technology.[27]

During the pandemic, reliable internet access became essential for many everyday tasks. Activities such as taking classes, attending doctors' appointments, accessing government services, ordering groceries, and working from home usually required a broadband connection. Many individuals were forced to park outside libraries or restaurants to get a usable connection.[28] The search for internet access created a new class of what *Texas Monthly* called "Wi-Fi nomads," who bounced from Walmart parking lots to McDonald's restaurants to local coffee shops to do their schoolwork.[29]

You'd be hard pressed to think of a state where providing widespread access to broadband would seem more difficult—and expensive—than North Dakota. It's the fourth most sparsely populated state in the United States, with just ten residents per square mile and hundreds of miles of wide-open spaces. Despite this, North Dakota's rural residents have better access to high-speed, fiber-optic internet than many American city dwellers.[30] The state has been ranked second for internet access by *US News and World Report*.[31]

How does a large state with a tiny population—the entire state of North Dakota has fewer residents than Charlotte, North Carolina—provide high-speed, low-cost broadband to its residents? North Dakota's success has been made possible by years of effort to form an effective public-private model that aligns financial and social incentives across business and government.

It began a quarter-century ago, in 1996, when fifteen telephone co-ops and independent companies formed a coalition called the Dakota Carrier Network to acquire rural telephone infrastructure for North Dakota. The acquisition paved the way for the future of high-speed connectivity in the state.[32] In 2009, the state used American Recovery and Reinvestment Act funds to expand the state's broadband infrastructure and lay hundreds of miles of high-speed fiber cable.[33]

North Dakota uses an "anchor-tenant" model to drive broadband infrastructure development. Just as a shopping mall developer seeks a large tenant to serve as an anchor store, North Dakota sought to partner with key tenants, such as colleges, hospitals, and state office buildings, to help justify its investment in fiber-optic deployment.[34] Through its partnership with the Dakota Carrier Network, the state leveraged this model to improve broadband infrastructure in the state, helping government and business find mutual advantage in developing internet access for North Dakotans.

Other states have similarly aligned economic and social incentives to expand connectivity. In West Virginia, Indiana, Ohio, Iowa, and Nebraska, for example, Facebook (now named Meta) subsidiary Middle Mile is laying hundreds of miles of fiber-optic cable to connect the company's data centers. The company plans to build about 275 miles of fiber-optic cable through West Virginia's western region, and another 160 miles in Indiana along the I-70 corridor.[35] These buildouts have been made possible through coordination among state agencies and legislatures, federal agencies, and Meta.[36] While the company will use the infrastructure to connect its data centers, its excess capacity can be used by local and regional broadband providers to improve access in previously unserved areas.

Similarly, the New Mexico Department of Technology created a $5 million public-private partnership with ExxonMobil and a regional internet service provider to build 107 miles of fiber infrastructure connecting its fields. As with the Meta buildout, this new infrastructure will help Exxon improve its operations while providing high-speed internet to local businesses, governments, and residents.[37]

The Infrastructure Investment and Jobs Act (IIJA) passed in November 2021 will provide further impetus to the broadband infrastructure buildout. It provides $65 billion for broadband expansion, much of which will go through states to underserved communities. The increase in federal funding creates a happy challenge for states. They have considerable discretion in how they spend these funds and should be poised to quickly identify the right investment choices. They can use some federal funds for grant programs to extend internet infrastructure, including middle- and last-mile infrastructure.

In many parts of the country, of course, laying miles of wired, fiber-optic-based internet cable simply isn't economically feasible. The US Department of Transportation, for example, estimates that laying fiber-optic cable can cost $27,000 per mile, a prohibitive cost for many communities.[38] That's where new connectivity technology comes in.

Low-earth-orbit (LEO) satellites, for instance, are creating new ways to connect. In March 2021, more than five thousand satellites were in LEO, and that number is expected to rise exponentially in the coming years.[39] Satellites and 5G can make high-speed connectivity in rural and mountainous regions much more feasible in the near future.[40]

The Hoh Tribe of western Washington, which has lived on a reservation since an 1855 treaty, lacked good internet connections. Tribal officials reached out to the state government, which connected them with SpaceX's Starlink team to discuss accessing its new satellite internet service.[41] The timing was perfect. Starlink was planning beta trials for that region and was able to provide early access to the tribe.[42] This tweet from the Hoh Tribe says it all:

> What a difference high-speed internet can make! Our children can participate in remote learning, residents can access #healthcare. We felt like we'd been paddling up-river with a spoon on this. @SpaceX Starlink made it happen overnight. Thanks @WAStateCommerce for introduction.[43]

Bridgebuilders who connect different people across governmental and sectoral boundaries can spur *big* changes, especially as they discover mutual advantages among the stakeholders.

Launching to Mutual Advantage

When NASA confronted growing problems within its space shuttle program, it made a stunning strategic decision. For fifty years it had run its launch program in close collaboration with private contractors. In 2019, the agency reported that about 81 percent of NASA's budget went to contracts for goods and services.[44] This model led to enormous successes, from putting the first American into space to landing teams on the moon.

After the "moon race" ended, however, NASA relied on the space shuttle, and it gradually became clear that this wasn't a sustainable strategy. NASA intended that the shuttle, first launched in 1981, would become a space truck, taking equipment, supplies, and people into orbit in a safe and cost-effective way. The shuttle program, however, never lived up to this promise, to the point that NASA decided to retire its aging shuttle fleet.

The cost for each shuttle launch soared to $450 million, much higher than NASA imagined at the beginning of the program. The agency was never able to match the quick turnaround times for which it had planned. Its fastest effort between launches was fifty-four days, rising to eighty-eight days after the 1986 *Challenger* disaster, when a minute after liftoff the vehicle disintegrated and killed everyone on board.[45] The shuttle was a vastly complex machine that required enormous ground resources and subjected its crews to considerable risks. The loss of the shuttle *Columbia* and its crew in 2003, in the words of space policy writer Doug Adler, "drove home that the Space Shuttle could never be truly safe."[46]

Ultimately, NASA decided to retire its aging shuttle fleet and pay for rides aboard Russian spacecraft to get Americans to the space station.[47] This left NASA with a dilemma: no one wanted to rely on the Russian government to meet American goals in space. But creating a new launch system through NASA's traditional practice—managing a design process for execution by private contractors—would take far too long and could prove to be much too expensive. How, then, could NASA produce new launch vehicles to take supplies and equipment into space?

NASA made a strategic decision to pivot from its first-generation system, in which NASA managed the space program, to a second-generation system in which NASA purchased its space vehicles through a competitive marketplace. Private companies were involved in both systems, of course, but they played a fundamentally different role in the second generation, with far more responsibility for system design and price. For its "Moon and beyond" project, for example, NASA chose seventeen different companies for 209 different partnerships.[48] It was a far cry from NASA's early days, when the agency relied on a few major companies for design and production. Market discipline never worked well when there was only one buyer and only a couple of sellers.

This quiet but revolutionary transformation ranked among the most fundamental shifts for any federal program in the last century. It caused a radical change in NASA's culture, bringing a host of new entrepreneurs as well as established mega-companies into close collaboration.

The NASA administrator steering this transition was Charles Bolden Jr., a retired Marine Corps major general and astronaut who flew on four space shuttle missions, piloting the one that deployed the Hubble Space Telescope. The leadership lesson he built on, he says, was "to get the rest of the team to adopt the ideas as their own," a daunting task for an agency with eighteen thousand of its own employees and forty thousand contractors.

"Rocket science is people," Bolden says, and building a team focused on the mission was the way to get the job done, "to find the optimal way of moving out together." The goal was to make NASA the best place in government to work—and to work closely with their commercial partners in pursuit of the shared mission. "Even the custodians," he says, "felt part of the team, helping Americans get to Mars."

These lessons, he says, came from his experience with Hoot's Law. In a launch simulation, he had been working with his commander, Robert "Hoot" Gibson, who gave him control of the shuttle. As with most of the simulations, it wasn't a "normal" launch, as the flight controllers tossed constant surprises at the crew. On this exercise, NASA's team triggered a lost engine, and Bolden quickly reacted by hitting a switch he thought would correct the problem. Instead, the switch shut down a second engine, which deprived the shuttle of the speed it needed to reach orbit, and the craft made a simulated plunge to the water below. As they were sitting on the imaginary floor of the ocean, Hoot told him, "Charles, remember 'Hoot's Law': No matter how bad things get, you can always make them worse."[49]

The way to avoid that, Hoot explained, is to also remember that "there's almost nothing in this vehicle that doesn't give you time to check with others." Profiting from the experience of the team, and integrating a disparate team as one, is the key. Being a "steely-eyed rocket man" (the biggest compliment one can give a space worker) means understanding the vast complexity of the systems that put astronauts into space, developing a shared recognition of the goal, and creating a shared community focused on mutual advantage.

This, Bolden explained, is the way that NASA accomplished its remarkable organizational metamorphosis. And it points to a fundamental lesson for finding mutual advantage: This is the way that rocket science really works, and it's the way that all smart managers can themselves become rocket scientists.

Wicked Opportunities in Complex Systems

What is it that connects wicked opportunities with the stories we have seen? It is the combination of hyperdynamic, super-complicated policy challenges that involve blended government. They are *complex problems* whose solutions require *complex systems*.

During most of the twentieth century, management experts relied on the quest for the "one best way" of designing and running organizations, an approach that dates from the pathbreaking work of Frederick Winslow Taylor.[50] It led to everything from the automobile assembly line to the typical hierarchical structure of most government agencies—and to the vending-machine model of government. But, as Danny Buerkli, co-director of the Swiss government reform lab *staatslabor*, put it, this approach is "not well adapted to many of the challenges public administrations face" around the world.[51]

This managerialist approach suited the problems of the twentieth century, even very complicated issues. Just a few decades ago, it was possible to pop open the hood of a car and tinker with the engine. These days, however, the world under the hood is mostly inaccessible to amateurs. Any work requires computer probes as well as wrenches. These engines have grown massively complicated while both their manufacture and their maintenance have become matters of routine.

But the functions of government have drifted far from even the most sophisticated engines and become increasingly complex. What is the difference? Complicated systems, from clocks to cars to ATM machines, are built of components designed to function in predetermined ways. Indeed, the ATM is a vending machine: insert the card, punch in the PIN, and wait for the money to come out. Complex systems, on the other hand, are made of interrelated elements. They work as more than the sum of their parts, toward an outcome that is the product of their interactions with the problem they are trying to solve—and with the environment. As Mark Foden suggests, clocks are complicated. In contrast, cats are complex. Clocks are composed of complicated elements. Cats derive meaning from their often unpredictable interactions with their environment.[52]

As problems have become more complex—that is, their solutions require the interaction of diverse streams of work—so too have the interactions of the organizations that seek to solve these problems. The impact of the stakeholders and problem solvers who pursue a solution is increasingly shaped by the interactions, interdependencies, and overlaps between diverse groups.

Complexity, in turn, rises with the diversity of the elements involved and the levels of interaction and interdependence between those elements. Public safety, for instance, is affected by the economy; job opportunities; transportation; education; physical and cultural aspects of neighborhoods; laws; and law enforcement and prisons, to give only a partial listing. These areas interact and even overlap. One cannot confidently disaggregate the problem, optimize the solution for each piece, and assemble a successful outcome. The interactions and relationships between the elements are as important as the elements themselves. This is why the behavior of complex systems is more than the sum of the individual parts.[53]

Indeed, government finds itself wrestling with problems that have increasingly blurred the once familiar boundaries that defined organizations and the ways they operate. As those boundaries have come down, new challenges have risen up. For example, to reduce recidivism, a county jail may have to work more closely with the state department of motor vehicles than with other parts of the department of corrections to provide driver's licenses needed for getting gainfully employed, but to solve another problem—say inmate contraband—it may find itself part of a different ecosystem of other prisons, state law enforcement, and even federal law enforcement.

That has led directly to the need for bridgebuilders, because they have developed the skills to create links across organizations where the existing structures and processes fall short. Bridgebuilders must step in where the traditional Taylor-style approaches aren't enough.

The collision of new boundary-spanning problems with boundary-bound organizations helps explain why so many problems seem so wicked. It also explains the large and growing importance of bridgebuilders, who can connect the players with the problems to be solved and make the whole much more than the sum of those parts. That is the lesson from the war against malaria, the work of Hoot Gibson, the other cases in this chapter—and throughout the book. Government problems are increasingly complex. They require increasingly complex systems to solve them. And to make these complex systems work, government needs bridgebuilders.

Ten Ways Bridgebuilders Pursue Mutual Advantage

Inside the Organization

- **Develop well-defined, unambiguous objectives.** To tackle the problem of veteran homelessness, the Obama administration established a clearly defined objective—to end chronic veterans' homelessness by 2017—and then provided funding and strategic resources. The administration didn't define what roles everyone would play; instead, the clear objective helped actors organize themselves.[54]

- **Develop your theory of change.** After defining the desired long-term goals, work back from these to identify all the conditions that must be present, and the interdependent relationships needed to achieve them. These should be mapped in an outcomes framework.

- **Ensure commitments from team members to a shared objective.** To ensure that all internal stakeholders have a common agenda and work collectively with external stakeholders, cross-sector leaders must communicate the objective to partners repeatedly to guarantee their commitment to the mission. Former NASA administrator Charles Bolden Jr. says the most significant factor in bringing about transformation is "to get the rest of the team to adopt the ideas as their own."[55]

- **Create a culture of knowledge sharing.** Bridgebuilders ensure a more open exchange of feedback, share stories of failures and successes, and suggest improvements that can inform future endeavors. By creating a mindset and culture of sharing and learning in real time, bridgebuilders can pave the path for future partnerships.[56] The Department of Homeland Security created its Procurement Innovation Lab to improve its purchasing processes. One important component of the lab is an online platform through which contract specialists can share new ideas, best practices, and lessons learned with colleagues.

- **Be flexible about organizational boundaries.** Crises often require a response coordinated across an ecosystem, one that is possible only if the groundwork of formal and informal rules, systems, and processes has been created and sustained *before* the crisis. The pandemic spurred many organizations to reexamine their processes, supply chains, and partner networks. For example, after personal protective equipment (PPE) and ventilator shortages became widespread in the United States, FEMA launched a supply chain stabilization task force that worked with US manufacturing companies, including nonmedical manufacturers, to expand PPE production.[57]

Across the Network

- **Reframe the wicked problem as an opportunity.** Any attempt to reframe a problem as an opportunity must begin with an understanding of its nature. "The key to making a difference in a diverse and complex ecosystem is to reframe the task at hand, not as an unsolvable set of wicked problems, but as interconnected opportunities," says Risa Lavizzo-Mourey, former CEO of the Robert Wood Johnson Foundation. "When we start to align across those linkages, we can kick off virtuous cycles of investment and beneficial results."[58]

- **Assign an ecosystem integrator.** How do you get disparate organizations to work together toward a common goal? It's vital to have central organizers capable of "holding the whole" and creating the space for aligned action by others. In the fight against malaria, several organizations, including the Bill and Melinda Gates Foundation, played a central role in bringing together multisectoral partners to tackle malaria.

- **Involve people closest to the problem.** Local community groups, with their firsthand experience of the problem, can provide deep, localized knowledge to help bridgebuilders gain a better understanding of unique challenges. "A key strategy was to keep it local," says Jamie Van Leeuwen, who oversaw Denver's "Road Home" initiative. "Let communities be part of the strategy."[59]

- **Leverage differences to create value.** Bridgebuilders turn different perspectives into strengths. "Generally, people start with a narrow self-interest, with what they think they really need to get out of each negotiation, but when you get different voices at the table, it's generally not that difficult to show people that they can benefit from a broader variety of outcomes," says US Senator John Hickenlooper.

- **Let partners play to their strengths.** Don't force everyone to pursue a solution favored by a single partner. "You have to go into this with a set of values that puts public interest at the core of what you're doing, and if that is the central value of the discussion, then you can find a solution or strategy that suits the situation that you're trying to address," says David Warm, executive director of the Mid-America Regional Council.[60]

Chapter 3

Nurture Private Partners

Effective Accountability Requires Building the Public Spirit into Private Operations

C limate models predict a future world in which tropical areas are so hot and humid that sweat doesn't evaporate, and outdoor conditions threaten human life.[1] The American West faces water scarcity, as the Ogallala aquifer, which supplies eight states and irrigates one-fifth of American wheat, corn, and cotton, runs low.[2] Some communities face a choice between migration or death. Maybe global warming won't mean global catastrophe. But responsible communities should prepare. At the very least, "nuisance flooding," which often puts roads and property underwater at high tide, has become a recurring problem in coastal communities like Annapolis, Boston, Charleston, and Miami. Such flooding, in fact, has increased by 300 to 900 percent in the United States compared to less than a century ago.[3]

The Plague on Forests

Take the example of forests, a key shield against global warming. They're also disappearing. The Earth lost 25.3 million hectares of tree cover in 2021 alone.[4]

The short-term economic incentives for clearing trees often conflict with forests' actual long-term value to humanity. Luckily, innovative financial approaches have proven it is possible to align the interests (and time horizons) of investors, communities, and forests. NGOs have led the way, showing how to negotiate the establishment of environmental protection areas, then funding their administration by using innovative finance structures to align interests of groups that may be at odds (forestry companies, local communities, national governments) and to bridge their time horizons—shorter-term for forestry companies, short- and long-term for communities, and longer-term for countries (depending on election dynamics).

The Nature Conservancy has long pioneered meticulous but bold strategies to protect important habitats from deforestation and destruction. The organization does everything from connecting wildlife migration corridors in the United States to funding research into sustainable cattle-grazing methods that might not require burning South American rainforests. Their longest running efforts, however, involve purchasing land to protect it.

Consider an effort in Belize. The Nature Conservancy purchased 236 critical hectares of jungle from a logging company. Carbon credits paid for half the purchase price and funded a $15 million endowment to maintain the park in perpetuity.[5] The Nature Conservancy figured out a transaction to bridge short-term returns from logging versus carbon storage that offers long-term environmental returns. They worked closely with local partners such as the Programme for Belize and Belize Audubon to engage the nine communities bordering the park.[6] "We bought the land, and now we have ten years of engagement ahead of us," said Elma Kay, one of the project's leaders.[7]

Costa Rica Forever, an environmental NGO that first started as a Nature Conservancy program, has made extensive use of "debt for nature swaps." Its vision was to incentivize the Costa Rica government to complete the national protected area designations required under UN commitments, and to then fund their management, using private-sector funding as an incentive for government action. To do so, they purchased and restructured parts of Costa Rica's national debt, directing new debt payments to administer forests and develop sustainable industry. Most recently, Costa Rica Forever partnered with Banco Promérica to invest $1 million from the swaps into green industries in Costa Rica.[8] They often invest in infrastructure to reduce the impact of ecotourism, like a solar-powered wastewater treatment plant for a backpackers' shelter in Chirripó National Park.[9]

A major catalyst for these efforts—and dozens more in which The Nature Conservancy has been involved—was the US Tropical Forest Conservation Act of 1998. The act offers developing countries the opportunity to repay debt to the United States by creating forest reserves. Instead of repaying the US Treasury, the country directs payments toward administering the protected lands and waters. The agreements have protected more than 67 million acres of tropical forests and generated more than $339 million for sustainable projects in developing countries.[10] In 2019, Congress expanded the act to include coral reefs.

NGOs like The Nature Conservancy and Costa Rica Forever contribute by purchasing forests, and developing nations then swap the cash for debt repayment. They also buy national debt privately and restructure similar financial arrangements. The US government hasn't negotiated a new swap since 2014, but NGOs continue to do so, having funded at least $22.5 million in swaps.[11] Then the cash, either from carbon markets or reinvested debt, funds the long-term upkeep.

These unique funding models produce results. The Nature Conservancy's debt for nature swaps secured protection for Cabo Pulmo National Park in Mexico's Baja Peninsula. After ten years, fish stocks rebounded by 400 percent.[12] In 2012, 1.6 million tons of carbon offsets helped the conservancy protect 100,000 hectares in Belize's Rio Bravo Reserve.[13] The same park earned $5.6 million from utility companies, and money from sustainable logging, to fund an endowment.[14]

The Nature Conservancy's Critical Role

The Nature Conservancy has been well positioned to take a global lead on conservation, not just because the organization has extensive scientific and technical expertise but also because it has developed proven approaches that align the public interest with private partners. That has helped to synchronize the long-term time horizon of public programs with the often short-term time horizon of private companies. With a $6 billion endowment, The Nature Conservancy can also be nimble, borrowing from itself to fund transactions and quickly hire local staff for key, long-term positions. Their work requires partnerships with a variety of government officials, politicians, community leaders, and business owners who have a stake in tropical forests.

While The Nature Conservancy may not have the weight of the US government behind it, neither does it have the government's complicated history in the region. No one can hold a grudge toward The Nature Conservancy about government's drug policy. The Nature Conservancy's mission is simple and altruistic, and that helps the organization build trust across the sectors.

The Nature Conservancy's project to create the world's first coral reef insurance in Quintana Roo in Cancun and Cozumel demonstrates its uncanny ability to align the economic incentives of different stakeholders. The Nature Conservancy worked with an insurance company to structure a new insurance product (coral reef insurance) and then convinced the hotel owners' association to not only recognize the protective value of the coral reef but be prepared to invest in it. "When we showed them the economic modeling and the physical modeling of how much physical protection that the reef provides and the fact that the damage of a storm would basically be doubled if you lost the first one meter or the top one meter of that reef, suddenly they understood there is an economic incentive," explains Andrew Deutz, The Nature Conservancy's director of global policy, institutions and conservation finance.[15]

The funding stream for the insurance is a bed tax the hotels pay to the government for the hotels and beaches. Along with The Nature Conservancy, the hotel industry went to the government and said they wanted a portion of that money to go to protect the reef. Why? Because the hotel industry came to understand the value of natural infrastructure and were prepared to see their tax dollars going to protect it because it protected them, their livelihoods, and their capital investments. "All of a sudden they became the advocates for the financing mechanism when they understood their self-interest in protecting the integrity of that coral reef ecosystem," says Deutz. This paid off. When the Delta hurricane hit the area in 2020, there was an insurance payout to restore the damaged corals.[16]

These initiatives require real buy-in from developing nations and private industry. Protecting forests and reefs requires community support, effective management, and enforcement of property rights. Countries must be willing to invest the income they realize back into conservation instead of other tempting uses for the cash. When Seychelles committed 30 percent of its ocean territory to conservation, as part of a debt-for-nature swap called a "Blue Bond," they positioned their economy toward ecotourism, suggesting they had turned their back on the political influence of foreign industrial fishing interests. This often is not an easy choice.

Over the past decades, such projects around the world have proved their worth. California's carbon market alone has saved vast tracts of rainforest. Debt-for-nature swaps are funding the protection of tropical forest and coral reefs. In some ways, these financial deals represent early social impact bonds. They help people protect valuable forest assets by helping them benefit financially. They don't always purport to make a profit for investors. The scientific metrics they've developed, however, can be built into more complex financial products.

To encourage industry to protect forests, the UN has spearheaded an effort to recognize generational and communal property rights. The goal: to create policies where more comprehensive property rights protect whole communities from losing ancestral forest resources. Done correctly, receiving property rights creates longer term stewardship incentives. The UN writes, "Land tenure, including a range of tenure types appropriate to local conditions and needs, such as community property rights and the protection of resource commons, creates certainty about what can be done with land."[17] That certainty allows merging with conservation projects, or even just sustainable community use.

The Business Push for Societal Impact

Government-to-business relationships have historically been predicated on negotiation, contracting, regulation, and enforcement. This is changing. Public-private relationships increasingly start from cocreation of shared interests. The shift requires government to rethink relationships with the private sector, especially around accountability.

Thanks to business's growing embrace of social and environmental values, more and more businesses have committed resources to address societal problems. Up until the 1970s and 1980s, business leaders were generally content to leave societal issues to government and NGOs. That approach has far fewer adherents today.

In 2013, Eggers wrote *The Solution Revolution*, a Harvard Business Press book detailing the new landscape of societal problem solvers. These leaders spearheaded new approaches, from social enterprises to huge foundations, and then to business's increasing focus on purpose and shared value. In the decade since, these trends have each accelerated dramatically.

More and more firms are pursuing a *triple bottom line*, in which companies seek to maximize financial, social, and environmental benefits. Most large companies now measure and publicly report their environmental, social, and corporate governance (ESG) impacts. In 2020, the Business Roundtable released a new "Statement on the Purpose of a Corporation." To date, 239 CEOs have committed to deliver long-term value to all their stakeholders—customers, employees, suppliers, communities, and shareholders.[18]

While customers and investors are driving much of this change, employees have also catalyzed the move to stakeholder capitalism. Internal pressure has influenced everything from hiring practices to ethical supply chains. A full 80 percent of employees in a 2021 16,800-person Edelman survey expected their employer to act on issues such as climate change and racism.[19] Moreover, the embrace of such core values is increasingly important for the next generation of employees, who want to find a job that advances their values alongside their pocketbook.[20]

In a world of blended government, the most successful governments acquire a deep understanding of this new landscape, then develop the skill sets, structures, and institutions to leverage the societal impact contributions of other sectors.

The Evolving Purpose-Driven Business Landscape

A 2019 global survey of 350 business leaders conducted by Deloitte and Forbes Insights explored companies' social responsibility initiatives. Respondents overwhelmingly believed that companies are not mere employers. They are, in fact, stewards of society. It's a role more business leaders embrace. Fifty-nine percent of companies devote one percent or more of their revenues to programs with a purpose.[21] Two-thirds increased budgets devoted to these programs from 2017 to 2019.[22]

Numerous studies have found that purpose-driven companies outperform their peers. The JUST Capital 100, a list of companies highly ranked on purpose in serving society, realized 56 percent higher total shareholder returns over five years compared to their peers.[23]

Banks and investment funds play a critical role in driving the growth of ESG practices. Their willingness to apply values-based judgments to investing could profoundly impact the pace of change in ESG by industry.[24]

An analysis of the world's largest one hundred commercial banks finds that commercial banks with good performance on material ESG issues outperform banks with poor performance on the same issues by 2 percent.[25] As emerging technologies such as AI enable better quality ESG data, investors are expected to demand that ESG factors inform a greater percentage of their portfolios. The Deloitte Center for Financial Services expects client demand to drive ESG-mandated assets to comprise half of all professionally managed investments in the United States by 2025, to total almost US$35 trillion.[26]

Meanwhile, another study showed that nearly nine in ten employees say working for a company with a strong purpose is more important to them now than ever before.[27]

That's no surprise, as high-caliber technical workers drive innovation and profits—and like anyone, they want their work to be meaningful. If the best minds of a generation ago might have been figuring out how to make people click links, the wisest minds today want something more. Businesses attract talent through social impact.[28]

The old wall between profit and purpose is collapsing (figure 3-1). A focus on societal impact can generate massive business opportunities. The potential business value of climate-related opportunities ($2.1 trillion), according to a Deloitte analysis, is almost seven times the cost of realizing them ($311 billion).[29] Through new sustainable products and services, companies in the financial sector can benefit most ($1.2 trillion), followed by manufacturing ($338 billion), services ($149 billion), fossil fuels ($141 billion), and the food, beverage, and agriculture industries ($106 billion).[30]

Purpose also attracts customers. Two-thirds of consumers say they are willing to switch to an unknown purpose-driven brand; 70 percent said they would pay premiums for more sustainable products.[31] Companies are changing their production and talent models to reflect this reality. General Motors introduced a Zero Crashes, Zero Emissions, and Zero Congestion plan. Intel committed to fill 40 percent of technical positions with women by 2030.[32]

Mastercard demonstrates how government agencies can enlist the private sector to societal benefit. In 2012, Mastercard teamed up with the UN to provide humanitarian aid in underbanked regions. Mastercard

FIGURE 3-1

The evolving purpose-driven business landscape

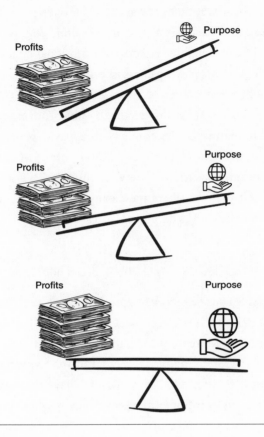

helped the UN monitor distribution of welfare grants using a smart card that can be tethered to an Android device. Mastercard's commitment allowed it to prototype new technologies while potentially reaching 500 million new customers.[33]

COVID-19 accelerated industry-to-government and industry-to-industry collaboration. Take the pharmaceutical industry's unprecedented collaboration in vaccine development. A public-private partnership led by the US National Institutes of Health (NIH) convinced industry partners to prioritize COVID-19 vaccine candidates, no matter who developed them. Subsequently, two pharma giants, Sanofi and Novartis, lent their manufacturing capabilities to produce the mRNA vaccine developed by Pfizer and BioNTech.[34]

Multisector collaboration has even entered foreign policy. In her book, *The Chessboard and the Web: Strategies of Connection in a Networked World,* Anne-Marie Slaughter rejects the traditional conception of foreign policy as diplomats playing chess in cold self-interest. She sees modern foreign policy as a matter of cross-sector networks that transcend government.[35] Terrorism has proven inextricable from energy policy, for example, and human rights in supply chains may depend more on Silicon Valley than the State Department. Power politics among decentralized networks require a shift to a "network mindset," Slaughter argues.[36] This implies that policy makers increasingly should be engaging with nongovernmental networks on global issues.

The Critical Role Foundations Play in Driving Social Impact

The massive wealth our economy has produced isn't just being reinvested in stocks. The drive for a social impact also fuels the growth of philanthropic foundations. More than 230 billionaires from twenty-eight countries have signed the "giving pledge," committing to give away most of their wealth in their lifetimes.[37] Foundations have the capital to shape markets around the solutions they seek. They might even seed whole industries.

Despite the pandemic, total charitable giving in the United States grew 5.1 percent in 2020, to $471 billion. Foundations led the way, giving $88.55 billion, 19 percent of total giving.[38] It's their largest share of giving ever.

Governments that partner with these foundations have powerful allies. Prominent foundations like the Bill & Melinda Gates Foundation, the Rockefeller Foundation, Bloomberg Philanthropies, and the Open Society Foundation played an outsized role in tackling COVID-19, providing funding for everything from enabling access to vaccines in middle- and lower-income countries to supporting low-income workers. Their influence extended to the informal sector, helping caregivers and undocumented workers weather the economic storm caused by the pandemic.

The Growth of Social Enterprises

Societal challenges force creative solutions. Sometimes, they inspire social entrepreneurs. These creative problem solvers realize that positive impacts need to be self-sustaining. Just as Amazon executives are encouraged to think of business as a self-propelling "flywheel," social entrepreneurs strive to change the world using business models that create their own momentum. Social enterprises engage in everything from protecting rainforests to operating businesses that consistently employ ex-convicts. Rather than use a triple bottom line, their primary bottom line is social. The finances help them scale.

Social enterprises have been growing rapidly. In the European Union, more than 2.8 million social enterprises provide around 13.6 million jobs.[39] Australia has over twelve thousand social enterprises that contribute more than $21 billion to the economy and comprise 1 percent of the country's GDP.[40]

Social enterprises rely on their business models to drive funding, giving them some independence from political winds. Yet the public sector is often a critical pillar of support. Some government procurement strategies favor social enterprises over purely commercial endeavors. Social enterprises might also be eligible to take advantage of microfinance services or to compete for social impact bonds.[41] Governments can use social enterprise to kickstart long-term, self-propelling societal change.

Old lines are blurring. Profit and purpose, public and private, business or charity: the more we understand them, the more we see inextricable connections. Consumers and employees are holding the private sector accountable for externalities, positive and negative. Nonprofits are learning that business models might sustain their missions. The public sector has the knowledge of these connections. They have the engines of business and nonprofit organizations to assist their mission.

Private Creation of Public Value

We tend to think of public programs as a set of forces under governmental control. The government often brings in private and nonprofit organizations as agents—under the government's steering mechanisms through grants, contracts, tax incentives, loans, and regulations—to pursue public goals. But it's also often the case that private and nonprofit organizations, through their pursuit of their missions, advance the public interest as well, without the government's heavy hand on the wheel. In fact, private organizations are often responsible for creating public value.

In his classic 1995 book, *Creating Public Value,* Mark H. Moore writes that a central role for government managers is to "create results that are valued" and that, at the same time, "are worth the cost of private consumption and unrestrained liberty foregone."[42] Government withdraws money from society, through taxes, and liberty, through regulations and restrictions. In exchange, it creates goods and services that citizens value. And that, Moore argues, is the great contribution of public managers.

But managers in the private and nonprofit sectors can create *public* value as well. Consider the case of Mobile Loaves & Fishes, an Austin-based nonprofit, that has become the single most effective force in the community's fight to reduce homelessness.

Austin's Mobile Loaves & Fishes: Improving the Lives of the Homeless

In 1984, Alan Graham, the founder of Mobile Loaves & Fishes, created an organization focused squarely on providing meals, housing, and training for those experiencing homelessness. For Graham, tackling the problem has been an article of faith, mixing his religious principles with a strategy to engage and improve the lives of the homeless.

Graham explained, "Our thought as Americans is that, to fix homelessness, we go build houses. But that dog don't hunt. What people need is community. We need each other. We have to look at it in a very different way."[43] To attack the problem, he put aside a prosperous real-estate career to work on the challenges of helping people escape homelessness.

He began "with a single gently used catering truck," as he puts it, in an effort to bring food to those on the streets. Over time, the effort has grown into a very large program that has served more than 5.5 million meals in Austin. His philosophy has grown into what he calls "Tex-Mex theology," which he celebrates in his podcast, "Gospel Con Carne."[44] His team calls him "one of the country's leading visionaries on issues involving homelessness." And, they add, "He's also a pretty cool dude."[45]

His strategy, Graham said, "is move people away from this transactional idea that you can fix this. If you really want to understand homelessness, you really have to understand what 'home' is." In Community First!, he created "an invitation to discover men and women we might have repelled from, but when we dive in, we discover something quite extraordinary."

Over time, Graham's effort grew into Austin's largest prepared feeding program, with the help of more than twenty thousand volunteers. On their rounds, the trucks bring sandwiches and baked goods, water, and coffee, as well as hygiene items, shoes and socks, clothing—and, as he puts it, friends as well. "Everything we do is about relationships," Graham said. "The biggest lesson we have learned over the years is that we are not a food ministry. We merely use food as a conduit to connect human to human and heart to heart."[46]

That belief led Graham to create a new "Community First! Village," a fifty-one-acre planned community that provides affordable and permanent housing for those experiencing homelessness. It began with an RV park with one hundred homes and then added 130 "micro-homes"—tiny houses for those who needed them. The community includes a bus stop, opportunities to learn new skills, and supportive social services. That evolved into 3D-printed houses, and an effort to solve one of the central problems of siting new housing units: "Not in my backyard. Never, ever in my backyard." Volunteers and staff live among those who previously were homeless. In fact, Graham and his wife live there as well, in a tiny home of their own.[47]

As Tracy Krause, a Community First! resident who had struggled with drug addiction and mental illness along with homelessness, told a *Washington Post* reporter, "It's a place where you can get dignity again." She added, "It's a place I could lay my head down and get some rest." The project won enthusiastic support from the county's sheriff, Sally Hernandez. "It's just pretty darn positive, if you ask me," she said.[48]

The Public Value Equation

Graham's Community First! program, along with many of the cases we've explored throughout the book, demonstrate that nongovernmental actors can create public value. They rely on a variety of tools, including private fundraising, partnerships, university endowments, company revenues, or clever financing mechanisms. And in many cases, they prove as effective as government organizations in pursuing public purposes.

There are, of course, private service contractors who provide everything from background studies supporting key policy decisions to public affairs work and engineering analysis. As private actors, they create public value by relying on work paid completely by public dollars.

In fact, there is a broad continuum of contributors to public value. On one end of the spectrum, the Social Security Administration provides 70 million monthly payments to individuals, thanks to the work of public employees who are supported by public money. On the other end, there is Mobile Loaves & Fishes, which creates public value with privately raised funds. In between, the US Patent and Trademark Office is managed by public employees, but fees charged to applicants for patents and trademarks fund the operations. America's airports are often operated by local governments or by quasi-governmental authorities and are funded both by tax dollars and fees charged to airlines and airport vendors.

The pursuit of public value thus emerges from a complex blend of public and private power, along with public and private resources. Government's role is vitally important. But government is not the only contributor to public value. And many of the most important forces for public value are hybrids.

There's no better example than Medicare and Medicaid, which operate in a peculiar world of public money and (mostly) private implementation. (We will explore these issues in more detail in chapter 9.) Indeed, in Medicare and Medicaid, there is no public budget for the programs. The government, to be sure, estimates how much the programs will spend, based on who is eligible for which services. But the key decisions about who actually gets which care rests on patient-practitioner discussions, which lie far out of the government's hands.

As figure 3-2 shows, creating public value happens in a large collection of programs, with a broad mix of public and private implementation strategies and just as wide an array of public and private funding. That, in turn, creates great complexity in programs that create public value. Two things are especially important here. One is that these complexities bring along with them a special need for bridgebuilders, like Alan Graham's efforts to connect his vision with the city's efforts. The other is that the role of private organizations like Community First! bring special challenges for ensuring performance and accountability in the effort to create public value.

FIGURE 3-2

The public value equation

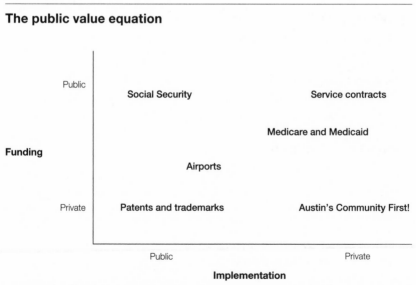

Government strategies to grow the public interest in private players

Governments around the world have developed a series of interconnected strategies to nurture the public interest among private players to create public value.

Convene important players

Forming partnerships can spur useful innovation. The government's role as a convener of important players can lead to impactful developments without ever advertising the public sector's subtle hand. Take urban mobility, an aspect of life that governments have always deeply influenced, from building highways and funding suburban home loans to installing public transit in an age of expensive gas. In a bit of a moon shot, NASA and the Federal Aviation Administration (FAA) are collaborating with industry stakeholders to develop a concept of operations focused on safe urban air mobility (UAM). As AI and drones make personal flight plausible, the FAA is working on standards that will encourage companies to invest in the industry. If suburban traffic jams dissolve into urban airspace, they'll be a major reason.[49]

Develop a business case that clearly lays out the value to potential partners

Governments must present a business case that clearly articulates the potential value of the given initiative project to private partners. The value can take different forms, from direct returns on investment to indirect benefits like greater economic development.

Establish a third-party entity

A third-party entity can encourage role clarity, promote political feasibility, and ease procurement. They can also help partners navigate the complex structure of both government agencies and private corporations.[50]

Bring greater transparency of ESG factors into the investment process

No matter what approach regulators adopt toward ESG, ultimately, investors stand to benefit from greater transparency of ESG factors in the investment process. In Asia, regulators have determined that increasing disclosure requirements about sustainability practices can encourage foreign investment. In 2018, the Chinese government, in a bid to increase transparency and investment, announced that listed companies and bond issuers will be required to disclose ESG-related risks. Singapore was an early adopter of ESG-related standards in Southeast Asia, which had a positive effect on the development of its capital markets. Investor confidence in the quality of ESG data was established in Singapore after sustainability reporting was mandated in 2016.[51]

Frameworks such as those created by the Sustainability Accounting Standards Board (SASB) can help companies report material information related to ESG in a consistent manner. Some companies have recognized that the increased value placed on transparency by investors can benefit them and have begun reporting performance on relevant ESG factors in much more detail than would be otherwise required by regulators.[52]

Provide greater regulatory flexibility

Innovative approaches may not fit well into regulations designed for older technologies and business models. When designing new methods of dealing with endemic societal problems, leaders should ensure regulatory flexibility to account for experiments and encourage growth. These could include simple regulatory carveouts, like for zoning laws, or frameworks for new technology, like the FAA's inquiry into standards for UAM. Many cities have experimented with special innovation zones.

Regulatory agility was increasingly important in the COVID-19 era, as governments eased restrictions to accelerate the development of new treatments and technology—such as autonomous delivery drones—to address the pandemic.[53] In other cases, governments have created experimental sandboxes that allow the private sector to test out new technology in a closed environment.[54]

Purpose and Positivity: Paul Polman and Unilever

When Unilever named Nestlé and Procter & Gamble veteran Paul Polman as its next CEO, press coverage focused on investors' positive reaction to his genial management style.[55] Few if any reporters mentioned
Polman's agenda beyond boosting the company's sagging stock price.

But he had a plan. In February 2009, a month after taking over,
Polman—the first outsider to run Unilever—told investors that the UK
consumer product giant would no longer offer short-term financial fore-
casts.[56] Henceforth, Unilever would take the long view.[57] And that outlook would extend far beyond quarterly reports: the next year, Polman
unveiled an ambitious plan aimed at raising both Unilever's bottom line
and living standards of customers—and society as a whole.[58]

Unilever had long staked out a position as a company aiming to do
well by doing good, tapping into "the fortune at the bottom of the pyramid" by offering low-cost cleaning and other products in traditionally
underserved markets.[59] But the Unilever Sustainable Living Plan (USLP)
went much further, aiming to halve the company's products' carbon
footprint, waste, and water use over the next decade while doubling
sales. "Continuing to increase our environmental impacts as we grow
our business," Polman said, "is not viable."[60] Unilever also pledged to
incorporate into its supply chain half a million small farms and distrib-
utors in developing countries—and even to improve consumers' health
by upgrading its food products' nutritional profile.[61]

Nearly every company of any size puts out a steady stream of pledges
and statements supporting goals for ESG and diversity, equity, and inclusion. Unilever's ten-year plan was different: not only more far reaching
but explicitly based on metrics rather than good intentions. The company
put detailed progress reports online and made transparency integral to
the effort,[62] even acknowledging that "finding robust and meaningful
ways to measure our impact across all our various social programmes
has proved harder than we initially anticipated."[63]

Did the USLP succeed? Has Unilever been able to thrive *because* of
sustainability, not *despite* it? Mostly. Financially, the company has done

well, and it can legitimately attribute much of that success to its broad sustainability efforts. But those efforts did not always hit every target. "Unilever has plenty of war wounds and mistakes to point to," Polman and coauthor Andrew Winston concede in their book *Net Positive*. "The pursuit of 100 percent sustainable sourcing covering thousands of ingredients has not yet fully materialized."[64]

Critics have noted that the green benchmarks Unilever met were ones the company itself set and that some initiatives—for instance, selling single-use sachets for shampoo—created new environmental problems.[65] But even skeptics credit Unilever with many wins as well as for raising both the bar and the floor for stakeholders' expectations and other companies' goals and plans.

Unilever also illustrates ways that multinationals can go about achieving far-reaching goals. Polman understood when launching the USLP that the company, with customers and suppliers around the world, would never reach its targets without partnering with governments and civil society. He explains:

> First and foremost, we worked for the interest of the countries that we were in. We figured out how to help them. We spent time on capability building with them. We trained food and safety inspectors. We worked with the OECD to put a fair tax system in place. We worked with countries as far away as Vietnam to put pension systems in place.[66]

Unilever worked with the Ethiopian government to build facilities and invest in school programs, encouraging oral hygiene while building a factory for oral care products—thus boosting health outcomes and the company's bottom line.

In Ivory Coast, Unilever wanted to produce mayonnaise locally and partnered with the government to build a supply chain from scratch, from encouraging chicken farming—creating both jobs and eggs—to creating local glass supplies for bottles. And in the Middle East, Unilever worked with governments to help alleviate water shortages through desalination projects and changed consumer consumption habits, viewing access to affordable water as good for a business selling toothpaste, shampoo, and soap.[67]

Of course, all companies need not develop a sustainability plan as comprehensive and ambitious as Unilever's to make a real difference. Purpose-driven organizations come in all shapes. But it's key that corporate leaders take a hard look at their companies' impact on the world and evaluate how to implement ESG policies—reducing waste, energy, and water consumption, as well as improving employee health—in ways that strengthen civil society and the planet without undermining profitability.[68]

Investors, too, can play a real role in building "an equitable, nature-positive, net-zero future." Polman, who stepped down at Unilever at the end of 2018, argues that shareholders can aid sustainability efforts by weighing a company's value by ESG criteria as well as financial performance.[69]

"Unlike the financial crisis, when business leaders returned to short termism and shareholder primacy, since COVID there has been a fundamental change," explains Polman. "We've seen more companies, triple the number of companies, signing up to science-based targets, including a $130 trillion commitment in Glasgow (the global climate summit) in private capital to get to net zero."

Unilever's practices, even beyond the USLP, offer many lessons for governments and agencies addressing greater societal issues. Partnering with private-sector companies can dramatically extend reach and resources, in terms of ideas, technology, expertise, and money. As more companies move toward a net-positive orientation, governments will more and more find partners with incentive beyond short-term profit to take action to improve health and environmental outcomes for customers and would-be customers. Increasingly, both private and public sectors share an ultimate goal of a broadly conceived sustainability for society in general *and* for the fortunes of any given company. Creating and nurturing public value is a shared responsibility. "Companies should answer two basic questions," says Polman. "One, how can you profit from solving the world's problems not creating them? And two, is the world better off because your company is in it, yes or no?"

Ten Ways Bridgebuilders Can Build Public Interest with Private Players

Inside the Organization

- **Gain an understanding of the private sector's emerging purpose-driven landscape.** Many companies are becoming more socially conscious; environmental, social, and governance criteria (ESG) are becoming important considerations in evaluating firm performance. A 2019 global Deloitte survey found that 59 percent of companies surveyed were devoting from 1 to 5 percent of their revenues to "programs with a purpose."[70] Such businesses increasingly link efforts to solve social and environmental challenges with their overall success and long-term profitability.

- **Create structures to cultivate private-sector participation.** Bridgebuilders develop the skills, policies, and structures needed to cultivate and support private-sector interest in creating public value. The Department of Homeland Security's Office of Partnership and Engagement, for instance, coordinates the agency's outreach efforts with stakeholders across the United States. Similarly, the FBI's Office of Private Sector coordinates efforts with private entities, while the US Agency for International Development (USAID) has designated a senior adviser to advise the administrator on private-sector engagement.

- **Reconsider rules and regulations that impede the free flow of ideas between sectors.** Bridgebuilders facilitate the open exchange of ideas among sectors. "We hermetically seal our government institutions against outside influence, and by doing so, we are hermetically sealing our government workers from outside ideas," explains Josh Marcuse, former director of the Defense Innovation Board, now with Google. "We have so many structures around acquisition rules in such a contentious and litigious acquisition environment that we make it extremely difficult to create the very institutions we would need to [support the] permeability of people and ideas."[71]

- **Adopt a "network" mindset.** The modern world is inherently interconnected. Counterterrorism is inextricable from energy policy; human rights in supply chains may depend more on Silicon Valley than the State Department. Anne-Marie Slaughter argues that policymakers must develop a "network mindset," as any policy action may be incomplete without the input of nongovernmental stakeholders.[72]

- **Create links between purpose and profitability.** Show companies how they can create public value by working with government while also attracting new customers and bolstering their bottom lines. When Mastercard teamed up with the United Nations in 2012 to provide benefit grants via a smart card in underbanked regions, it allowed the company to prototype new technologies and potentially reach 500 million new customers.[73]

Across the Network

- **Facilitate the cross-sector pursuit of public purpose.** Bridgebuilders can use government authority to set favorable regulations, create new standards, and develop procurement strategies that support the private-sector creation of public value. The US Tropical Forest Conservation Act has allowed organizations to purchase debt owed to the United States by a variety of developing nations in return for environmental actions on their part.[74]

- **Align the interests of diverse stakeholders.** Bridgebuilders recognize and support private efforts to align the economic interests of diverse sets of stakeholders. The state of Quinta Roo, Mexico, for instance, supported The Nature Conservancy's effort to develop the world's first coral reef insurance. This novel insurance project

addressed the economic interests of the insurers, the local population, and the hospitality industry.[75] Payments from this policy were
used to repair damage to reefs and beaches caused by Hurricane
Delta.[76]

- **Build local support to improve private appeal.** Bridgebuilders
  engage with the local community to build meaningful relationships
  and attract private players. Projects with positive social outcomes
  can appeal both to community members and businesses with social
  responsibility goals. Ghana's Mining Health Initiative partnered with
  Newmont Mining, which operates two mines in the country, to reduce
  malaria among its employees, contractors, and the local population.[77]

- **Maximize funding resources.** Bridgebuilders find innovative ways to
  team with investors, foundations, and businesses on projects benefit-
  ing the public good. The $44.5 million alliance between USAID and
  the Skoll Foundation brought a venture capital approach to fueling
  innovation in the areas of health, energy, governance, and food
  security.[78]

- **Create an equitable environment for potential partners.** Bridgebuilders treat partners as equals and facilitate an environment in
  which they feel heard. "The executives at the US Department of
  Agriculture were really comfortable and very skilled at bringing
  together farmers and agribusinesses and NGOs into a room and
  figuring out where's the common ground and what can we do
  together," explains Andrew Deutz of The Nature Conservancy.
  "USDA was super comfortable facilitating the milieux that brought
  all different stakeholders to the table."[79]

Chapter 4

Build Trustworthy Networks

Improving Trust in Government Depends on Excellence in Cross-Sector Collaboration

The brutal death of George Floyd in Minneapolis on May 25, 2020, set off huge protests throughout the United States—and throughout the world. The unrest spilled over the border into Canada, where many police forces already faced rising hostility from the people they are intended to serve.[1]

Minneapolis was not alone in its problems—or efforts to tackle the tough challenges of policing. A year and a half before, in February 2019, Dale McFee was sworn in as chief of the Edmonton Police Service (EPS), backed by a police commission committed to change. McFee had an extensive background in policing, including twenty-six years as a police officer in Prince Albert, Saskatchewan, nine years as its chief of police, and six years as the deputy minister of corrections and policing in Saskatchewan's Ministry of Justice. McFee's thirty-plus years of experience gave him a strong belief in the policing profession and a vision of how it can be improved.

In his first few months as chief, McFee developed a fresh approach. He issued a formal apology—"On behalf of the Edmonton Police Service, I am sorry and we are sorry"—for a legacy of mistreatment of LGBTQ2S+ communities, including bathhouse arrests and public shaming in the early 1980s. "For a long time, the community has not felt listened to by many different organizations," said Clayton Hitchcock, cochair of the Edmonton Pride Festival Society. "And so, to hear feedback that we've given, and to hear that reflected back to us in his speech today, makes me trust that we will move forward, and change will occur."[2]

But such gestures were only the beginning. While public apologies and blue-ribbon commissions can lower temperatures and generate ideas, real change requires cultural change, new systems, and new ways of working. In short, it requires building communities of trust.

Soon after becoming police chief, McFee launched a thorough overhaul of EPS based on dozens of interviews with officers, civilians, and community groups. With these data in hand, McFee and his team drafted a blueprint for change called Vision 2020, intended to rebalance police efforts between traditional enforcement and social assistance—and to rebuild public support.[3] Vision 2020 called for the police to collaborate with external social service agencies to break "the arrest-release-remand cycle" that officers and just about everyone else found so exhausting.[4] "The two things we really focused on were reducing intake and making sure that every 'offramp' works," McFee says.[5]

He pointed out that 80 percent of police calls typically concern "antisocial" behavior that can be more of a minor crime but can lead to more crime if not stopped. In many if not most cases, the individuals involved would be better served through other government services rather than the criminal justice system. "The focus should be on getting somebody with mental health and addiction issues the help and supports they need before they go off the rails," McFee said. "Moving money around from one agency to another has never worked. The right partnerships such as LEPH (Law Enforcement Public Health) show more promise. Working as teams gets better results—much safer, quicker, and can significantly reduce intake into the justice system."

McFee put engagement and trust at the forefront of his approach. In contrast to police departments that struggled to repair trust during crises after the George Floyd protests, McFee made trust a priority from his first day as commissioner. "You build trust in the good times," he explained. "That's what you need to rely on to get you through the bad times."

He characterizes his LGBTQ2S+ apology, for example, as part of a reconciliation process, in which he asked for "advice, guidance and partnership." McFee followed his statement by surveying community members on how they felt the department should engage with them and created an online portal to discuss the survey results and ongoing engagement efforts.[6]

This was only one of many communities McFee engaged with in his listening tour. He also formed the Nîsohkamâkewin Council, named for the Cree word meaning "the act of helping," and invited indigenous community members to join and help develop policing changes. "It's one thing to go into a community and tell them top-down what they need to do," said McFee. "It's another to stand by their side with the research and the data to drive sustainable change."[7] Trust, he believes, grows out of a partnership with the community.

McFee also worked closely with academia and the business community to build community trust and pilot innovative approaches to reduce crime. In February 2020, he unveiled an information hub dubbed the Community Solutions Accelerator, with the goal of using artificial intelligence (AI), machine learning, and big data to develop solutions for crime, homelessness, mental health, and other issues, particularly methamphetamine addiction.[8] The hub was intended to assemble academic institutions and frontline practitioners to examine new policing approaches. Corporate partners such as ATB Financial, TELUS, and Motorola Solutions Canada assisted with funding, lab space, IT infrastructure, technical support, and marketing.[9]

One goal of the accelerator was to reduce Edmonton's average toll of 9,600 annual liquor store thefts, which often feature an organized crime component. "We looked at the data and turned that over to the accelerator, saying let's solve this problem," McFee said. Working with its business partners, EPS developed solutions including storefront scanners that require customers to show their driver's licenses to enter a liquor store and GPS tracking devices on bottles. A pilot program in five stores reduced thefts and robberies by more than 95 percent. "We basically took the market away from the criminals," McFee said. "You could do the same with auto thefts, catalytic converters, and other areas. By engaging with your private partners to take away criminal markets, you build trust and reduce the need for police interventions."

In summer 2020, as the George Floyd protests shook trust in police around the world, McFee unveiled a "Commitment to Action" to repair community relations, pledging, "This is not simply just another consultation or listening campaign, we want to move into action and change immediately."[10]

Through all of this, McFee faced a challenge common to reform-minded chiefs: pushback from police officers anxious about receiving adequate backing from the top. Building trust required strengthening relationships both with the community and with the officers who interacted with members of the community. His years in the rank and file helped him to retain support by quickly acknowledging "discipline fatigue" within the service, and the need to bolster accountability among officers without "using discipline as a sentence."[11] He also focused on changing the binary "either-or" conversation he saw in other cities. "It's not about hard on crime, arrest and incarcerate, versus soft on crime, hugs and second chances," he explains. "We need to do both well."[12] Trust, it turns out, is an asset that should be nurtured both within organizations and between organizations and the citizens they serve.

Why—and How—Trust Matters

Distrust in government is one of the biggest challenges faced by the public sector around the world. A 2020 Organization for Economic Cooperation and Development (OECD) study found that fewer than half of citizens surveyed in twenty nations trusted their governments—a problem that cuts to the heart of effective governance. Trust matters, the OECD concluded, calling it "the foundation for the legitimacy of public institutions and a functioning democratic system. It is crucial for maintaining political participation and social cohesion."[13]

And according to OECD, this trust depends on each government's values (especially integrity, fairness, and openness) and competence (including responsiveness and reliability in service delivery).

Distrust drives down political participation, increases political polarization, makes government programs more expensive, encourages noncompliance with government policy, fuels corruption, slows policy innovation, and erodes the foundation of government itself.[14] Distrust, Francis Fukuyama has contended, makes it harder and more expensive for governments to do almost *anything.* It "imposes a kind of tax on all forms of activity, a tax that high-trust societies do not have to pay," he says—and the rising global wave of doubt is making high-trust societies rare.[15]

It's practically a truism that Americans don't trust their government. The Pew Research Center's data shows that only a quarter of US residents count on Washington to do the right thing even most of the time, a dismal finding that has scarcely budged since the mid-2000s.[16]

If distrust is so dominant, what can we do? Its political roots go very deep, often stretching back for generations. Much of it flows from broad social and economic factors, especially the deeply rooted problems of income inequality, racism, and other social forces. In a global survey, the OECD found that disadvantaged groups had lower levels of trust in government.[17] Moreover, distrust has been baked in from the first days of the American republic, when the founders fought a war to rid themselves of the power of the British king and then worked that distrust into barriers to restrain the power of every part of American government. For government managers, these issues cast a very long shadow indeed.

Wholesale and Retail Trust

Kettl calls this the problem of "wholesale trust," issues that strike at the broadest social and political questions and over which individual officials—even presidents and prime ministers—often have little control.[18]

A 2021 Deloitte survey concerning issues related to COVID-19 found that trust tended to fall with increasing age; Baby Boomers had less trust in government than Gen X, while Gen X had less trust than Gen Z and Millennials. Trust was highest among urban dwellers, followed by suburban residents and then rural residents. Trust was highest for public health agencies at all levels of government. State and local political officials ranked lower, while federally appointed or elected officials ranked lowest. Just 13 percent of Baby Boomers trusted Congress and the White House.[19]

But there's also the concept of "retail trust," concerning the direct relationships between individuals and the government programs that serve them (figure 4-1). Here there are signs of hope. As political scientist Amy Lerman points out, a core issue of trust is simple: "Can government do the things I want it to do? Is it going to do them well?" In addition, she says, it's not enough to pass a new piece of legislation. "Passing policies that have potential to meaningfully impact people's lives is a first step. But there has to be follow through." All these steps, she argues, are important to "have an impact on this persistent belief that government doesn't actually do anything helpful or useful."[20]

It's the connection between government's promises and its outcomes that matters most, as research points out. A 2019 McKinsey study concluded that customers are nine times more likely to trust a government agency if they're satisfied with the services they receive from it. Immigration, Refugees, and Citizenship Canada has found that its clients are

FIGURE 4-1

Retail versus wholesale trust

Trust in individual agencies, government programs

Versus

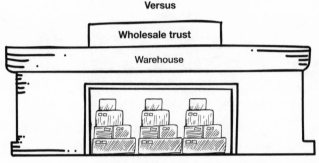

Trust in government as a whole

twenty-six times more likely to trust it when they're satisfied with its services. From 2015 to 2018, the US Department of Veterans Affairs (VA) aimed to improve veterans' experiences. The work paid off: trust in the agency rose from 47 percent to 70 percent.[21]

OECD has found that citizens tend to trust individual service agencies more than government itself, and that this trust varies across different policy areas. Among the twenty nations OECD surveyed in 2020, trust was highest for local police (at 78 percent), followed by health care (71 percent), education (68 percent), and the judicial system (57 percent). National governments as a whole, by contrast, were trusted by just 51 percent of respondents.[22]

Between 2020 and 2022, Deloitte surveyed more than ten thousand Americans to understand their levels of trust in government at the federal, state, and local levels. At the federal level, citizens were asked about

FIGURE 4-2

Trust signals: Aggregate of thirty-nine federal agencies versus US government as a whole

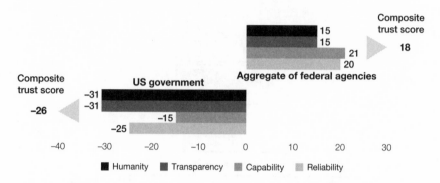

Respondents were asked to rate thirty-nine federal agencies and overall US government separately on the four trust signals.

Source: Deloitte analysis of TrustID survey data.

their views on how thirty-nine different federal agencies and departments performed on four "trust signals": humanity, transparency, capability, and reliability. As with the OECD survey, respondents' trust in the federal government was *significantly* less than their trust in the aggregate of the thirty-nine agencies (figure 4-2).

Clearly, then, government can't address trust issues with a one-size-fits-all approach. Understanding how different agencies interact with their customers—a spectrum Deloitte calls *retail to regulator*—can help them begin rebuilding trust (figure 4-3).

Citizens tend to have higher trust in agencies that provide them with direct services, at the "retail" end of the spectrum. At the other end of the spectrum, "enforcers," such as federal law enforcement agencies, were trusted least (figure 4-4). This stands in contrast to the role of enforcers elsewhere in the world, where police and the judiciary often generate more trust, in comparison with the national government.[23]

Such results actually are a hopeful sign. Citizens can and *do* differentiate among different government agencies. And agency leaders who seek to earn the trust of their citizens can do so—if they take the right steps.

FIGURE 4-3

Six types of government actions

Retailer	Retailer-like	Innovator	Educator	Regulator	Enforcer
Offer goods and services to external customers or staff in a competitive environment, e.g., US Postal Service	Provide a service, often for a fee, but no competitive alternative exists, e.g., Passport Services, Department of Motor Vehicles	Drive new ways of thinking and doing; or support the innovation of others through investment, e.g., National Institutes of Health, National Aeronautics and Space Administration	Impart knowledge, skills, and resources to inform, influence, or drive an outcome, e.g., Census Bureau, Voice of America	Develop rules and regulations that effectively deter undesired or illegal behaviors, e.g., Food and Drug Administration, Federal Aviation Administration	Enforce rules and regulations by detecting wrongdoing and enacting consequences, e.g., US Customs and Border Protection, law enforcement agencies

FIGURE 4-4

Trust signal scores across six agency types

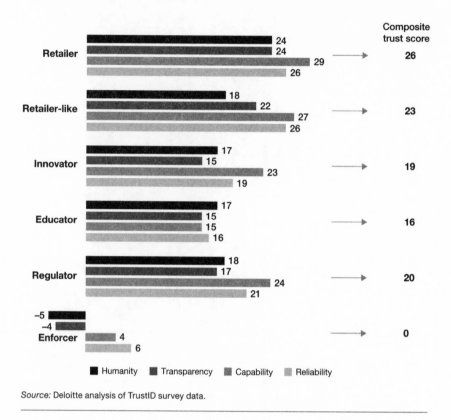

Source: Deloitte analysis of TrustID survey data.

It All Starts with Measurement

Without trust, regulations are less effective, services suffer, and citizen dissatisfaction climbs. Yet the complexities of government trust relationships and the invisible nature of trust can lead agencies to pay it too little attention.

But the wind is invisible, too, and still we have learned to measure it and use it. Government agencies *can* measure trust and use it to improve their functions. The first step is simply to begin to measure trust in all its complexity. Surveys, feedback tools, and network mapping can help agencies build a picture of the different stakeholder groups with which they interact. This can help them fine-tune their understanding of their trust networks and increase transparency by providing greater opportunity for stakeholder feedback, a proven driver of trust for commercial brands. With this information, government agencies can identify and prioritize their problems and coordinate their trust networks to maintain the standards citizens expect.

Measurement in government is often very tricky, of course. That's even more the case for measuring trust. It can be very challenging to design and calibrate surveys. It can be difficult, as well, to develop sophistication in using proxy measures of citizen trust and satisfaction, like complaints funneled through legislative or local council offices. Assessing who trusts whom to do what is a deceptively complicated issue. Focusing on complaints alone, for example, can easily create a distorted picture of government's success because managers risk hearing only isolated pockets of bad news.

Even more fundamentally, "trust" as a stand-alone concept is not very useful. Its true meaning lies in charting the relationship between the people and the government that serves them. It is a concept shaped by the competency of government employees, the humanity they demonstrate in serving the people, and the integrity with which they do their jobs. Measuring trust, therefore, is a matter of developing metrics for these underlying concepts. And it is a matter of understanding the way these concepts fit together to define a government program's relationship with the people. That, in turn, can provide insight into whether trust is improving—or undermining an agency's ability to accomplish its mission.

Measuring trust is essential for improving it. But developing good measures is not for amateurs.

Trust and Digital Transformation

Proximity to public services and officials is certainly a factor in trust. Citizens obtain services locally and can speak with public officials at town halls, school board meetings, or the supermarket, while their federal representatives, seen mostly on television and social media, seem far less connected to their daily lives. When citizens can feel some connection with government officials, they're far more likely to trust them. Surprisingly, though, the quality of the *digital* services governments provide may be even more important in engendering trust.

Deloitte survey respondents who said they were pleased with their state government's digital services also tended to rate the state highly on measures of overall trust. Those unhappy with digital services scored government much lower on trust; dissatisfaction essentially wiped out any inherent loyalty to local institutions. Respondents tended to disagree—strongly—with the statement, "My state government's internet and digital services are easy to use."[24] At a time when state and local officials are looking to bolster trust, improving the digital experience seems critical.

But today, an effective digital experience involves much more than cleaning up a glitchy interface or reducing superfluous clicks. It must be part of a broader digital transformation that provides a more seamless service experience, with services that are:

- *Personalized*—tailored to individual needs, interests, and circumstances. The service provider genuinely tries to understand its customers and create an increasingly customized experience.

- *Frictionless*—requiring little effort on the consumer's part, with no demands for information or frustrating barriers. Think of "one-click" shopping or other apps that make it easy for citizens to get what they want quickly.

- *Anticipatory*—anticipating customer needs and offering them proactively, just as Netflix anticipates its viewers' wishes, queueing a new video as the credits roll. However, Leslie K. John, Tami Kim, and Kate Barasz warn that personalizing services can also raise risks. "With personalized ads" in the private sector, they write, "there's a fine line between creepy and delightful," because of the way they nibble away at individual privacy.[25]

Achieving these innovations at scale requires citizens, businesses, and employees to trust the technologies as well as the government behind them. It's a high barrier to clear. "We figured out that if we want to pro-vide services digitally, we obviously have to have a trusted interaction from both sides," says Siim Sikkut, former chief information officer for Estonia, widely considered the world's most digital government. "Gov-ernment needs to know who's entering the service, and the citizen needs to know if the other side is actually [trustworthy]."[26]

Of course, the success of *every* technology depends on individual deci-sions about whether to use it, based on the belief that its benefits will outweigh the cost and inconvenience of adopting it. But as technology becomes more complex—and less understandable to the ordinary user—the level of trust it demands rises.

Digital technologies involving many components and interactions require new levels of trust. Both organizations and end users need to trust a whole network of technologies supported by an ecosystem of often-unseen players.

Consider one high-profile example: the growing use of facial recogni-tion technology at airports. For such a system to function effectively, pas-sengers and employees alike must implicitly trust the government agencies, airport authorities, and technology providers behind the cam-eras and scanners. Studies suggest many travelers aren't sold on the idea precisely because they *don't* trust these entities. A 2019 *PCMag* survey found that just 28 percent of two thousand respondents supported the use of facial recognition in the airline industry, even though the tool could save time, increase security, and reduce hassle.[27] Technology is cre-ating opportunities for a more seamless customer experience in dealing with government, but often those opportunities come at the cost of a surrender of individual privacy. We are a long way from resolving that tension.

Convincing users not only to adopt but embrace new systems is a chal-lenge even when stakes are low, especially because they might rightly be suspicious about how their personal data might be used. Understanding individuals' decision-making processes requires us to consider their viewpoints, often by employing human-centered design and a focus on customer experience.[28]

Veterans: Gaining Trust with Better Service

All these issues of trust surrounded the VA's effort to transform its services for veterans with computer-aided health care. The VA pioneered the initiative in the early 1980s, with its decentralized hospital computer program, and then again in the 1990s, with its health information system and technology architecture. Despite such innovations, the agency's problems with scheduling and access to care continued to grow.[29] In 2011, an internal VA study identified *nineteen* veterans who had died due to delays in medical screenings. In 2014, some veterans were being forced to wait up to *seventy calendar days* for routine care—more than double the thirty-day standard mandated by federal law.[30] Such revelations dramatically undermined the trust of patients, VA staff, and everyone else.

By 2019, however, the VA had undergone one of the more remarkable turnarounds in the federal government's recent history. A May 2020 survey put veterans' trust in the VA's outpatient services at an all-time high of 90 percent, even with the pandemic.[31] In the same month, the VA's Connected Care telehealth program won a prestigious Samuel J. Heyman Service to America Medal.[32]

How did the VA's leaders pull off this transformation? It began with a cultural shift throughout the organization, focused on leading with trust.

In 2015, the agency launched a Veterans Experience Office to drive the effort. Two years later, the VA launched its Veterans Signals program, which collects online feedback after outpatient services from veterans and their dependents, caregivers, and survivors.[33] By April 2020, Veterans Signals had collected more than 4 million survey responses and 1.8 million comments.[34] These data allowed the VA to measure service attributes linked to trust signals, including transparency, empathy, effectiveness, and ease of use, and use the resulting insights to improve its customer experience.

The program proved especially useful for identifying veterans in crisis. The VA intervened in a total of 691 suicide crises, using AI-based tools that analyze comments in real time and route concerns to local VA offices and crisis hotlines.[35]

Surprisingly, veterans' most common complaints about health care involved not their medical treatment per se but the digital infrastructure *around* care: scheduling and rescheduling appointments, confusion over which part of a hospital to visit, and a lack of facilities in waiting rooms. "[One] veteran had to click seventeen times to find a PDF file, which they then had to download, print, fill out by hand, and mail," says Tom Allin, who served as the VA's first chief veterans experience officer at the VA. "Clearly, that's not the type of experience we're looking for. When people are going online, the goal is to get something done."[36]

Veterans Signals leaders studied such feedback and responded by making changes to appointment scheduling, reorienting waiting rooms, and having volunteers greet and guide veterans upon entering a facility. "There previously were over five hundred veteran-facing websites," Allin says. "We collapsed them into one where they could get everything done on one site with one ID, one password, one sign-in." These simple tweaks went a long way toward improving the patient experience. VA's success suggests several important lessons for agencies:

- *Focus on customer experience.* The online and offline experiences both play a vital role in driving trust in public services. A focus on customer experience can help provide a consistent and reliable experience across the system.

- *Measure what matters.* "The problem was what we were measuring was not important to the veterans. For measurement to work, it needs to be accurate in terms of what's important to the customer," Allin says. "Our goal was to try to understand how we can measure an experience in real time." By measuring and focusing on the attributes that drive trust, the VA improved its ability to use new tools and digital technologies, as well as to support its broader efforts toward patient-centered health care.

- *Deliver services with empathy.* Demonstrating empathy can go a long way toward improving trust. The Veterans Signals program has helped the VA focus tightly on veterans' experiences and well-being. Connecting with customers as people can both improve the connection between customers and agencies but also strengthen the foundations of trust.

Earning trust, it turns out, depends on improving the customer experience, with that improvement built on metrics and empathy.

Census: The Count That Really Counts

Every decade since 1790, America has successfully conducted the nation's constitutionally required census, despite a civil war, major depressions, and two world wars. In 220-plus years, there's never been a significant delay. The predictability of the process, along with the communication that surrounds it, is crucial to making the census work. After all, the census doesn't work unless people trust the forms they get in the mail, the security of the information they provide—and, if all else fails, opening the door to strangers to provide information about the household.

Once a decade, April 1 is the traditional "Census Day," when the US Census Bureau officially kicks off the once-in-a-decade effort to count the nation's population. On April 1, 2020, though, the pandemic had effectively closed down much of the country. Census Day literally couldn't have come at a worse time.

For years, census workers had been planning, coordinating, and modernizing their systems for the 2020 count. They needed to complete data collection by July 31 to produce legally required apportionment counts by December 31. The pandemic, however, forced the Census Bureau to delay door-to-door counts during this crucial time to protect its field employees as well as the public.

The significance of this delay can't be overstated. Census data shapes everything from congressional representation to the allocation of hundreds of billions of dollars in program areas such as health, education, disaster recovery, and infrastructure.[37] If the census didn't work, virtually everything about government could have found itself on a rickety foundation.

But the pandemic wasn't the only crisis at hand. The 2020 census was being conducted amid a near collapse in public trust in the federal government, which fell to a near-historic low of 20 percent in 2020.[38] The Trump administration's attempt to add a citizenship question to the census further politicized the debate, as online rumors reported that the bureau would share data with the Immigration and Customs Enforcement Agency (ICE). That rumor continued to plague the census, likely leading some people to refuse to complete the form.[39]

The trust problem didn't appear suddenly, however. In a 2018 census survey, a fourth of all respondents were worried about the privacy of their data, with racial and ethnic minorities expressing the most concern. And a quarter of those surveyed said that the odds were low—or zero—that they would fill out the census form when the time arrived.[40]

The Census Bureau faced a monumental challenge—and then got to work.

The bureau launched a "Trust and Safety" team led by Zack Schwartz, a young Census Bureau technologist. Schwartz and his team assembled a network of partners and experts, both internal and external, to mitigate threats to census employees and combat misinformation about the 2020 count.[41] While the bureau hadn't planned for a global pandemic, their wargaming for a host of other potential crises—from cyberattacks to major staff shortages—gave them a head start when the pandemic hit. "We had planned for various crises, knowing how to react, knowing the types of resources that were available to us, with a focus on being nimble," says Schwartz.[42]

The team used social listening tools and analytics to identify threats to census workers and misinformation that could jeopardize the census's credibility. This allowed the bureau to identify trends and get ahead of false narratives that gain traction rapidly in social media.

To counter this, in a first-of-its-kind initiative, the Trust and Safety team worked closely with all the major social media companies—as well as other partners—to combat misinformation and disinformation (figure 4-5). Partners adapted their policies to protect the census, highlighted violations, and took a multitude of mitigation actions, such as content demotion and labeling.

FIGURE 4-5

Leveraging partnership networks to detect, mitigate, and respond to mis- and disinformation about the census

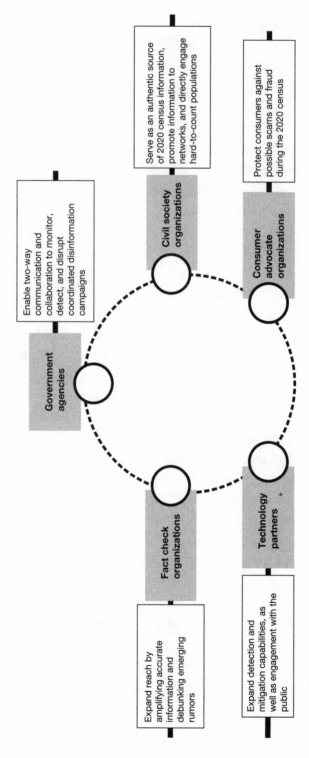

Source: Deloitte analysis.

"When we went out and saw information out there that was inaccurate, we were able to quickly react, the platforms knew what to do," Schwartz said in a 2021 interview. "It was just a whole shebang of making sure that information that was out there about the census was accurate, and therefore encouraging people to respond online, over the phone or by mail."[43]

The census team realized that partners were vital to ensuring a complete and accurate count. It also realized that it needed to get information *directly* to the public. To do this, it tapped into a massive ecosystem of tribal, state, and local governments as well as more than four hundred thousand national and grassroots partners including the American Association of Retired Persons, the American Library Association, and the social platform Nextdoor.

These partners distributed accurate and reliable information about the census and its importance and told people how to avoid potential scams. "The corner store on the street where I live in Downtown DC had a huge 'Participate in the 2020 census' sign up," says Schwartz. "My barber up the street had the same sign up. That gives you some idea of the breadth of our partnerships." The bureau recruited dozens of specialists to facilitate these kinds of partnerships.

To boost partner participation, the bureau visualized outreach efforts with a daily census response rate map. "Local communities could see how they were doing compared with their neighbors," Schwartz says. "It provided friendly competition. These groups and the work they contributed kept the census moving forward."[44]

One of the big challenges facing the census was reaching minority communities, especially where distrust in government was high, and where COVID-19 compounded the problem. Many groups were concerned that historically hard-to-count populations would be undercounted due to their concerns about confidentiality and because of earlier proposals, which had been rejected, to include citizenship questions on the census and possible uses of census information for deportation. "We worked hard to understand at the hyper local level what was the issue or concern for that particular hard-to-count community," Schwartz says. "Much of it was triggered by misinformation floating out there that we then worked with our partners to counter."

One of the most important partners were churches. "The coronavirus has added to the already existing fear that people had about a number of questions," explained the co-convener of the National African American Clergy Network, Reverend Barbara Williams-Skinner.[45] In response, the clergy network created an "Everyone Counts" website to encourage participation.[46] Black churches organized block parties, recruited DJs to promote completion of the census, and developed online chats for those who wanted to avoid close contact during the pandemic. Reverend Leslye Dwight, one of the program's leaders, said, "The challenge of Black participation in the census is a moral issue, not just one of civic engagement."[47] A major impediment to completing the census was distrust. One of the most effective strategies for connecting with the Black community was through the institution trusted the most, the churches they attended.

The result? According to the Census Bureau, 99.98 percent of all housing units and addresses nationwide were accounted for in the 2020 census.[48]

Using "Trust Networks"

The 2020 census illuminates one of the basic facts about trust in government: To improve trust, government's managers have to consider the large number of intermediaries that deliver its services or otherwise influence public perceptions.

As we've shown, governments today rely on networks of providers to deliver services to citizens. Government actions are "interwoven" with those of vendors, contractors, other levels of government, and private industry to provide citizens with what they need. Thus, trust in government doesn't concern citizens alone; there's a whole range of stakeholders who must trust government and that government and constituents must trust (figure 4-6).

But the mechanisms of transparency and accountability haven't kept pace with the complexity of this interweaving of public and private enti-

FIGURE 4-6

Government stakeholders

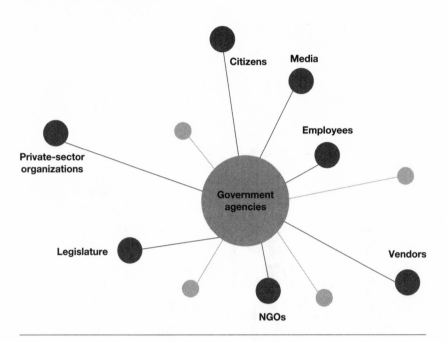

ties. If any stakeholder involved in a process fails to behave in a trust-worthy manner, it's likely to harm the reputation of government as much as, if not *more than*, that of the service provider.[49] If government is to be trusted, it must hold an entire ecosystem of players to the same high standards (figure 4-7).

Consider the financial stimulus programs enacted during the pandemic. Such programs were executed by a combination of government employees, website vendors, financial institutions, and more. For the program to be trusted, each stakeholder had to work to the same standards of competence and intent. If vendor incompetence led to security breaches, or if banks acted in bad faith by prioritizing loans to their existing customers, their actions could have damaged trust in the program and in government at large.

When executed well, a network can actually help *improve* trust for government services. Consider again the use of facial recognition in air

FIGURE 4-7

Trustworthy government services: An ecosystem held to common standards

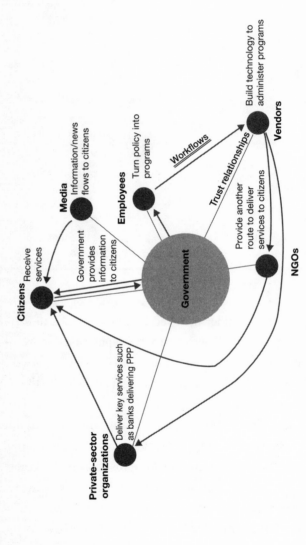

travel. Government agencies coordinated with airlines and airports to deliver efficient facial recognition services without maintaining a large apparatus for capturing and matching faces.[50] But while working through networks can help build trust, it also introduces greater risk and variability to the trust relationship. A citizen's final perception of trust in facial recognition now depends not just on government but on hardware, algorithms, the airlines that use them, the airports that may own them, other government agencies with databases that need to be checked (such as no-fly lists), and so on.

So how do you coordinate large networks of trust?

- *Understand stakeholders' needs and perspectives.* You can't improve trust unless you know its current state. Surveys and other instruments tailored for different stakeholder groups represent a key first step toward that understanding. Then, too, agencies need a mechanism for learning what stakeholders value, to make sure actions move in the direction they want. Understanding their values and driving toward consensus can cut through polarizing social trends that undermine trust. Even when finding strong consensus is impossible, demonstrating respect and ensuring due process to all involved in the system can significantly advance trust. As we have seen, this process is highly complex and requires seasoned experts.

- *Define and communicate the mission.* Research has demonstrated a clear link between employee engagement and trust in government—and perhaps the most important element of engagement is workers' perceptions of how and how well their skills support the agency mission. For this reason, government agencies can build employee engagement by clearly defining the mission and how success is measured, linking each employee's job to the mission, and communicating these to employees repeatedly. This can build employee engagement and a more cohesive organization, which in turn helps employees counter corrosive factors in the wider trust environment.[51]

- **Work through networks of real people.** People aren't abstractions. They're flesh and blood and live in the physical world. If managers want to affect their behavior, it's best to reach them through those they know and trust.

  In Exeter, New Hampshire, for example, the fire department managed COVID-19 vaccinations at a well-known senior center a stone's throw from downtown. The fire chief ran the program and used his extensive network in town to ensure doses weren't wasted. He recruited neighbors to watch residents' dogs while they got vaccinated and drove seniors to and from their appointments. When a neighbor said she felt unsure about the vaccine, he urged her to visit the senior center to see what it was like. She got her vaccine in the next week.[52]

  This approach isn't just for vaccines. Working through a community's social networks can help government build trust on any number of issues, from building confidence in government services to countering misinformation.

- **Reimagine experiences with stakeholders.** New technologies and stakeholders create opportunities for government to reimagine how citizens experience services. The possibilities are almost endless, from a single sign-on to log into your bank and pay taxes, to personal digital assistants assisting you in seeking government services. But with so many different stakeholders in so many different roles, it's important to align incentives for all players to ensure everyone pulls in the same direction. Government agencies should consider arenas such as aviation safety, in which bilateral, multilateral, and international organizations have successfully aligned incentives across whole industries.[53]

- **Make collaboration someone's main responsibility, not just a secondary duty where no one is in charge.** It is important, of course, for everyone to contribute to the collaborative enterprise. But unless coordination is someone's job, not just a sidelight to everyone's job, better collaboration is likely to be a dream.

- *Build structures and processes to advance collaboration.* Smart managers can do a great deal through their own leadership to advance trust. But the right structures and processes can make that job easier, especially strategies that make it easier to identify citizens' concerns and how well the organization meets them. That's especially important because, as the 2023 Edelman Trust Barometer found, trust in private and nonprofit organizations ranks significantly higher than in government.[54] Government can borrow trust from its partners to enhance its performance.

Trust in government is essential. It's complex. But it can be improved. Chief McFee's work in Edmonton, as well as the VA and census examples, demonstrate just how much progress trust-centered leadership can bring.

Ten Ways Bridgebuilders Can Cultivate Networks of Trust

Inside the Organization

- **Communicate a clear vision for change and connect it to a shared purpose.** Bridgebuilders connect the organizational vision to a shared purpose to drive collective action. Once the VA made improving the veteran experience a top priority, Tom Allin established the Veterans Experience Office to guide collective action toward realizing this vision.

- **Use data-driven systems and processes to measure trust.** The Veterans Experience Office collected online feedback from millions of veterans, dependents, caregivers, and survivors after they received outpatient services.[55] These data allowed the VA to measure service attributes linked to trust, including transparency, empathy, effectiveness, and ease of use.[56]

- **Understand that trust and accountability are interlinked.** Accountability and trust go hand in hand. If the community trusts you as their leader, it is easier to get their buy-in for the execution of programs, even during times of crisis. "That's when you get community leaders saying, well, wait a minute, you know this person has worked with us," explains Michael A. Nutter, the former mayor of Philadelphia. "We don't need to tear up our town or burn the place down because of what's happened. . . . We're going to let them handle their business, and we're going to hold them accountable."[57]

- **Develop diverse, multidisciplinary teams.** Chief McFee recruited epidemiologists, economists, data modelers, and clinical psychologists to join his department and help to reimagine the police force.

Across the Network

- **Build trust during good times.** In contrast to police departments that struggled to repair trust after the George Floyd protests, Edmonton Police Chief McFee made building community trust a priority from his first day as commissioner.[58]

- **Identify pain points.** Bridgebuilders should understand the different perspectives important to stakeholders. Tom Allin set out on his journey to reimagine the veterans experience by measuring what really mattered to veterans—what was working and what wasn't—and engaged them in the conversation about how the experience could be improved.

- **Understand the root causes of trust problems.** Bridgebuilders delve deep to understand the root causes of trust challenges. In 2010, the New Orleans Police Department aimed to reduce taboos around sexual assault reporting and make the process more empathetic. To tackle the problem, the department worked with advocacy groups and academics to create training that encouraged detectives to display more empathy to sexual assault victims.

- **Build bridges with diverse groups of stakeholders.** The 2020 census tapped into a large ecosystem of tribal, state, and local governments as well as more than four hundred thousand national and grassroots partners who could advocate on its behalf. No organization was treated as too small or too unimportant. "The biggest and the most important thing we did in bridgebuilding was to make sure we had a diversity of groups and organizations and legislators that we worked with," says the Census Bureau's Zack Schwartz.[59]

- **Achieve buy-in by cocreating solutions.** Engaging beneficiaries in a challenge creates ownership for solutions. The principle is "no change without us"—don't do it "to" us, do it *with* us, tapping the collective wisdom of diverse groups. Bridgebuilders can use cocreation approaches, including human-centered design, to design, develop, and deploy new solutions to improve adoption. A partnership between the city of Minneapolis and Nexus Community Partners works to improve racial equity in the membership of government boards and commissions, which in turn influences major policy decisions toward more equitable outcomes.[60]

- **Be human and sincere in communication.** The more people can see the implementers as real people rather than a nameless bureaucracy, the greater trust they will have in the process. Constituents should see the communication as a "dialogue" instead of unidirectional information flow.

Chapter 5

Grow Catalytic Government

Government Often Doesn't So Much Manage or Deliver as It Shapes and Integrates Solutions

- Governmental Catalysts
- A Toolbox for Managing Government's Catalytic Strategies and Tactics
- Catalyzing Defenses for the Cyberworld
- Catalysts by Design
- Government Leaders as Catalysts
- Ten Ways Bridgebuilders Can Catalyze Innovation

The next time you take a flight, think of the marvel transporting you—and consider that almost everything from the jet engines to the radar came from government-sponsored projects.

The first jet engines emerged during World War II, with British and American engineers working on one side, and German experts on the other. While the German Me-262 saw limited combat in the war, all of the earliest jets had little use because they were enormous gas guzzlers. But in the postwar years, the Pentagon worked with Pratt & Whitney to create the J57 engine, which powered the B-52 bomber and some of America's most formidable jet fighters. Later, a variant of that engine was used in the Boeing 707, the first commercially successful jetliner.[1]

Radar also emerged from wartime efforts, with each government operating under tremendous secrecy. The US Navy's Signal Corps worked on a project labeled Radio Detection and Ranging—or RADAR, for short.[2] (It's an example of an important lesson: good acronyms are pronounceable.) The Allies' advantage in developing and deploying radar—the acronym turned into an ordinary word in short order—made a huge difference in the outcome of the war.

The construction of airline seats is another product of federal research, with regulations set to make them sturdier and flame resistant in crashes. So, too, are the floor-level lights leading passengers to the exits in case of an emergency—and the design and location of the exits themselves, which federal rules stipulate must be able to help all passengers evacuate in ninety seconds. The requirement that window shades be open on takeoff and landing comes from accident research by the National Transportation Safety Board. Airplane radios were the product of considerable military research. Federal investigators explored how best to reduce the fire risk and studied the dangers that handheld lasers pose to aircraft. And of course, federal research led to tougher air travel security through hardened cockpit doors, more stringent airport security, and the background computer screenings none of us ever see.

Governmental Catalysts

During the fierce race for advanced weapons during World War II, the US built the first nuclear weapon by assembling the nation's best minds in a far-flung research and manufacturing network, all under the leadership of the legendary Army general, Leslie Groves, who managed what became known as the "Manhattan Project." The name might seem a puzzle, but its first offices were at 270 Broadway in Manhattan, and that worked well as a code name.

Groves managed the extraordinarily complex $40 billion project.[3] At its launch in 1942, the engineers and scientists developed four different ideas for the bomb—but they were not sure which of them might work or, indeed, whether *any* of them would work. Moreover, secrecy was essential, to prevent any of the country's wartime enemies from stealing the secrets—and gaining strategic advantage. Groves dealt with the secrecy aspect of the program by using different manufacturing modules around the country run by universities, private companies, and the military.

When Groves and his team prepared the first test of the weapon in New Mexico during mid-1945, some scientists feared it wouldn't work. Others feared that it would. At the zero mark of the countdown, the bomb lit up the early morning sky with a blast of humbling intensity.[4] The test director, Kenneth Bainbridge, said, "Now we are all sons of bitches."[5]

Government's role as a catalyst spilled over to medical policy as well. When Congress created Medicare and Medicaid in 1965, the federal government provided funding but relied on private companies—and in the case of Medicaid, on state governments as well—to implement the programs. And then there's the case of Operation Warp Speed, which used the government's leverage to coordinate the private companies that produced the COVID-19 vaccine. (We will explore these cases in greater detail in later chapters.)

State governments have been active catalysts as well. Regulations by the state of California created the market for catalytic converters in cars. At the local level, improved building codes have made buildings far sturdier and dramatically reduced losses from fires.

What do all these efforts have in common? Each employed a strategy of *blended government*, with government's policy woven together with public, private, and nonprofit organizations to achieve results. In each case, government's role was not that of a direct service provider but instead to serve as a *catalyst* to assemble the players who, together, could attack these problems.

FIGURE 5-1

Government's toolbox for catalyzing innovation

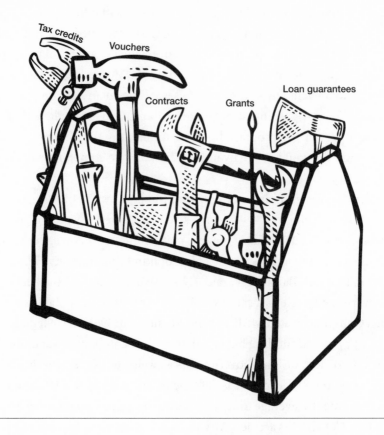

The term "catalyst" comes from chemistry, describing a substance that increases the rate of a reaction without being consumed by it. And that's the key for leadership in complex public policy problems: to find individuals and organizations who can lead solutions across organizational boundaries while sustaining their influence over time.

Twin forces are accelerating the role of governmental catalysts. One is the reality at the core of this book: the increasing interconnection of government agencies and private partners. The second is government's funding of public programs, without the government actually delivering them, through the growth of *indirect* government tools (figure 5-1).

Indirect Government

In 1980, Frederick C. Mosher wrote a pathbreaking article for *Public Administration Review*, "The Changing Responsibilities and Tactics of the Federal Government." Since the New Deal and World War II, he argued, changes "have been of such magnitude as to alter fundamentally the nature of federal responsibilities and modes of operating." As a result, "in virtually all functional fields," the US federal government is "carrying out those responsibilities through, and interdependently with, nonfederal institutions and individuals."[6]

Today this phenomenon operates at a very different scale and with broader implications than what Mosher wrote about decades ago. It has emerged at all levels of American government, and in many governments globally—but it has been a particular phenomenon of the US federal government.

Consider a snapshot of the federal government's activities. In 2021, for example, the federal government budget was $6.8 trillion. Its overall financial footprint, however, was nearly twice that size (table 5-1). The financial cost of tax breaks and loan programs was about $1.5 trillion each, and the cost of complying with federal regulatory programs was about $1.9 trillion. Moreover, most of the federal budget went for entitlement programs, grants, contracts and acquisitions, and interest on the federal debt. That left 4 percent of the budget for programs the federal government directly administered, for programs ranging from air traffic control to forest management. Although some of these numbers are estimates, one point is clear: the vast majority of the federal government's activities—more than 95 percent—occurs through blended government.

At the state and local levels, direct government accounts for a larger share, for programs like police and fire and transportation (although, because of the way they report their budgets, it is not possible to produce good estimates of the scale of their blended government). But state governments also rely heavily on contracts for programs ranging from road construction to child welfare. They regulate everything from

TABLE 5-1

The federal government's financial footprint

	Amount (billions of dollars, 2021)	Percent of total
Total outlays	$6,822	58%
Entitlement programs	$4,629	39%
Grants (except mandatory programs)	$551	5%
Interest	$352	3%
Contracts and acquisitions	$832	7%
Other discretionary spending	$458	4%
Tax expenditures	$1,500	13%
Loans	$1,539	13%
Regulatory compliance	$1,900	16%
TOTAL	$11,761	100%
Direct government	$458	4%
Blended government	$11,303	96%

Sources: Office of Management and Budget, "Historical Tables," 2021, https://www.whitehouse.gov/omb/budget/historical-tables/; USASpending, "FY 2022 Spending by Object Class," 2022, https://www.usaspending.gov/explorer/object_class; Bloomberg Tax, "Tax Expenditures—The $1.5 Trillion Elephant in the (Budget) Room," Daily Tax Report based on Treasury data, September 7, 2021, https://news.bloombergtax.com/daily-tax-report/tax-expenditures-the-1-5-trillion-elephant-in-the-budget-room; Congressional Budget Office, "Projected Costs or Savings from Federal Credit Programs in 2021" (table), 2020, https://www.cbo.gov/publication/56315#_idTextAnchor006; Clyde Wayne Crews, "Ten Thousand Commandments 2021: An Annual Snapshot of the Federal Regulatory State," Competitive Enterprise Institute, June 30, 2021, https://cei.org/studies/ten-thousand-commandments-2021/.

insurance to beauty salons. They have their own entitlement programs, and in most state budgets Medicaid spending is the largest and fastest-growing item. They provide tax breaks for economic development, as do many local governments. Indirect government, then, may not be as prominent at the state and local levels, but it's a large financial force there as well.

Of course, the dominant ideas, both in academic theory and in the practical imagination of policymakers, build on the notion that the federal government actually *manages* the programs on which it spends money. So, there is a significant and growing gap between concept and reality. What we need are modern tools for managing these *indirect* levers of government power. Developing them begins with understanding the role of catalytic government and how it has evolved.

Catalytic Government's Evolution

Reinventing Government, the classic 1992 book by David Osborne and Ted Gaebler, begins with a focus on catalytic government. They recognized government's growing reliance on complex networks to pursue public goals. Governments' most important roles, they argued, involve steering policy. "Rather than hiring more public employees," they wrote, "they make sure *other* institutions are delivering services and meeting the community's needs."[7] In short, governments are *catalysts for action*.

The big question, of course, is *how* to catalyze action—and to choose which actions to catalyze. Research since Osborne and Gaebler's book suggests that complex problems require cooperation both among organizations and across sectors of society, and that government can catalyze these relationships.[8] A central idea of catalytic government is that members of networks come together in their shared pursuit of common goals—that problems *define* the members of the network and bring it cohesion; that network members work collaboratively toward solutions; and that catalytic leadership guides and fuels the process.

For example, COVID-19 created a crisis that was powerful in "unlocking significant activity with governments," in the words of the OECD. But "there are important questions around the sustainability of this and what governments need to do to build a deeper and more entrenched capacity to allow for transformation not only in response to a crisis, but a transformation that fits with the values that governments aspire to."[9]

Policy crises and governmental transformations have always been linked. As Samuel Johnson put it, "When a man knows he is to be hanged in a fortnight, it concentrates his mind wonderfully."[10] But how can transformation be made part of government's routine, in the absence of a major external crisis?

The answer is to focus on government's catalyzing role. And while the idea has been around for decades, there are few practical guides for how to do it.

A Toolbox for Managing Government's Catalytic Strategies and Tactics

Catalytic government is about much more than building complex networks. It's also about catalyzing those networks toward *outcomes*.

Every innovation has three elements—funding, regulating, and doing. Every innovation needs someone to play each of these roles. It need not be the same player, and the players aren't necessarily the same for each innovation. Changing dynamics among the players can be easily seen in the funding role, where the private sector increasingly plays a central role in funding basic research and development (R&D).

Governmental Funding

The Manhattan Project was an initiative for innovation as much as for production. Its weblike structure maximized its potential for both security and creative thinking. Different companies and universities produced the discrete components necessary to make the nuclear bomb. A private company ran the plutonium project; Union Carbide developed gaseous diffusion; Chrysler produced diffusers; and the University of Wisconsin supplied the electrostatic generators needed to measure nuclear constants. In some cases, General Groves assigned the same task to several entities to spur innovation.[11] But at the core of this effort was the surprising fact that the federal government was a very small operational part of the research and development of the bomb.

The federal government maintained this model for the nuclear weapons program in the years following the war. In 1951, all but five thousand of the sixty thousand people working for the Atomic Energy Commission (AEC) were contractors.[12] Building a nuclear industry, however, took much more than federal contracting money. It required a *commercial* market for nuclear power—and that in turn meant substantial financial and regulatory risks for private companies.[13]

The federal government used regulation and policy levers to help build this market. The Price-Anderson Act charged the AEC (later the Department of Energy) with maintaining a commercially funded insurance pool to provide liability coverage for nuclear companies.[14] In effect, the act removed a major barrier to commercial participation in the nuclear industry while protecting consumers, and at no cost to taxpayers.[15]

The long-term outlook for nuclear power generation was and *is* hotly debated, as the industry finds itself caught between safety concerns and the push for green energy. But there's no disputing the fact that, from its roots in the Manhattan Project, the industry grew into a network of ninety-four operating nuclear plants accounting for about 20 percent of US electricity generation—and it developed because of the government's catalytic action.[16]

Not all governmental seeding leads to success. In the 1960s, the federal government invested $1 billion in supersonic transport, but the country never got an SST into the air.[17] The British and French, however, financed the development of the Concorde, a true technological marvel and a plane of genuine beauty. *Popular Mechanics* in 1960 hailed commercial supersonic vehicles as the plane of "tomorrow."[18] But so far, this particular tomorrow still hasn't arrived.

Government seeding thus can prove extraordinarily valuable in fueling innovation, but there are no guarantees.

Private Funding

Obviously, the private sector also is a significant and growing source of investment in innovation. Since the late 1980s, business R&D spending has exceeded the federal government's (figure 5-2). In 2019, the commercial sector accounted for the largest shares of funding for applied research (55.0%) and development (85.5%).[19] Just the top five "big tech" firms individually now spend as much on R&D as NASA or the Department of

FIGURE 5-2

Business and federal funding for R&D as share of GDP

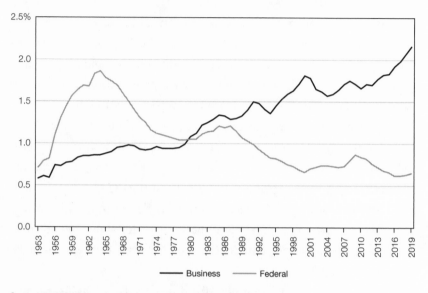

Source: National Center for Science and Engineering Statistics, 2021.

Energy.[20] In addition, foundations and private individuals are investing massive amounts in the search for major innovations.

Philanthropies have likewise fueled societal innovation. *Forbes* reported that the top twenty-five US philanthropists have donated $169 billion in their lifetimes.[21] Foundations led the way by giving $88.6 billion, 19 percent of the total.[22] The Gates Foundation *alone* spends more on health issues around the world than the World Health Organization—and more than most nations. Its impact on the fight against diseases ranging from HIV/AIDS to malaria has been truly impressive.[23]

Blending the Streams

Catalytic action has fueled remarkable successes and, increasingly, much of it has been supported by blended streams of public and private capital.

In the 1970s, for example, as oil prices skyrocketed and government officials worried about American dependence on foreign oil, DOE's Energy Research and Development Administration launched a project at Lawrence Berkeley National Laboratory to develop window coatings that reduce the emission of heat ("low-E"), saving energy in both cold and hot weather. Simultaneously, students from the Massachusetts Institute of Technology were trying to spin a research project into a company to produce low-E glass film. They couldn't raise private funding, so they reached out to DOE, which granted them $700,000 on the condition that they partner with a national lab. The new company connected with Lawrence Berkeley National Laboratory and, with its support, produced the first low-E film that could be installed in windows.

It was one thing to *produce* the film, of course. It was quite another to convince private industry to install it. DOE authorized an industry council to create uniform standards to test, label, and rate windows so that consumers could make informed decisions about them. Since then, many states have made it mandatory to label and rate windows according to the standards of this council. DOE also created the ENERGY STAR program, which allows energy-efficient products to be labeled and marketed with its logo. To further accelerate the installation of energy-efficient windows, the federal government offered tax credits based on the ENERGY STAR program. Local governments also added ENERGY STAR standards to building codes to drive the use of low-E (energy-efficient) windows.[24] These measures created a robust market that rose to $13.4 billion in the United States alone by 2020.[25]

Different stages of innovation often involve different players. In the very early stages of technological innovation, for example, government agencies are likely to fund academia to conduct basic research. As the science matures, they might take on a more direct role in testing or creating demonstration projects, through the military or the fabled Defense Advanced Research Projects Agency (DARPA). Private industry often becomes more involved as research matures to the point of product development (figure 5-3).

FIGURE 5-3

Different stages of innovation involve different players

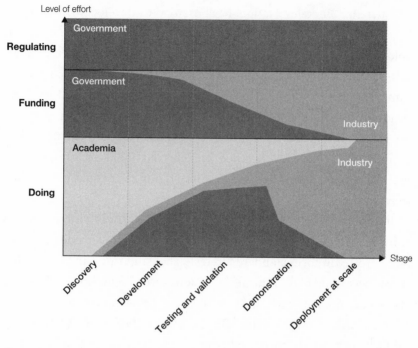

Source: Deloitte Center for Government Insights.

The same is true in social innovation. Different players tend to be involved in different stages of the development of social innovation (figure 5-4).

In general, different players excel in different roles. Government can jump-start new ideas and insulate them from social and economic risks; academia can help develop and test those ideas; and the private sector can scale them into production (table 5-2).

Consider the different roles played by government and the venture capital industry. Venture capital is skilled at funding certain early-stage innovations, but it is unlikely to fund extremely high-risk activities, such as deep space exploration, so those will typically fall to government. Further, because venture capital is sensitive to returns, it will tend to invest in less capital-intensive innovations (hence the preference for software

FIGURE 5-4

Stages and players involved in social innovation

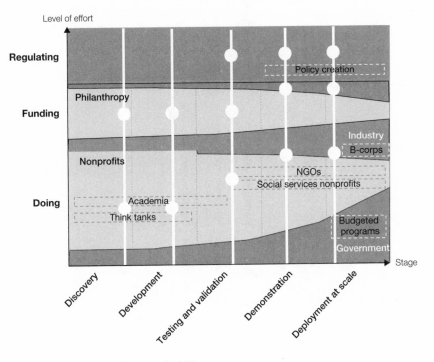

Source: Deloitte Center for Government Insights.

or service-based businesses). So when capital-intensive innovations get to the scaling stage (on projects like mass transit), the funding role may fall to government (as a single large buyer) or to established industry players.

Blended governance has led to blended *roles*. Instead of waiting for government to fund research and early-stage innovation, other players have become more active, which has increased the pace of innovation and reduced barriers between the various players' roles.

The more government tries to navigate these transitions, the more it needs new indirect tools to shape the behavior of the other players. That, indeed, is the story of the exploration of space, as the federal government pays for the development of deep-space projects but engages in closer collaboration with private companies in manned space flight.

TABLE 5-2

Roles played by key players in the innovation life cycle

	Discovery	Development	Testing	Demonstration	Deployment at scale
Government	Project funding	Convening and connecting players	Additional funding	Standards, educational programs	Tax credits, voluntary standards
Academia	Funding from university endowments	Researching ideas and products	Comparing results with scientific research	Creating partnerships with nonacademic organizations for demonstration projects	
Private sector	Investments in product development	Prototype development	Market testing		Scaling from R&D

TABLE 5-3

Government tools can support innovation either indirectly or directly

	Authority	Finance	Delivery
Direct	• Enforcement • Rulemaking • Intellectual property rights	• Grants • Contracts	• Government delivery of public goods and services • Government supply of information
Indirect	• Labeling requirements • Codes of conduct • Voluntary standards	• Government patents provided to all • Vouchers • Tax credits • Loan guarantees	• Blockchain development • Coordination • Convening of interests • Public-private partnerships

The Changing Role of Governmental Tools

Whether it is doing, funding, or regulating, government has a clear role to play in supporting innovation, especially when policymakers conclude it's in the public interest. But the changing innovation landscape means that the role of government's tools is always changing as well.

These tools can be categorized by the type of government tool involved—commands through authority, incentives through finance, or delivery through different instruments—and whether that power is exerted directly or indirectly (table 5-3).

Catalyzing Defenses for the Cyberworld

This combination of roles sets the stage for one of the biggest challenges facing policymakers in the twenty-first century: cybersecurity, with new threats that can come from anywhere. Yet government can't simply secure every organization's networks and systems. So, what can it do? Catalyze *others* to build effective defenses themselves.

On May 1, 2021, a cyberattack disabled the network of Scripps Health, the San Diego area's second-largest health system, and crippled five hospitals for a full month.[26] Patients and staff couldn't access online records or images. Medical teams had to rely on old-fashioned paper records. Smartphone apps stopped working. When patients were unable to book urgent appointments, neighboring hospitals were overwhelmed.[27]

Less than a week later, on the other side of the country, drivers along the East Coast encountered hastily shuttered gas stations, long queues at those with working pumps—and gas prices that rose by the hour. A ransomware attack was executed against the Colonial Pipeline, which provided gasoline to stations along the coast.[28] The company's CEO hurriedly paid the ransom that the hackers demanded, but it didn't come quickly enough to prevent airlines from grounding some planes and four states from declaring states of emergency.[29]

Both incidents illustrated how cyberattacks on companies, institutions, and systems can quickly disrupt the lives of average citizens. Aggressive cybersecurity demands not only heighten the need for vigilance, but also for collaboration of public- and private-sector players—and a sense of collective defense.

For both ransomware cases, the US Department of Homeland Security and the National Institute of Standards and Technology developed both direct and catalytic strategies for preventing attacks, if possible, and fighting back if necessary.[30] Months later, Russian officials arrested the hacker who had staged the attack, in a rare case of cooperation between intelligence and law enforcement officials in both countries.[31]

Complex, interconnected problems require complex and interconnected strategies. Cybersecurity is no exception. Physical assets, including much critical infrastructure, have converged with digital systems. This convergence—and the increased opportunities for attack it creates—have made governments and private industry more vulnerable than ever.

Cyberthreats are growing ever more sophisticated. State actors have found cyberattacks a useful threat to brandish. Criminals have discovered a lucrative market in cyberattacks for hire. Nations have learned that bargaining over intervention into cybercrimes has become an important diplomatic issue.

Building Israel's Cyber Strategy

The Israeli government has found itself amidst a cyber battleground, and it has made cybersecurity an essential part of the nation's strategic posture.

In 2002, Israel established a National Information Security Authority to protect the vital computer systems of public and private organizations. A decade later, it established the Israeli National Cyber Bureau to formulate cyber strategies and strengthen the nation's cyber defenses. In 2017, Israel merged these functions in its National Cyber Directorate.[32]

The government's focus on cross-sector cybersecurity, including training for K–12 students and new university research centers, has helped catalyze an astonishing level of private investment.[33] Israeli cybersecurity startups raised US$8.8 billion in 2021 alone; as of that year's end, one-third of the world's cyber unicorns (privately held startup cyber companies valued at more than $1 billion) were Israeli.[34] "We took our existing innovation ecosystem and nudged it into cybersecurity," a senior government official said. "We went from startup nation to cybersecurity nation."[35]

Most of those startups were incubated in the same place, the Israel Defense Forces' legendary Unit 8200, a not-exactly-secret national hub for cybersecurity and intelligence research.[36] Tech-savvy young Israelis perform their mandatory military service with the unit and emerge as sought-after employees and entrepreneurs.[37] This expertise has built up Israel's capacity for executing cyberattacks of its own, apparently including the 2021 Stuxnet "worm" that undermined production at an Iranian nuclear facility.[38]

Cybersecurity has become part of a vibrant Israeli innovation ecosystem, with cross-pollination among business, government, civil society, and leaders comfortable with sharing information and responsibility. Even young people performing their military service who *don't* end up in Unit 8200 come away with advanced technical training and a sense of responsibility for cybersecurity and preparedness, boosting employee competence across the nation's workforce.[39] And the broad emphasis on innovation helps the nation's institutions, from agencies to companies to nonprofits, make creative moves when economic, political, or security circumstances shift.

Keeping Estonia Online

Israel isn't alone in pursuing a catalytic cyber strategy. Estonia went digital before its neighbors—and before most other nations.[40] Its state-funded push to put everything online, however, created more points of attack for hackers. In 2006, the government established a national center to monitor threats and assist organizations across sectors in cyber defense and response.

These moves came none too soon. In the following year, nation-state hackers, ostensibly furious over a relocated Soviet-era statue, targeted government networks and infrastructure with the aim of crippling the entire nation.[41] "The attacks were aimed at the essential electronic infrastructure of the Republic of Estonia," said Minister of Defense Jaak Aaviksoo. "All major commercial banks, telcos, media outlets and name servers—the phone books of the Internet—felt the impact, and this affected most of the Estonian population. This was the first time that a botnet threatened the national security of an entire nation."[42]

A Ministry of Defense working group, tapping a network of cyber-security experts in nations such as Finland, Germany, and Slovenia, quickly tackled the assault, at one point taking the drastic step of temporarily severing Estonia's internet connections with the rest of the world.[43]

In the next few years, the government formally established entities to assess and counter cyberthreats—and expanded the nation's national-security posture to include the cybersecurity of civilian sectors. Estonia's national cybersecurity strategy requires vital private service providers, government networks, and critical infrastructure sites to map their downstream dependencies and links to help maintain "an active and cohesive cybersecurity community," with information-sharing and joint exercises.[44] Today, all sectors in Estonia sees cybersecurity as a team effort.

Battling Botnets

Law enforcement officials around the world have battled "botnets," networks of computers infected by hackers and then used to attack a target. In a "distributed denial of service" attack, the bot sends enormous numbers of digital requests through email and other media to overload a targeted computer network. Computer experts have managed to take down some botnets, but others have flourished, giving cybercriminals a tool with which to mount debilitating offensives.[45]

Every successful campaign to take down botnets has required a global coalition—and someone to lead it. Law enforcement agencies usually spearhead these efforts, but the private sector also has stepped up.

Consider Necurs, the botnet that infected more than 9 million computers worldwide after its appearance in 2012.[46] It was an especially nasty botnet because its operators rented it out to criminal clients. Some hackers using Necurs appropriated the name "Legion of Doom," the collection of supervillains who organized to counter DC Comics' Justice League. The Legion of Doom participated in ransomware, pump-and-dump scams, and the theft of banking information.

Necurs was a particular threat to computers running Windows 7 without updated virus protection. In 2020, however, Microsoft led a global counterattack in coordination with internet companies and law enforcement organizations around the world. Microsoft and its partners essentially shut Necurs down and closed the door to that particular attack.[47]

It wasn't the first time that Microsoft—whose Windows system is a favorite malware target—initiated a collaborative takedown, and it likely won't be the last. But two things are certain: catalytic leaders will be at the forefront of the battle against bots; and governments certainly will play a major, but not exclusive, role as catalysts.

We see a similar pattern in efforts against many of society's biggest challenges, where the catalyst and convening roles of the major players—including government—are remarkably fluid and intertwined.

Catalysts by Design

Government agencies that have been successful at using a variety of tools to catalyze innovation have one thing in common: individuals with deep savvy and expertise working across boundaries.

NASA's Catalytic Innovations

OpenStack software, emergency foil blankets, cordless drills—NASA keeps catalyzing innovation. Spin-off technologies that began at NASA include memory foam, the computer mouse, and many cell phone cameras. NASA intentionally encourages commercial innovation, welcoming it from all comers.

NASA understands that innovation can come from anywhere. The agency has a plethora of programs—Small Business Innovation Research, Small Business Technology Transfer, Technology Transfer, Space Technology Research Grants, Center Innovation Funds and Early Career Initiative, and NASA Innovative Advanced Concepts as well as prizes, challenges, and crowdsourcing—all to support emerging capabilities in space-related technologies.

NASA's Space Technology Mission Directorate supports a wide range of companies, including small businesses that aspire to supply innovative solutions to NASA. In 2021, for instance, NASA partnered with five US businesses selected to receive nearly $20 million in NASA funding to create lunar capabilities. In the same year, NASA selected six university-led lunar research projects to pursue advancements in in situ resource utilization and sustainable power. NASA's Artemis mission to return American astronauts to the moon will also require breakthroughs from the commercial sector. More than three thousand US companies are lending their support.

"There is a recognition and appreciation that commercial partnerships, international partnerships, university partnerships are absolutely critical to getting work done in our current environment," explains Jenn Gustetic, NASA's director of early stage innovations and partnerships.

"So the default is to have considered what partnerships with those sectors could look like in order to solve a problem."[48]

NASA also uses public procurement to drive innovation and help scale and sustain companies that support its mission.[49] NASA's grants and contracts helped to catalyze the commercial space economy, which is expected to rise to more than $1 trillion in value during the next two decades.[50] "NASA is very thoughtful about our acquisition strategy process," says Gustetic. "NASA is constantly asking: 'Is there a service or a capability that we believe is important for the agency to have access to?'"

For all the catalytic tools it has available, NASA's most critical ingredient just may be its people—and the encouragement they receive to engage with other sectors to further NASA's mission. NASA's organizational structures are critical to its success in its employees engaging the private sector. For example, it closely tracks emerging technologies to identify potential partners. NASA dedicates dozens of principal technologists and system capability leaders to such market sensing.

NASA executives also have external collaboration featured prominently in their annual evaluation criteria. "NASA doesn't have just two or three senior executives at the top that are the ones that are always out there talking, forming these partnerships and prizes," says Gustetic. "The agency really does encourage everyone to see themselves this way. This allows you to get far more exposure to potential partners and interface points."

DARPA's "Fail Fast, Fail Forward" Research

DARPA, the US Defense Advanced Research Projects Agency, pioneered strategic technological innovation in the late 1950s. Its "fail fast, fail forward" approach intentionally gives innovators sufficient room to experiment. Since its inception, DARPA has played a foundational role in the development of the internet, stealth technology, GPS, and important advances in semiconductors and deep learning; in 2013, the agency supported research on the first mRNA vaccines.

Main features of catalysts-by-design organizations

- **Focus on getting the best people.** DARPA program managers have some of the best jobs in government; they're a quintessential archetype for bridgebuilders. And NASA has a well-deserved reputation for being a great place to work.

- **Identify goals and track progress.** Both DARPA and NASA program managers focus tightly on their objectives and measure their progress along the way.

- **Cultivate scouting capabilities.** NASA employees have the curiosity and baseline knowledge to watch for new developments in technology—and the creativity to see how they might be useful.

- **Use powerful catalytic tools.** Funding and program flexibility allow DARPA and NASA to shape markets and sustain innovation. Their tools include grants, contracts, procurement, seed funds, offices of technology assessment, prizes, challenges, joint ventures, and various creative financing mechanisms.

- **Maintain strong institutional channels for engaging with the private sector and academia.** Whether through offices of public-private partnerships or innovation, nearly all catalyst-by-design agencies have dedicated channels for cross-sector engagement.

Unlike a Skunkworks, which experiments internally, DARPA funds research at outside institutions (public and private) and integrates the most successful findings into new technologies. When a technology looks promising, the agency spins it off to a business or another agency, so that DARPA can maintain its focus on innovation.

DARPA program managers (PMs) are responsible for creating connections among innovators—often academics and corporate scientists who jealously guard original research. DARPA, however, requires these partners to present their work to one another as a condition of funding. Research on parallel tracks finally overlaps when a PM decides it's time for everyone to compare notes. DARPA thus not only seeds research, but through its PMs keeps an eye out for relevant inventions that can be drawn into the agency's fold.

J. C. R. "Lick" Licklider, one of the twentieth century's most prominent computer scientists, was a legendary DARPA PM in the early 1960s. Sometimes called the "Johnny Appleseed of computing," Licklider used his time at DARPA to identify brilliant techies who might be excited by the idea of interconnected computers. The projects he funded, including MIT's AI research, Stanford's computer lab, and Xerox PARC, accelerated multiple American businesses while laying the foundation for what would eventually become the internet.

DARPA seeds projects to move them "from disbelief to mere doubt."[51] Former DARPA director Regina Dugan described how this process begins with a specific challenge: "In 2010, we were contemplating new programs, and a program manager by the name of Dan Wattendorf asked two big 'what ifs.' He said, what if we have a global pandemic and it's a novel pathogen? That will be catastrophic. . . . And what if instead we could use mRNA to create a vaccine in days and weeks instead of years?" The challenge eventually became even more specific: design vaccines that could "produce antibodies for any virus in the world" within sixty days of obtaining a blood sample.[52] These seemingly impossible challenges led to seed funding for Moderna when it had just three employees, and mandatory information sharing among other mRNA researchers.

The economy's incredible complexity demands cross-sector coordination to ensure that innovations have the supply chain needed to move them from idea to production. One industry vendor quoted in a book about DARPA said, "You just can't make anything happen in industry [today] on your own, because it's completely impossible. You have to find a partner, you have to convince your competition. . . . They ask, 'Why are you helping me with this?' and the fact is you give them information so the suppliers are in the right place to help you."[53]

DARPA can hire the best and brightest as PMs because it offers an amazing experience. DARPA hires in direct competition with finance or tech jobs, and since it can't offer a competitive salary, it instead offers workers the freedom to develop solutions to some of the world's toughest challenges, with real-world stakes. Hiring red tape is waived for these employees. PMs are hired for three- to five-year terms so they'll know they aren't stuck in a slow career track. The five-year limit also prevents the creation of bureaucratic fiefdoms.

Similar approaches have mushroomed in the US government and across the globe. Given the rapid pace of technology, traditional R&D methods relying on long gestation periods are making way for more agile approaches. Inspired by DARPA, Italy established ENEA Tech and Biomedical with an endowment of €500 million. The organization fosters economic development and competitiveness in the Italian biomedical, green-tech, agri-tech, and deep-tech industrial sectors by supporting research, development, and industrial reconversion.

Similar strategies have been developed across the world. One analysis suggests that 81 percent of OECD nations have launched initiatives to bolster innovation through public procurement. In 2021, the UK government announced the creation of an Advanced Research and Invention Agency (ARIA) with a four-year budget of £800 million. Like DARPA, ARIA will remove multiple layers of approvals across the R&D life cycle. While DARPA's objectives are tied to defense, ARIA will serve multiple government departments to address cross-cutting societal challenges.[54]

DARPA and other like government agencies catalyze by building cross-sector connections. DARPA's relatively flat hierarchy empowers PMs, who fund and oversee research teams *anywhere*, from universities to small business to large corporations.

This isn't to say they're networking without a plan. "DARPA PMs network in the literal sense of creating networks, not just plugging into them," says information technologist Benjamin Reinhardt. "The idea of focused networking is important. DARPA program managers have a clear purpose for building the network."[55] Building networks is *essential* to their missions.

Government Leaders as Catalysts

From the Manhattan Project to DARPA, there's a long and truly distinguished history of catalytic action by public agencies.[56] Yet relatively few public organizations have truly understood their potential as catalysts.

But that's changing. As more governments rely more on indirect tools, the opportunities for a far broader array of catalytic roles are growing rapidly.

Two major themes have shaped the book so far: no single organization can manage and control the biggest challenges we face, and blended government is an ideal vehicle for developing public value. With catalytic government, a third theme emerges: we need leaders who *understand* their role as catalysts, who develop the capacity to play that role, and who are ready to *use* the leverage provided by the indirect tools of government. Increasingly, it's a central role for public leaders. Our NASA and DARPA examples demonstrate that if you get the rewards and incentives right, the result will be employees who work at the intersections of societal sectors. And these bridgebuilders are the key to catalyzing the messy human process we call innovation.

In short, bridgebuilders are catalysts by design, with a clear vision of what they want to accomplish and a broad view of how to do it, in collaboration with the partners they need to achieve the goals they share.

Ten Ways Bridgebuilders Can Catalyze Innovation

Inside the Organization

- **Build dedicated scouting and sensing capabilities.** Catalyst organizations continually track emerging market capabilities. NASA has dedicated sensing and scouting teams to track the latest technological developments that can complement or supplement its missions. "We have principal technologists and system capability leaders that are responsible for understanding a vision state, a current state of the art, and current investments that can help us to achieve that future vision state across a variety of technology areas," explains NASA's Jenn Gustetic.[57]

- **Develop foresight abilities.** Scenario planning, strategy, and tracking can help governments address uncertainty and disruption in their broader ecosystems in the near *and* long terms. Bridge-builders use foresight not simply as an intellectual exercise but as a mechanism to build an organizational bias toward action in the face of uncertainty.

- **Use the right tools to spur action.** Bridgebuilders choose the right tools to incentivize and catalyze outcomes at different stages of the innovation life cycle. For the low-E project, the US federal government initially provided funds and later used tax credits to create a market for energy-efficient windows.

- **Balance risk and returns.** Bridgebuilders strike a balance between risk and return to catalyze outcomes. The US federal government used its regulatory powers to lower the market risk to commercial participation in the nuclear industry.

- **Reshape internal incentive structures.** Reimagine processes such as performance evaluations and bonuses to encourage leaders to make external connections and try new things. External collaboration is an important performance indicator in NASA's annual evaluation process. Project managers are empowered to run and fund research projects with universities and large and small businesses.

Across the Network

- **Tap into diverse perspectives.** Bridgebuilders identify and build on synergies by leveraging cross-sector competencies. The BRAIN Initiative, profiled later in the book, assembled an eclectic mix of partners including the Food and Drug Administration, DARPA, the National Science Foundation, and industry.[58]

- **Create markets to cultivate innovation.** Building a nuclear industry in the 1950s took more than government dollars. It required the creation of a commercial market for nuclear power. To catalyze the commercial nuclear industry, the US government employed various tools including regulation, policy, finance, and funding for demonstration projects. In the case of malaria from chapter 2, creating markets for mosquito nets, diagnostic equipment, and medicines through government and philanthropic funding helped lower costs enough to serve hundreds of millions of low-income people and incentivize companies to develop solutions.

- **Identify the right player for each role across the innovation life cycle.** Every innovation needs someone to do the work, whether it's research, testing, production, financing, or regulation. It's important to choose the right player for each role. "Depending on the problem you're trying to solve, and which partners you want to engage with, there's a certain expertise or flexibility that's needed to customize initiative by initiative," says NASA's Jenn Gustetic.[59]

- **Beware the "valley of death."** The transition from small-scale research funding to full-scale acquisition has been called the valley of death because it has killed so many innovative concepts.[60] Pay special attention when ideas move from research to market or implementation; innovations are most at risk at this point.

- **Align incentives to achieve shared goals.** Incentives outside the organization can support or crush innovation. For example, while everyone recognizes the importance of cybersecurity, many critical infrastructure sectors still lack adequate cyber defenses due to competing incentives. Industry-spanning efforts, such as various cyber defense collaboratives globally, can help build bridges among different industry players and reshape incentives toward collective goals.

Chapter 6

Focus on Outcomes

Internal Procedures Can't Dominate the Search for Multisectoral Success

In the opening months of the COVID-19 outbreak, public health officials saw that the disease was spreading at hyper speed. They knew that they had few of the tools they needed to slow it down—a new vaccine, strategies for treatment, and efforts to improve indoor air quality. At the end of April 2020, the *New York Times* ran a sobering article asking, "How Long Will a Vaccine Really Take?" In the piece, Dr. Anthony Fauci from the National Institutes of Health (NIH) suggested that developing and deploying a vaccine would take *at least* twelve to eighteen months, perhaps arriving by the end of 2021.

The *Times*' Stuart A. Thompson, however, called this a "rosy forecast" and said that "A vaccine probably won't arrive any time soon," because science had never before moved at such a rapid pace. "Clinical trials almost never succeed. We've never released a coronavirus vaccine for humans before. Our record for developing an entirely new vaccine is at least four years—more time than the public or the economy can tolerate social-distancing orders."

Getting a vaccine within months, Thompson said, would require scientists to "achieve the impossible." One cell biologist said a fast-track process was "worth the try—maybe we will get lucky." The *Times* concluded that the best hope for "how life could continue even without a vaccine" might lie in developing treatment drugs to help people recover faster. The prospects for a quick escape from the pandemic seemed bleak.[1]

The previous record for new vaccine development was indeed four years in 1967, for mumps.[2] With the COVID-19 vaccine, however, scientists shattered the old record; inoculations began reaching health-care professionals in December 2020. During the first month of 2021, millions of older Americans received the vaccine in what was quite simply one of the most astonishing medical advances in world history.

The story of the COVID-19 vaccine is a tale of how scientists focused squarely and powerfully on the outcome they were trying to achieve—a vaccinated populace that could get back to something approaching normal life—instead of allowing red tape to gum up research and production. A laser-like focus on the goal brought together a complex partnership of governmental and private organizations, both in the United States and abroad, to fight the biggest public health crisis of a century.

Operation Warp Speed

In the past, vaccine development typically required years to master the science, test the vaccine's efficacy, and receive governmental approval.[3] The vaccine had to be "safe"—that is, it couldn't inflict *greater* health problems on individuals than it prevented—as well as effective. Yet no vaccine is entirely risk-free; one early measles vaccine put some children in the hospital. Another developed for dengue fever produced complications and several deaths.[4] No scientist wants to make people sicker with a vaccine they developed, and no public health expert wants to undermine confidence in vaccination. The need for speed thus had to be tempered by safety concerns.

But as the pandemic paralyzed the global economy, the world couldn't wait years. Pharma companies were moving ahead with possible vaccines, but it quickly became clear that a government-led initiative would be critical to drive robust manufacturing and distribution, while ensuring safety and public confidence in the process.[5] So the Trump administration launched an ambitious partnership with private companies to develop a COVID-19 vaccine under the name "Operation Warp Speed." (The term comes from science fiction, especially the *Star Trek* television show and movie series, and means travel faster than the speed of light.)

Everyone applauded the idea, but relatively few observers thought it was likely to work. "Trekkies know that when a spaceship travels at a high warp factor, things can go wrong," two *Bloomberg Businessweek* reporters quipped.[6] Even Fauci, champion of the fight against COVID-19, wondered if the name conveyed a sense of recklessness.

And some feared that *anything* the government touched might get bogged down in endless red tape. Contract fulfillment, with its innumerable reporting requirements, can be such a chore that some biotech companies have gone bankrupt while negotiating contracts with federal agencies.[7]

From Lab to Arm in Record Time

The United States—and the world—couldn't wait for interdepartmental jockeying and a long testing regimen. But neither could anyone risk safety shortcuts. So, decision makers in government, public health, and medicine convened to rethink the vaccine development process on the fly. Operation Warp Speed aimed at dramatically accelerating the development, manufacturing, and distribution of COVID-19 vaccines, therapeutics, and diagnostics. "Innovation toward our end state is our only concern," said General Gustave Perna, the former chief operating officer of Operation Warp Speed. "It is about how to solve this complex problem."[8]

By any measure, Operation Warp Speed was a resounding success.[9] Tasks that normally would have required seven years—or longer—were completed in six months.[10] The program proved to be a genuinely successful public-private collaboration, with tangible and important results.

Operation Warp Speed pushed hard to guide the development, approval, and manufacturing of vaccines at scale, expanding from a single US manufacturing facility to a nationwide network of laboratories and factories.[11] By backstopping pharma companies financially, it freed them to invest heavily in vaccine development. It's rare for any project mission to have such clarity or such clear markers of success: hundreds of millions of doses of safe and effective vaccines, distributed as quickly as possible.

An Integrated Command Structure

Making this partnership work—and getting the incentives right—demanded strong leadership. Led by chief adviser Moncef Slaoui, former chairman of global vaccines at GlaxoSmithKline, and General Gustave F. Perna, the project's chief operating officer, Operation Warp Speed set out clear objectives for participants. An integrated command structure held teams to timelines and addressed issues as they surfaced.[12] Under tremendous time pressures, an agile approach allowed groups and companies to perform essential tasks, such as safety and efficacy testing, in parallel.

The operation became an interagency and intersectoral program involving numerous federal entities. The CDC, the Food and Drug Administration (FDA), Department of Defense (DoD), and the NIH comprised the public side of a large-scale public-private partnership.

Making it work at warp speed also demanded a different approach to contracts—specifically, the use of "other transaction authority," a class of contract used often in defense involving much less red tape. Such agreements, which got their start when NASA was created in the 1950s, have been used for advanced research projects for decades and more recently have been employed frequently by DoD. Their use dramatically streamlines the contracting process and can attract companies that might not otherwise choose to work with the government.[13]

Unprecedented Regulatory Flexibility

Operation Warp Speed streamlined the process of doing business with the federal government and protected firms from the unexpected consequences of regulatory roadblocks. With unusual regulatory and contractual flexibility, project leaders were able to get all the parties moving in the same direction in an integrated system.

The ultimate goal, of course, wasn't just to develop effective vaccines but to get them into human arms, and regulators kept that in mind when planning for manufacturing and distribution. The distribution plan was a bit ragged, but it provided a foundation for the logistics needed to get the vaccine to communities around the country.[14]

The logistical problems were especially complex because some of the leading vaccines required super-cold refrigeration during delivery—a problem exacerbated by substantial shortages of truck drivers and limits on the number of hours they could drive. To aid the effort, the Federal Motor Carrier Safety Administration waived limits on driver hours when delivering COVID-related supplies, while the Federal Aviation Administration (FAA) issued an alert warning of safety risks for those transporting super-cold materials, including dry ice.[15]

Operation Warp Speed contracted for hundreds of millions of doses— more than enough to vaccinate the entire US population—and collaborated closely on distribution with UPS, FedEx, and McKesson, each with extensive experience in transporting temperature-sensitive pharmaceuticals. A web-based IT system tracked the entire vaccine supply chain from purchasing to distribution.

The US government actively encouraged pharmaceutical companies' work by reducing their financial exposure, funding clinical trials at NIH sites, and purchasing hundreds of millions of vaccine doses. The FDA sent staffers to monitor and evaluate vaccine candidates throughout the trial process. In all, the operation "completely took away R&D risk and regulatory risk," said Dr. Michael Callahan, special adviser on COVID-19 to the assistant secretary of preparedness and response at the US Department of Health and Human Services.[16]

In a *Politico* interview, French President Emmanuel Macron praised Operation Warp Speed's "extremely innovative model" and American officials' flexible approach. He lamented that "Europe had a slower strategy," citing in particular the US public-private effort to compress clinical trials.[17] "Warp Speed has transformed the investment and R&D cycle for public health using biotechnology," Callahan said.[18]

A Model for Public-Private Partnerships

Operation Warp Speed benefited from the coordination of all the participants. By ameliorating risk for pharmaceutical companies and lowering regulatory barriers for other players, federal officials made it easy for agencies, companies, and nonprofits to produce results without becoming stuck in process concerns. And a clear, universally desirable goal helped to unite the players.

Only a broad federal program could have rallied so much funding and authority, but Operation Warp Speed left plenty of room for innovation by individual companies. For instance, pharma research teams competed fiercely for successful vaccines. While government guarantees meant that companies wouldn't have to write off failed efforts as total losses, success would be extremely lucrative down the road.

Operation Warp Speed can serve as a model for future crises, offering a clear way forward for problems ranging from climate action to homelessness. The federal government sets the goals and then clears the way for private enterprise to use its capabilities to achieve them.

Challenges for Accountability in Blended Government

Operation Warp Speed was a remarkable success story for blended government. It is a story of the integrated work of organizations across all the levels of government, and especially between government and its private-sector partners. Such efforts very often stumble on the internal rules and procedures of different organizations, which can create tall barriers to

FIGURE 6-1

Aligning different players on the end goal is key to success

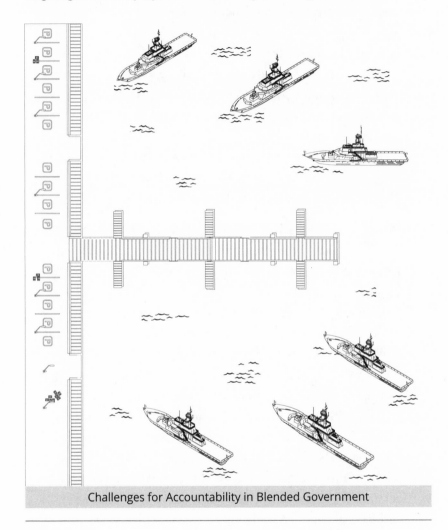

Challenges for Accountability in Blended Government

collaboration. The lesson of Operation Warp Speed is that identifying a common objective and ensuring that everyone works toward that goal is the key to success (figure 6-1). It is a case where outcomes trumped process.

The closely integrated partnership, however, also presented major challenges for accountability.

- *Who's in charge?* The more cooks involved, the harder it is to determine who's the chef in chief. It complicates the challenge of achieving the goal, but also makes it *far* harder for government to steer the project, since so many outside experts have a hand in shaping the strategy—and since so many of them have greater expertise and competence in their fields than do the government officials who supervise them.

The problem is what economists call *information asymmetry.* When one or more parties in a transaction have more or better information than others, it's hard to hold them to account.[19] The blended government strategy of Operation Warp Speed succeeded, but it was painfully obvious to all players that the private companies' superior knowledge in research and manufacturing gave them the upper hand in the relationship.

- *Private benefit at public expense?* The outsized role of private pharmaceutical companies in Operation Warp Speed stirred frequent concerns about whether they were using their role to increase their profits.

  In mid-2021, for example, the companies that had created the most successful vaccines argued that a third shot would provide stronger protection. Some experts suggested that directing initial vaccines to less-developed nations could do more to stop COVID-19—of course, it wasn't an either-or choice, since it was possible both to vaccinate Americans and to ship more doses abroad. But the boosters quickly put billions of dollars more into the companies' hands.[20] The boosters undoubtedly improved public health, but the fact that private companies could profit by creating ongoing demand for their products led to some public suspicion about their motives.

- *How much should government pay?* A strong case for blended government is that reliance on private partners brings market discipline into governmental financial decisions. In the 1980s, leading thinkers such as E. S. Savas and Stuart Butler argued that relying more on private companies was "the key to effective government," calling it "a strategy to eliminate the deficit."[21] But market discipline works best, of course, when there are large numbers of buyers and sellers. If consumers want to buy a refrigerator or a new printer, they can choose among many stores and many different products.

For many governmental programs, though, there's only one or two buyers, whether it's for a new municipal sewage system or hundreds of millions of vaccine doses. A market with a single buyer is what economists call a "monopsony," which gives sellers an enormous advantage.

- *How can we build the bridges we need across different organizations?* A major challenge for building information systems across government agencies, across levels of government, and across sectors is that data systems often have a very hard time talking with each other. The way data are coded, who collects the data, and different hardware systems organizations used to manage the data can all create enormous challenges for linking blended government through information systems (Chapter 7 will address the data challenges in-depth).

Such issues often play an important role in blended government. Efforts to reform the Rhode Island child welfare system show how smart management can solve for these problems.

Reforming Rhode Island's Child Welfare System

Soon after becoming governor of Rhode Island in 2014, Gina Raimondo faced a daunting challenge: transforming one of the nation's most deeply troubled child welfare systems. The state had the nation's fourth-worst share of youths living in group settings rather than with families, and the second-worst share of children reentering state care after family reunification.[22]

On Twitter, Raimondo promised that her administration would "turn around" and "strengthen" the state's Department of Children,

Youth and Families (DCYF).[23] Within a few years, DCYF had boosted its number of contracts with family-based foster homes by 66 percent and cut the share of foster children living in group settings by nearly a quarter.[24] Thanks to improved preventive services, DCYF also reduced the number of children entering state custody in the first place, and dramatically expanded its portfolio of family-based services and supports.

As with most child welfare systems in the United States, DCYF still has a long way to go in its transformation. Even so, the strategies it used offer broader important lessons for improving accountability and getting better outcomes from service providers.

Closing the Knowledge Gap

Governor Raimondo tapped Jamia McDonald, Rhode Island's director of emergency services, to turn DCYF around.[25] One of McDonald's critical early decisions was to enlist the help of the Government Performance Lab (GPL), an organization within Harvard's Kennedy School of Government. Founded by Jeffrey Liebman, a former high-ranking official in the US Office of Management and Budget, GPL made a name for itself by tackling difficult social problems and working with human service agencies to help them improve services and increase budget efficiency. Liebman's team specialized in reforming procurement processes— and, in particular, shifting the organizational focus from outputs to outcomes.

McDonald and the GPL team soon realized that DCYF's problems went well beyond a simple lack of funding.[26] The main issue was a dysfunctional contracting system. Despite spending about 40 percent of its budget on contracted services, ranging from residential care to family supports, DCYF knew very little about the actual interventions for which it was paying—or whether they were effective.[27]

Why the knowledge gap? The information either wasn't collected or wasn't shared. With little emphasis on coordination, different units—case management, contract and fiscal compliance, and program evaluation—

couldn't share performance data. No single unit within DCYF was accountable for improving outcomes.

Restructuring the Procurement Process

The first order of business was to listen. McDonald's team interviewed frontline caseworkers, department supervisors, and care providers on what needed fixing and how to do it. Stakeholders highlighted services facing lengthy wait lists—and programs where excess capacity made it difficult for providers to cover their fixed costs. Some services had failed to evolve to meet the shifting needs of at-risk children and families, such as the rise in human trafficking and sexual exploitation among young women. And too much money was going into residential care and not enough into *preserving* families and foster care.

"It was clear that there was a big structural problem," Liebman says. "The agency needed to fix the service mix, rebid the service array, and get more resources into supporting intact families."[28] McDonald adds, "I said to the providers 'you are selling us services that you have, but we don't want to buy those anymore.'"[29]

Instead, McDonald and GPL moved to structure each of the agency's services around fifteen outcome categories and link each to specific performance objectives, such as safely preventing unnecessary reentry into congregate care and preparing youths for independence. Then they incorporated these outcomes into 116 new contracts worth about $90 million annually. Under these, providers would have to meet certain *goals* rather than simple output metrics.

"Government contracts typically aren't structured to have anyone on the hook for outcomes," Liebman says. "Having even a small portion of a contract dependent on outcomes can make a big difference. It locks in a focus on results by making sure the outcome gets regularly measured and reviewed"[30] And instead of dictating exactly *what* services providers must deliver, the new process asked them to propose the services, supports, and resources that would best help children and families achieve the outcomes sought.

Providers at first had mixed reactions about such a radically new approach. Margaret MacDuff ran Family Service of Rhode Island, one of the state's largest child welfare providers. With thirty years of experience in the field, she knew the system from the inside out and was a strong supporter of the overhaul. Not all the providers were as positive, however. "There was a lot of resistance from some of the residential providers who had been doing a lot of work without a focus on outcomes," she said. "But we had to come up with a way to get to evidence-based practices where there hadn't been such a focus before."[31]

Six lessons from Rhode Island's child welfare system transformation

The shift away from an output mindset isn't easy, considering inflexible timescales and the complexity of outcome measurement. But the Rhode Island case provides several important lessons:

1. **Invest time in getting to common outcomes.** Governments and providers often get off track when moving to outcomes models, said MacDuff, because "they don't recognize the amount of time and partnership it really takes to get to common outcomes."[34]

2. **Agree on shared outcomes with your vendors and service providers.** Rhode Island had open and honest conversations with child welfare providers to achieve a shared understanding of outcomes.

3. **Convene stakeholders regularly.** Hold frequent check-ins to ensure better outcomes. "These meetings help to troubleshoot things, to spot opportunities to reengineer the systems, and to get better performance," said Harvard's Jeffrey Liebman.

4. **Weave pay-for-performance into contracts.** Bridgebuilders incorporate pay-for-performance clauses into contracts to help

An approach called *active contract management* was essential to the new system.[32] The idea behind this was regular, biweekly, or monthly check-ins with groups of providers at which they could share lessons learned and participate in honest conversations about what was working and what wasn't. "You need a mechanism to have the dialogue," McDonald said. "We needed to create a conversation about how to incentivize the right outcomes and share risk in a way that was workable."[33]

The sessions were set up to encourage honest dialogue, not as a stick to beat providers. "One of the challenges," Liebman says, "was getting

create and track achievable targets. "It locks in the focus," said Liebman.

5. Get the incentives right. One of the trickiest and most important pieces of successful outcome-based contracting is to choose the right incentives. Getting this wrong causes such contracting to often go off course. "No one knew how to incentivize good behavior in a way that is healthy," McDonald said. The incentives need to be both workable and trackable, with an emphasis on shared risk.[35] For example, cost-plus contracts, where contractors are paid a fixed rate on top of whatever their costs might be, create strong incentives to run up the bill because that generates more profits (although in cases where the goals are vague, it might be impossible to specify the goals more precisely). Every set of relationships has incentives built within it. Aligning the incentives with the objectives provides the clearest route to success.

6. Bring the end user into the process. Early in the process of reform, Rhode Island brought in parents, foster care providers, and other members of the system and invited hundreds of staff to listen in. "That was new [for] parents," explained MacDuff, "to ask them 'what is the menu of services you need and how can we make the system easier for you to navigate?'"

providers to believe that government was looking for something other than compliance management—and that these sessions were aimed not at *punishing* but at getting to a shared understanding."[36]

Child welfare in the United States and many other nations is delivered by a blend of public, private, and nonprofit providers as well as foster parents. They operate in an ever-changing environment in which children's lives and futures are at stake. It's among the most challenging of public-private programs for bridgebuilders to master; it can be improved but probably never perfected. What the Rhode Island reforms demonstrate, however, is that a culture of continuous communication and improvement can make a *profound* difference.

What made Rhode Island's reform truly distinctive was its focus on outcomes. Its bridgebuilders, like McDonald and MacDuff, focused both on running their agencies and, just as important, on building consensus around the policy goals, creating incentives to reinforce those goals, and weaving the broad network of service providers into a concerted whole. The focus on goals was not a top-down strategy but an effort to listen carefully to the needs of customers and make those needs the center of the strategy, from the bottom up.

All too often, governments equate *activity* with success, regardless of its actual impacts. We wouldn't try to evaluate a person's health by counting the number of trips they've made to the doctor—and agencies shouldn't measure their impact on citizens' lives by the number of interventions or services they offer.

To be sure, output measures matter and should be tracked to assess the timeliness and accuracy of service delivery. But the emphasis should be on *outcomes*, from policy design and procurement to delivery and evaluation.

Policy experts have argued for an outcomes approach for decades, but it remains relatively uncommon. Most human services programs, for example, still use metrics that tally processes, tasks, and outputs (checks issued, referrals made, and so on) rather than the quality of engagement and tangible improvements in the lives of those they serve.

Ten Ways Bridgebuilders Can Focus on Outcomes

Inside the Organization

- **Develop a culture of agile leadership.** Bridgebuilders adapt their approaches as needed to achieve positive outcomes in highly complex and dynamic situations. For example, health-care regulators in multiple nations reformed their authorization processes to bring COVID-19 vaccines to market in record time.

- **Don't conflate inputs and outputs for outcomes.** Governments shouldn't just measure their progress by the number of interventions or services they provide. To be sure, output measures matter and should be tracked, but to truly improve the well-being of families and communities, the focus should be on outcomes.

- **Shift the mindset from compliance to collaboration.** Bridgebuilders provide the freedom to design solutions without insisting on rigid practices. Instead of dictating what services providers must deliver, Rhode Island's procurement process asked providers to propose services and resources that best enable children and families to flourish.

- **Act on performance data.** Much program information is reported for regulatory purposes. Use these data to measure outcomes, hold partners accountable, and tweak programs to achieve desired outcomes.

- **Practice horizontal service delivery.** Bridgebuilders build programs, capabilities, and delivery teams to deliver outcomes across government partitions. "Vertical accountabilities naturally lead to siloed efforts, siloed policy and siloed systems in government," said Pia

Andrews, who has held senior governmental roles in Australia, Canada, and New Zealand. "Too often, government executives are driven to continually narrow the scope of their efforts. Teams are asked to stay within budget and 'minimize risk,' but we end up with gaps emerging between functions at the cost of whole programs or realizing policy intent. This creates a systemic barrier to holistic program and policy delivery."[37]

- **Proactively identify risks to devise longer-lasting solutions.**
  Bridgebuilders constantly scan their working environments to identify issues and challenges *before* they explode into major policy disasters. They identify their root causes to devise stable solutions.

Across the Network

- **Maintain flexibility about outcomes.** Jamie Van Leeuwen, the official we met in chapter 2, recalls how the city of Denver contracted with a faith-based homeless services provider that struggled to meet its outcome targets with the city. "They were afraid to tell us it wasn't working," explained Van Leeuwen. "The contract said two months, but they really needed six months, so we had to reinvent the model."

- **Develop problem-based procurement.** Contracts should describe problems and seek solutions rather than establish rigid requirements. Move from traditional, cut-and-paste contract renewals to results-driven contracting focused on performance improvement.[38]

- **Build markets around desired outcomes.** Jason Saul, executive director of the University of Chicago's Center for Impact Sciences, says one of the best ways to improve outcomes for government grantmaking is to create a market for "purchasing" social outcomes, ranging from getting kids school-ready to reducing the number of food-insecure individuals and families. "Each outcome should be binary and observable, competed among lots of providers who can bid on how many people they can help achieve a desired outcome," said Saul. "Now all of a sudden the provider is empowered to be a market participant, a producer of a product called impact that they can price and deliver."[39]

- **Focus on *personal* outcomes.** Wales has a national outcomes framework that describes how government agencies will measure improvements in social care and support services. This framework focuses on *personal* outcomes, improving well-being by aiming to understand what people want to achieve—a person might want to find stable employment, regain independence at home after a hospital stay, or reconnect with estranged parents.[40] By acknowledging people's goals and aspirations and giving them some control over their care, agencies and providers can help them find the best path forward. Scotland's self-directed support program, for example, gives beneficiaries a budget to plan their own services as equal partners with social care staff.[41]

Chapter 7

Make Data the Language

Data Creates Not Only Information but the Shared Grammar for Acting on It

In February 2020, Johns Hopkins University researcher Beth Blauer was planning a trip to India and Israel. As she was sketching out her itinerary, however, she began seeing multiple reports of individuals ending up in hospital with dry coughs and sore throats—indications that a new virus might be spreading very fast. Given the reports, Blauer decided to stay home and focus instead on this new "flu."

Her decision turned out to be pivotal to our understanding of the COVID-19 virus. Instead of getting aboard the plane, she turned to creating a dashboard to track and communicate the threat and spread of the new COVID-19 virus.

From her previous work with Martin O'Malley, mayor of Baltimore and then Maryland's governor, Blauer knew that real-time data would be crucial in understanding the new disease. She teamed up with Johns Hopkins colleagues to develop a new COVID-19 tracking system that soon dominated news coverage.

Disease tracking traditionally had been handled by federal, state, and local public health agencies. The public health system, however, found itself squeezed between its traditional culture of proceeding cautiously through careful research and a virus traveling at lightning speed. The system quickly fell behind in the fight against COVID-19.

Data has always been at the core of the public health system's work. CDC's website states that "Data drives decisions in public health, and especially at CDC. Good data across our nation's public health system is critical." But it recognized the mounting criticisms of its work. "Years of under-investment in our data" weakened its response, the agency claimed. "The central challenge of public health is to take these vast data—delivered at different times, through different channels and intermediaries, and of different quality and completeness—and turn them into useful, actionable information to improve the nation's response."[1] COVID-19 clearly presented a significant challenge to the public health system's traditional approach.

A senior CDC official spoke anonymously to a reporter to describe how its research struggled in the face of a pandemic. "It's done in a very academic way," the official explained. "Cross every 't,' and dot every 'i,' and unfortunately, we don't have that luxury in a global pandemic. There's going to be a need to have a significant cultural shift in the agency."[2] The academic approach put the agency—and with it the nation—behind as the virus spread.

As the public health community struggled, though, Blauer and her Johns Hopkins team proved to be fast and nimble. She knew immediately that the pandemic required a different approach. "This is the first time data has been such a central part of the narrative," she told the *Washington Post*.[3]

First-year doctoral student Ensheng Dong played an important role on the team. A visiting student from China, he talked with his adviser Lauren Gardner, an associate professor in the university's engineering school. Concerned about reports of a mysterious disease quickly spreading across his native country, he began tracking and mapping the reports. Dong and Gardner concluded that following cases in real time could give public health officials a leg up in combating the disease. Soon, Lainie Rutkow, a health policy professor, joined the team, as did Blauer. The Johns Hopkins Coronavirus Resource Center was born, and quickly became a staple of news coverage throughout the world.[4] Blauer added a political and policy eye to the public health, engineering, and web management skills of the other team members.

According to team member Sheri Lewis, a public health and disease surveillance expert, "The first 6 1/2 weeks, we were building the plane as it flew, and we were flying at supersonic speeds."[5] One of the first things they found was evidence that minority communities were suffering most from COVID-19; posting the relevant data helped shape the ensuing public debate. The team also highlighted the absence of important data—some states simply didn't *know* the disparate impacts of COVID-19 on their populations—and thus provided these jurisdictions with strong incentives to begin measuring the full range of COVID's awful impact. But rather than wait for all these questions to find answers, the team launched the dashboard determined to refine it over time. The quick launch and rapid adjustments made it even more useful.

As COVID-19 continued spreading, the data problem became increasingly important. Around the world, cases and deaths tended to be underreported. When data did arrive, differences in tracking methods and the time periods analyzed often made it hard for public health analysts to conduct systematic comparisons. As Johns Hopkins professor Nilanjan Chatterjee pointed out, "If the data is not as good, then our forecast in the future [will be affected by] underreported deaths . . . and that will lead to under preparation [as these predictions] help governments to prepare how many hospital beds will be needed, ICU beds, and ventilators." A news story concluded, simply, that "data around COVID-19 is a mess."[6]

In short, experts and the world's leaders lacked the basic data they needed to develop and align their strategies to fight the virus. That's why the Johns Hopkins project was so important—it helped make sense of numbers reported from around the world. Blauer and her colleagues provided what the public health system couldn't: information collected through rapid-fire data collection, displayed as it arrived. In fact, users of the Johns Hopkins website often used updates only an hour or two old.

Data as Language

The global war against COVID-19 depended on understanding the enemy, identifying where it might surface next, and determining the most effective strategies against it. Especially in the first months, the Johns Hopkins effort led by Blauer and her colleagues was vital because it provided a common base for understanding the problem across the United States and around the world.

Just as importantly, shared data provided a *common language* for the fight.

Blauer and her teammates were bridgebuilders, not in *creating* policy but by helping leaders *communicate* about strategies and their effectiveness. Sometimes, bridgebuilding is about creating the "glue" that holds the policymaking process together. Of course, having the data doesn't necessarily lead to the best policies and implementation. And different states, like California and Florida, often measured COVID-19 very differently. But without the foundation of data, decision makers were blind. The information gave them the raw material for improving their policy actions.

That was true also for Houston's remarkable efforts in the last decade to house its homeless residents, as we saw in chapter 2. When Houston's leaders set out to transform its services in 2011, the city had one of the nation's largest homeless populations.[7] The system was disjointed, with duplicative services and service gaps. "Different organizations were all working in their own lanes, according to their own rules and procedures, doing what they wanted to do. There might be 100 open shelter beds on a given night designated for mothers with kids, but we didn't have mothers with kids who needed beds," said Annise Parker, the city's former mayor.[8] It was hard to house people because it was hard to pull a disjointed system together.[9]

"Somebody could be feeding lunch at one corner and, right across the street, feeding lunch as well," said Marilyn Brown, former CEO of Houston's Coalition for the Homeless.[10] The challenge: "Nobody was looking at duplication of services or where gaps in services were based on geography."[11]

This problem was hardly unique to Houston. Government agencies and nonprofit service providers around the nation have struggled to coordinate, communicate, analyze data, and relay information effectively. Houston's sprawl made the problem far worse. It's a metropolitan area of vast complexity, larger than New Jersey, with residents who speak more than 145 languages.[12] These factors made effective delivery of services for the homeless difficult at best.

Houston's service providers had no way of knowing what services an individual had already received, or where. They had no way to share case plans or track outcomes. Some individuals received services that might not be appropriate for their needs but happened to be provided by the door on which they knocked.[13] This led Houston to make "an organized effort to look to solutions, as opposed to [just] managing the problem," recalled Mike Nichols, CEO of Houston's Coalition for the Homeless.[14]

A new, more effective system was glued together by the coalition's Homeless Management Information System (HMIS), which helps its users understand each homeless person's individual needs and concerns and share that information with others in the system.[15] Many cities have HMIS hubs, but few cities have been as effective as Houston in *using* it to attack the problem.[16] Since 2011, Houston's homeless population has been reduced by 63 percent, with the city placing more than twenty-five thousand homeless residents in housing, with a majority of them staying off the streets after two years.[17]

The most important element of the HMIS is its ability to track individuals from their first encounter with the system through all the services received—and to gauge the ultimate outcome, especially whether those helped remain off the streets.[18] A real-time collection of housing options allows service providers to visit homeless encampments, assess needs, and offer permanent housing through voucher programs. The system also helps social workers create action plans for each individual by identifying their challenges and program eligibility and then connecting them with the right service providers. Each client's HMIS record tells his or her story; each agency that provides services to a given client adds to it.[19] These data allow the coalition to identify which people need the most ongoing help—and which entities are the most appropriate to provide it.

SEARCH Homeless Services, one of the coalition's service partners, offered additional help, including daycare and preschool services, so parents could safely leave their children while visiting prospective employers and applying for jobs.[20] After Houston resident Michael Collier, a military veteran, lost his telecommunications job in 2009, he was evicted from his apartment, had his car repossessed, and ended up homeless. SEARCH helped him find a new job and housing. "I went from living under a bridge to attending Rice University," he says.[21]

The Houston initiative illustrates that government leaders and their partners increasingly recognize data as critical to success. However, while a tranche of information might be interesting on its own, it could also prove problematic if the data is of poor quality, if data is missing, or if individual numbers fail to paint a clear aggregate picture. Its real value lies in the insights it generates from data aggregation, integration, and analysis. And the data also provide a scorecard for tracking what works.

All too often, government entities don't share data sources to advance the overall mission. In many communities, information becomes siloed, underutilized by antiquated analysis tools, and managed by specialized teams that fail to connect with others. It's impossible to solve complex problems without building connections among the players—and the most important of those connections is *data* (figure 7-1).

FIGURE 7-1

Data as common language

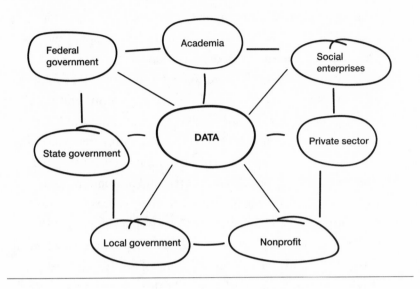

Data as a Roadmap to Collaboration

As Blauer showed, COVID-19 forced leaders to *quickly* break down information silos, coordinate with public and private entities, and expand their own pools of data talent.[22] They *had* to act quickly, because the virus wouldn't wait for them. Data sharing among agencies and within a wider ecosystem allowed cities, states, and nations to identify and track infections, develop and authorize vaccines and antiviral medications, and serve especially vulnerable citizens more effectively.

Better data collaboration requires a series of steps:

- *Make data-sharing the default.* One of the biggest problems with data is that, by default, information tends to be closely held by the agencies that create and curate it. Precisely the opposite ought to be the case. Collaboration is much easier if data are widely available. That not only reduces the hassle factor in tracking down important pieces of information. It also nourishes trust among those in the service network if the assumption is that everyone is on an equal, dependable footing.

- *Multisector data-sharing capacity.* Data Across Sectors for Health (DASH), a Robert Wood Johnson Foundation–funded program, collaborated with organizations across industries including housing, health care, and education to build a multisector data-sharing capacity aimed at improving community health and promoting health equity. Public Health Seattle and King County, Washington, used DASH to link administrative housing data with Medicaid claims to inform and implement targeted interventions, such as diabetes control and prevention classes among subsidized housing residents. "The goal was never just to stop with health and housing data," said King County DASH Project Director Amy Laurent, "but to try to build it out as much as we can to really have a robust picture of health—not just physical health, but also behavioral health—so that we can see the impacts of various programs."[23]

  DASH's learning network, All In, offers a platform for sharing experiences, ideas, and best practices.[24] From February 2017 to February 2020, 193 community collaboratives across thirty-four states and covering twenty-one social sectors participated in All In. "When people have the opportunity to get involved in projects where they're really passionate and can see how data-driven planning and evaluation allow for more effective decision-making, then they really start to understand the power of data," Laurent says.[25]

- *Integrated data systems.* In Oregon and Washington, integrated data systems connect data across various public programs to generate a comprehensive picture of individuals' needs for health and social services. An integrated data system can improve public administration and policymaking by enabling data analytics for program monitoring and evaluation, business operations, and case management. For example, researchers can use integrated data systems in longitudinal, population-based studies to examine service and program usage and utilization costs.[26]

- *Crowdsourced data gathering.* With a population of more than three million spread over seventy-eight square miles, Buenos Aires has long struggled to maintain its public infrastructure. A call center allowed citizens to log complaints or service requests for everything from fixing a pothole to removing graffiti, but delays rendered the program ineffective. In 2010, with complaints taking an average of six hundred days to resolve, city leaders aimed to streamline information flow and improve departmental coordination.[27] The city launched a mobile app that citizens can use to register complaints, with geolocation features linking problems with nearby vendors. The data acquired through the app quickly built a detailed picture of the city's infrastructure problems, and the average time needed to resolve individual complaints plunged by 93 percent.[28]

  "The dashboards can identify bottlenecks," said Rodrigo Silvosa, a Buenos Aires city official. "If we find that claims in one area of the city are not being resolved within a certain period of time, we can decide to either increase the investment and strengthen the work team or change the execution priorities so that indicator goes back to normal."[29] The very process of creating such a crowdsourced system also strengthens bridges and improves unity of effort.

- *Data-sharing agreements offering incentives for all participants.* Such agreements form the basis of any effective public-private data-sharing effort, but partners may be less enthusiastic if it seems that participation could leave them at an economic disadvantage. For this reason, it's critical to *carefully* assess costs and benefits up front, to ensure that the agreement benefits all participants. Take the time needed to develop these agreements.[30] Managing these understandings in advance can save valuable time when big problems demand quick action.

- *A streamlined interface.* Boosting the well-being of children in low-income families is one of the toughest social challenges precisely because it involves so many steps that are difficult to manage and hard to integrate. Individual providers, whether agencies or nonprofits, must partner widely to have real impact. In 2008, forty Los Angeles–area nonprofits, agencies, and faith-based organizations formed a social innovation network called the Magnolia Community Initiative (MCI), aimed at improving educational and health outcomes for children in low-income neighborhoods.

The MCI now comprises more than seventy-five partners. But getting them all moving in the same direction hasn't been easy. "Nonprofits aren't really good at collaboration," says Ronald E. Brown, a sponsor of MCI. "Our competition really isn't each other—it's poor health, social injustice, and the whole concept of systemic injustice. When we look at each other, we need to see what value we can bring to the table. It is important that organizations see the value of that, to look beyond themselves and align with the bigger vision."[31]

To that end, the MCI streamlines duplicative and cumbersome paperwork and closes gaps in social service via shared information. The organization built a dashboard for providers that includes measures of childhood health and outcomes; the parental actions (such as daily sharing of books) and family conditions (such as food security) that influence outcomes; and the specific care processes MCI member organizations offer.[32]

Data Stewardship: The Human Genome Project

In 1990, the National Institutes of Health (NIH) and the US Department of Energy launched one of the most ambitious research programs ever. As the NIH later put it, "Rather than an outward exploration of the planet or the cosmos, the Human Genome Project was an inward voyage of discovery led by an international team of researchers."[33] In concept, the goal was simple: to map the entire genetic blueprint for human beings. At the technical level, it was one of the most complex scientific efforts ever attempted.

Two years earlier, the team sketched out an ambitious project they expected would last for fifteen years. At its launch, NIH picked James Watson, one of the world's most revered molecular biologists and geneticists, to lead its part of the project. Watson won the Nobel Prize for medicine in 1962 for the work he and three collaborators conducted that established the central role DNA molecules play in shaping the genetics of human life and charted the molecule's now-famous double helix structure. Watson kicked off the project and then handed it off to Francis Collins, a human genetics researcher at the University of Michigan.

The Building Blocks of Life

By 2000, the team had produced "a working draft of the sequence of the human genome—the genetic blueprint for a human being." The research team had identified four DNA fragments of the genome. The breakthrough required putting these fragments in the right sequence.[34]

Human Genome Project researchers ultimately deciphered the human genome in three major ways: determined the order, or "sequence," of all the elements in our DNA; made maps showing the locations of genes for major sections of all our chromosomes; and produced "linkage maps," through which inherited traits (such as those for genetic disease) can be tracked over generations.

The consequences were enormous, leading to new diagnostic tests and new treatments for a host of diseases. Perhaps nowhere has the impact been more dramatic than in cancer treatment, where genomic testing has helped identify the particular risks each cancer patient faces, leading to specialized treatments directed at the individual's own cells.

Strategic Puzzles

Collins succeeded Watson as head of the Human Genome Project in 1993. He produced remarkable results through two basic strategic initiatives.

The first was Collins's leadership of a vast international consortium. NIH provided about half of the funding for the project, but government agencies and public charities financed work in other countries. In all, sixteen institutions comprised the "International Human Genome Sequencing Consortium," with three research centers in Germany; one each in France, Japan, the United Kingdom, and China; and nine scattered across the United States, from California to Massachusetts. Additional research came from the private sector.

Collins's strategy built on what NIH called a "hierarchical shotgun" approach, in which scientists took the human genome apart, assigned different groups to determine the right sequence for portions of the genome, and then reassembled the combined results. Studying parts of the genome was relatively easy, and essential to identifying gene components that might provide clues for human health. But reassembling the whole was much more difficult. Scientists worked to identify the places where one bit of the shotgun-produced genome overlapped with another, and then painstakingly put things back together.

The genius of the project wasn't just in its bold vision. It also lay in the broad public-private network Collins led to ensure that everyone worked together. It would have been impossible to reassemble the bits of the genome if the language they were using got in the way of conversations among members of the team. This led to Collins's second key strategic decision: to use an open-data approach for the research. Many researchers traditionally keep their work under wraps until they're ready to publish it. For private companies, the incentives to maintain secrecy are even greater. Their leaders knew that vast amounts of money could be made in creating new tests and cutting-edge treatments. In fact, some private companies tried to *avoid* government funding to control access to their results.

The Transformation of Research

But Collins's transparency strategy won out, with a mutual agreement that all new information be posted online within twenty-four hours of discovery. Some experts worried that the quick-release policy might introduce errors—and that other scientists, armed with the public data, might beat them to the punch in publishing new research findings. In the end, though, the twenty-four-hour model won out. And contrary to many of the scientists' fears, the open-data approach produced vastly better insights for things such as new diagnostic tests. One study found that 30 percent more new tests emerged from the study of sequenced genes in the public domain versus those closely held by private companies.[35] That underlined the importance of making data open as a tool for promoting collaboration.

"There it was, going out into the whole world," said David Haussler, who directed the University of California Santa Cruz Genomics Institute. This made it possible for scientists everywhere to explore the human genes and chromosomes, one at a time—an enormous step forward. The standard previously "was that a successful investigator held onto their own data as long as they could," Haussler said.[36]

At the beginning of the project, scientists hoped they would identify one hundred thousand "single nucleotide polymorphisms"—genetic variations that could help us understand the way in which the human genome affects health, both now and in the distant past. The researchers blew past that goal with a catalog of *one million* variations by the end of 2000. The Human Genome Project had produced a shared language for identifying the building blocks of the human body.

In the fifteen years in which he led the National Human Genome Research Institute, Collins skillfully navigated a vast assembly of scientists, multiple streams of funding, a large collection of research centers throughout the globe, and ever-present incentives for researchers to keep their data under wraps until they could release it for their own benefit.

Before the project's launch, scientific projects were frequently closed and hidden. In the wake of its enormous success, science was forever changed, not only in genomics research but in other fields as well. Researchers, even in the social sciences, began making their data openly available following publication, allowing others to build on their work more quickly. Research progress vastly accelerated. Collins succeeded in beating the target for sequencing the genome because of his skill in assembling a vast scientific network of thousands of scientists throughout the world and coordinating their work so that the pieces fit. It was a marriage of leadership with data.

Collins received a host of recognitions for his work, including the Presidential Medal of Freedom and the National Medal of Science. Some medical patients found their treatments transformed. Furthermore, the economic benefits were stunning. Between 1988 and 2010, the federal government invested $3.8 billion in the effort. A 2013 study by the Battelle Technology Partnership Practice estimated the total economic impact of the project at $796 billion, a return on the federal government's investment of 141:1.[37] In 2009, President Obama recognized Collins's success by appointing him director of the NIH, a position he held until the end of 2021.

Open-source data about the building blocks of the human genome allowed researchers everywhere to probe the role of chromosomes in causing and curing disease. The result was a new, vast, *global* network using the genome to understand health problems and create new treatments.

Data Networks Propel Taiwan's COVID-19 Response

Taiwan earned global recognition for its quick, effective response to the COVID-19 pandemic. In September 2020, as the disease raged around the world, Taiwan had reported only 496 confirmed cases.[38] Much of the credit for that early success goes to an army of civic technology "hacktivists" and to the country's digital minister, Audrey Tang. Despite her title, she doesn't run a ministry. As one of nine "horizontal ministers," she advises other parts of the government on all things tech—and, because of her passion for the United Nations' Sustainable Development Goals, environmental considerations as well.

Appointed in 2016 at the age of thirty-five, Tang was the youngest person and the first transgender individual ever to join Taiwan's cabinet.[39] Her background in the private sector included computational linguistics, crowd lexicography, and social interaction design.

She was also an active participant in g0v ("gov zero"), a civictech community.[40]

In February 2020, a crowdsourced website created by technologist Howard Wu went viral and provided the public with mask inventories at individual pharmacies, giving them accurate, up-to-date information on where to find masks. The next day, Tang engaged the government to support the effort. She suggested the nation distribute masks through pharmacies affiliated with the National Health Insurance system and open the agency's real-time database to track their availability.

Tang then invited the nation's civic tech activists to use the data in any ways they wanted. "Our civic hackers, our civil engineers in the digital space, built more than 100 tools," explained Tang. "We codesigned this distribution system with the pharmacies, with the whole of society."[41] She also created her own website as a clearinghouse for future mask information apps.[42]

This citizen-government data partnership, which quickly produced a variety of mask location apps, serves as a prime example of Taiwan's forceful response to the coronavirus. Taiwan's success highlights how a government can combine historical evidence with evolving information about current events and data-based predictions to build effective public-private responses to crises.

This pattern was seen from the beginning of the crisis. In December 2019, when a whistleblower report about a new SARS-like virus in Wuhan started circulating on internet message boards, Taiwan's medical officers took immediate action. Past experience with the 2002–2004 SARS outbreak prompted them to act quickly, while crowdsourced, real-time data allowed them to provide a fast and agile response. Scenario planning conducted after the SARS outbreak guided them as they implemented travel restrictions and health screenings for people traveling from Wuhan.[43]

In its response to COVID-19, and in other digital civic initiatives, Taiwan applies the same principles that guide open-source software communities: working from the bottom up, sharing information, improving on the work of others, seeking mutual benefit, and taking participatory collective action. Taiwan's success depended on strong two-way trust between government and the civic tech community.[44]

Tang called Taiwan's approach the "all of society model." Instead of obeying instructions issued at the top, people felt empowered to follow their own ideas, to innovate, and to remix current government policies.[45]

As with nations the world over, Taiwan had to tackle misinformation swirling around social media about the pandemic. "In the very beginning of the pandemic, what was really difficult was the twin of the pandemic and the infodemic," said Tang. "Because when people buy into conspiracy theories and buy into the fear, uncertainty and doubt as amplified by anti–social media platforms, then it becomes almost impossible for science to thrive."

Tang convinced the government to adopt a unique approach to countering misinformation. The country's 2-2-2 "humor over rumor" strategy provided a response to misinformation within twenty minutes, in two hundred words or fewer, along with two fun images. When people were panic-buying cartons of toilet paper early in the pandemic due to a rumor that it was being used to manufacture face masks, supplies started running out. The Taiwanese premier, Su Tseng-chang, released a cartoon of him wiggling his bum, with a caption saying: "We only have one pair of buttocks." The post went viral, showing how effective humor can be in stanching misinformation.[46]

Under Tang's leadership, Taiwan's civic hacking initiatives have extended far beyond the pandemic, bringing innovation into many aspects of public life. "In social innovation, democracy happens literally every day," said Tang. "When your idea goes viral, the whole society changes."[47]

Each year, Taiwan runs a three-month Presidential Hackathon, inviting everyone in the nation to suggest new ideas connected with any of the government's 169 Sustainable Development Goals. Through a process called "quadratic voting," twenty proposals were ultimately chosen for incubation. Examples of ideas to emerge from the process include using machine learning to quickly detect water leakages and using drones to detect oncoming marine debris before it reaches the coast.[48]

The teams that developed the twenty chosen ideas from beta collaboratives then owned the mechanisms for data collection, computing, and governance. "The government supports but does not control such data collaboratives," said Tang. After further developing their ideas, the top five teams receive a trophy from Taiwan's president—a microprojector that shows the president promising to turn the efforts of the past three months into national policy in the following year. "That's politically binding power as the prize, instead of any monetary prize," said Tang.[49]

During one Presidential Hackathon, Tang helped facilitate the development of a solar-powered device that can measure and log water pollution levels on an open-source blockchain. Citizens worried about industrial waste, for instance, could buy a few of these relatively inexpensive monitors, drop them in water, and create a data set that could be used to hold businesses and officials accountable for environmental regulations.[50]

Data so often appears in the policy world as a challenge for measurement. But, as we have seen in this chapter, it is far more powerful—indeed, essential—as a tool for creating a shared understanding of the policy problems that governments face, as an instrument for understanding what works and what doesn't, and as a force for building trust and confidence in the often far-flung partnerships that determine whether a program actually produces good outcomes.

Ten Ways Bridgebuilders Can Create Shared Grammar through Data

Inside the Organization

- **Build a business case for data sharing.** Bridgebuilders articulate the need to share data among *all* participants. They develop specialized structures, mechanisms, and incentives to facilitate data sharing. This entails understanding regulatory issues that conflict with data sharing and finding approved data-sharing mechanisms to realign incentive models.[51]

- **Rethink data governance.** Bridgebuilders should revisit data governance policies, redefine the parameters of data ownership and data quality standards, and strengthen data protection. "We have been very keenly focused on making sure that we have the proper privacy and cybersecurity arrangements in place in terms of procedures, protocols, but also technology," said Siim Sikkut, Estonia's former chief information officer.[52]

- **Move away from the "don't ask, don't tell" data-sharing model.** Bridgebuilders should build broader accountability in the ecosystem, especially where data aren't freely shared across organizational boundaries. The focus should be on building a "share-first" organization. "We tried to make it the culture where, if you don't share information, you can be held accountable for that," said General Stanley McChrystal, former commander of Joint Special Operations Command. "If somebody didn't know something they needed to know, and you had that information, then they shouldn't have to ask you the question: if you know they need it, you need to make sure they get the information."[53]

- **Use data as a tool to inform decision-making.** Getting the greatest value from data is a top priority for cross-sector leaders. "We need to get our data in a place where obviously it not only can be used, but it actually can mean something to somebody," says Edmonton Police Chief Dale McFee. "It boils down to not only having data, but also to be able to effectively build a team. That team will give you a lot of leverage in driving that change in your organization."[54]

- **Establish the role of data steward.** New York University's GovLab advocates creating the position of data steward in the public, private, and nonprofit sectors. These stewards collaborate across sectors to protect sensitive data while acting on the insights generated by shared data.[55]

- **Develop an appropriate talent mix.** The data team should include technical skills such as statistical analysis, data science, and data management as well as soft skills such as communication, critical thinking, and business acumen.

Across the Network

- **Build exchanges to accelerate data sharing.** Public agencies have established specialized data portals to share data with other government agencies, community groups, and industries. UNICEF invested in a data-sharing platform called Magic Box, through which private partners can share real-time data to improve humanitarian responses. The platform's applications include school mapping, household poverty, epidemic response, and natural disaster mitigation.[56]

- **Codesign data partnerships.** Taiwan's COVID-19 response highlights how cocreation can enhance effective cross-sector responses to crises. Audrey Tang invited the nation's civic tech hackers to use open government data in any way they wanted. "Our civic hackers, our civil engineers in the digital space, built more than 100 tools," Tang said. "We codesigned this distribution system with the pharmacies, with the whole of society."[57]

- **Facilitate FAIR and standardized data.** Findable, accessible, interoperable, and reusable (FAIR) principles can help ensure public data can be accessed efficiently in a standardized manner to allow for greater interoperability. The European Open Science Cloud, a digital platform that promotes data-driven science, is guided by FAIR principles. It provides the scientific community with open access to data in a variety of disciplines including medicine, arts, and agriculture, while supporting the interoperability of data sets from multiple providers.[58]

- **Adopt best practices from the broader network.** Bridgebuilders learn from each other. The NIH launched the National COVID Cohort

Collaborative cloud-based data sharing and analytics platform to study COVID-19 and identify possible treatments, helping government experts, researchers, and commercial organizations exchange data, ideas, and observations, arguably revolutionizing how clinical research is shared.[59]

Chapter 8

Redefine Accountability

We Need a New System to Replace
Traditional Top-Down Authority

When California isn't fending off atmospheric rivers, it's fighting enormous wildfires. Six of California's seven largest wildfires on record erupted between 2020 and 2021.[1] Weather extremes have made the state ever more vulnerable to catastrophic events—and they've created ever bigger collaboration challenges for the state's emergency responders.

When a wildfire burns in California, the nearest resource may be a Forest Service hotshot crew, a shiny red municipal fire engine, or a state of California CAL FIRE helicopter. Command of the fire may swiftly transfer to a different agency, and will continue to transfer as the incident grows in size and complexity. A major wildfire can utilize thousands of firefighters and support personnel. Government contractors increasingly fill gaps in manpower, and some protect individual homes on behalf of wealthy clients. The nation's number of private fire contract companies grew from 197 to 280 in the 2010s.[2] Despite this bureaucratic diversity, a fire's command team must ensure each unit gets paid, fed, and resupplied according to their contracts.

Interagency collaboration generally runs smoothly. People share a clear goal—stop the fire.

Zoom out, and wildfire budgeting gets harder. Unlike municipal firefighting, where the fire department sends a fire marshal to ensure all structures are fire resistant, the agencies responsible for fighting wildfires are not always the ones responsible for wildfire prevention. Fire prevention may require clearing brush around houses, thinning trees, or lighting controlled burns. The cost of prevention then falls on cash-strapped homeowners, indebted municipalities, private power companies, or tightly funded ranger districts. Politicians endure political discomfort from inevitable complaints about smoke, killing trees, or expense.

The cost of *suppressing* wildfires, on the other hand, usually falls to state and federal agencies, or federal disaster relief funds. During a megafire, locals are less likely to punish elected officials for the smoke.

This incentive mismatch reflects the interconnectedness of major societal challenges. In the roughly 250th year of our nation, if a problem has survived departmental attention, it's intertwined with factors beyond departmental authority. Complex, interconnected problems require collaboration. Fighting fires shows collaboration is possible. Preventing fires shows it has a long way to go.

The difference between the successful collaboration and the unsuccessful is accountability. It's incredibly difficult to know who to hold accountable for the myriad factors that contribute to megafires. It's relatively easier to hold crews accountable for extinguishing them.

Accountability in Blended Government

The complex tale of firefighting in California captures the core problem of accountability in blended government: our existing system of accountability, with its laws and rules and procedures, doesn't fit the problems our system of government is trying to solve.

While this example concerns firefighting agencies, it captures the core problem of accountability in blended government: our existing system of accountability, with its laws and rules and procedures, doesn't fit our system of governance as it's evolved.

In that system of accountability, decision makers—legislators and chief executives—create policy and delegate its execution to administrators. It's a top-down system, in which responsibility flows down the hierarchy from senior officials to the frontline personnel charged with executing the law faithfully (figure 8-1). Everyone knows their place in the policy chain and, therefore, everyone can be held accountable for their contribution.

It has the virtue of clarity—but it doesn't fit the way in which much modern governance actually works. As we've seen throughout this book, governance is increasingly blended, with different organizations and

FIGURE 8-1

Traditional structure of authority versus system of accountability in blended government

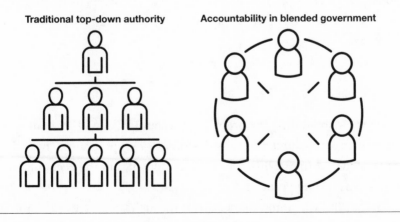

Traditional top-down authority   Accountability in blended government

individuals playing different roles in taking a policy idea to actual results. Virtually every case in this book, in fact, is part of an evolving system of blended government, driven by grants, contracts, regulations, and other forms of collaboration.

Blended government has become both a virtue—it assembles loose but effective coalitions with the expertise needed to get the job done—and a political necessity. It shares the power in making and implementing decisions to build support. Blended government makes more ambitious government possible in an era when many citizens don't want and don't trust a bigger government.

And there's the problem of accountability. Both our laws and popular expectations are based on the notion that accountability flows from the top down, through hierarchy. But the vast majority of public policies aren't executed through hierarchies and don't work from the top down. So how do we introduce accountability in a system when it is impossible to clearly know who's responsible for what?

We have a system of laws and public policy that doesn't match the governance system we want to hold accountable. When people look out their windows and see flames heading their way, they don't care about who puts them out—they just want to protect their property and their lives. But with firefighting responsibilities shared over multiple organizations, public and private, it's hard to know whom to hold accountable, or how accountability ought to work.

And if this collection of government agencies and private firefighters posed a problem of accountability, consider what happens when private players become even more deeply involved, as we shall see in the case of Medicare.

Government Programs That Aren't

Further compounding the problem of accountability is that many government programs aren't actually *government-only* programs. They might be created and (mostly) funded by government, but the accountability chain runs through other entities.

In the 2000s, a famous meme swept through senior citizens' protests about government. At a South Carolina town hall, a man stood up and told Representative Robert Inglis (R-SC), "Keep your government hands off my Medicare." Exasperated policy wonks and government officials tried to explain, to no avail, that Medicare *was* a government program. Inglis later told a reporter, "I had to politely explain that 'Actually, sir, your health care is being provided by the government.'" But, Inglis added, "he wasn't having any of it."[3]

In fact, however, the senior citizen at the Simpsonville, South Carolina town hall meeting was at least partly correct. Government doesn't actually *provide* health care under Medicare. And for many seniors, the government's role is anything but clear. Seniors contribute to the cost of the program through a monthly charge and taxpayers contribute as well. But Medicare clients visit private or nonprofit hospitals and clinics to actually receive services, and generally they have little or no contact with federal employees. The federal Centers for Medicare and Medicaid Services (CMS) runs the entire program—which serves 140 million people—with just 4,800 employees.[4] The University of Texas at Austin, by contrast, has 4.5 times as many employees as CMS to serve about 50,000 students.[5]

Then, of course, there are the Medicare Advantage programs, which look like and are advertised as full-service insurance programs, offering everything from prescription drug coverage to health club benefits.

Recipients and providers alike have long worried that government would swoop in and destroy their freedom to make their own health-care choices. At the same time, just about everyone connected with these programs has worried that they're unaccountable to *anyone*. The US Government Accountability Office has had Medicare on its "high-risk list" of programs prone to fraud, waste, abuse, and mismanagement since 1990.[6]

Medicare is a premier example of the ways in which government and its private partners work together to create public value—and how private organizations play a huge role in shaping the outcomes. Such complex partnerships, however, require a new system of accountability to guide them. Often, where power is blended, there's neither clear accountability nor a clear alternative for creating it.[7]

Modern democracies operate under a rule of law that protects the rights of individuals, restricts the power of officials, and promotes accountability for government administrators. This has generally played out in top-down hierarchies, the traditional pyramid shape of government organizations. The tradition has all kinds of pathologies, including complaints that bureaucracies have become inflexible, rulebound, and unresponsive. The American scholar Philip K. Howard has described this as the "rule of nobody," in which problems abound and bureaucracies are everywhere but, all too often, *no one* has the power to actually get things done.[8]

Despite its manifest problems, hierarchical authority has an enduring virtue: it provides both a theory and practical tools to control the power of bureaucrats. Administrators have only those powers granted by elected officials and those officials can, at least in theory, hold administrators accountable. But blended government confounds our understanding of accountability.

The Private Parts of Public Programs

The firefighting and Medicare stories open a window into the broader question of who controls the government's work—and its purse strings. Professor Paul C. Light has examined the "true size of government," and he found that the federal government's "blended workforce" of civil servants, postal workers, active-duty members of the military, contractors, and grantees amounts to about 10 million persons. Federal civil servants account for just 20 percent of the federal government's total workforce, while grantees and contractors make up 62 percent of the total.[9]

This isn't as large an imbalance as is the case with Medicare (and its sister program, Medicaid), but it's impossible to miss the fact that outside actors play a decisive role in governmental program delivery. Moreover, just a few federal programs account for a very large number of federal employees: air traffic control (48,000), transportation security (65,000), Social Security (60,000), tax collection (74,000), and the civilian side of the Defense Department (732,000) account for 44 percent of the total.[10] A close corollary of the proposition that no one agency controls anything that matters is that the responsibility for managing almost *everything* is shared by a very large number of nongovernmental employees.

The Multiple Challenges of Blended Government

Many nongovernmental employees are contractors involved in the creation and delivery of public programs, from the construction of spacecraft to the provision of advanced computing systems. More than twenty thousand scientists, technicians, and engineers, many of them government contractors, were involved in the development and construction of the $10 billion James Webb Space Telescope. In information management, technology companies like Amazon Web Services (AWS) provide cloud computing resources for thousands of government agencies. Even the CIA has contracted with commercial technology providers for tens of billions of dollars of contracts involving the management of supersecret information.

In fact, the federal government spends more than $400 billion a year on contracts, split about equally between purchases of products (such as computers and military gear) and services (such as architectural and engineering services). The federal government, of course, has been buying products since George Washington was a general. But it increasingly relies on contractors for a very wide range of services.

The relationship has been reciprocal. Many companies earn the majority of their revenues from the government, supporting military operations, the intelligence community, homeland security, veterans' affairs, and human services. Booz Allen Hamilton's involvement in some of the nation's most sensitive defense and national security challenges is reflected in the fact that 69 percent of the company's employees held a security clearance in 2019.[11] The clearances make it much easier to share critical information and to establish deep, ongoing partnerships with industry.

Governments rely on contractors because they don't have enough employees to do the work; because contractors often have experience that's hard to acquire in government; because contractors aren't locked into the government's pay system; and because contractors give the government more flexibility in increasing or downsizing staffing as needed. The private role has grown significantly over time, establishing an important private voice in public programs.

Public Risks in Private Power

Increasing public reliance on the private sector, however, also poses significant risks:

- *"Inherently" governmental functions.* Since 1955, the US federal government has had policies in place to avoid competition with the private sector; in that year, the Bureau of the Budget (the agency later reorganized into the Office of Management and Budget) stated that the "federal government will not start or carry on any commercial activity to provide a service or product for its own use if such product or service can be procured from private enterprise through ordinary business channels."[12] On the other hand, "inherently" governmental functions are to be performed only by government employees.

   OMB Circular A-76 defines "inherently governmental" as "an activity that is so intimately related to the public interest as to mandate performance by government personnel."[13] The policy may seem clear, but its implementation is anything but. The Federal Activities Inventory Reform (FAIR) Act of 1998, for example, cites functions that "significantly [affect] the life, liberty, or property of private persons."[14] Many government agencies, however, contract for private security and substantial analytical advice for policy. This contracting certainly does affect the "life, liberty, or property" of private individuals, but government agencies often find this help invaluable in pursuing their mission—or saving money—or both.

   Drawing the line between commercial and inherently governmental activities turns out to be extremely difficult, and over the years the GAO has regularly highlighted conflicts. Private organizations unquestionably can create public value but ensuring that they don't perform work that should be done by government is an exceptionally difficult problem. As GAO put it, the growing reliance on contractors risks the government "losing control of its mission or contractors perform functions reserved for federal employees."[15]

- **"Smart buyers."** GAO's report highlights the need to have enough governmental oversight capacity—and to overcome what Kettl calls the "smart buyer" problem: building enough competence to know what it can and should buy from contractors; to discover who best to buy it from; and to determine whether the government is getting its money's worth.[16] When governments don't invest enough in overseeing and guiding the work done by contractors, it confounds the pursuit of the public interest.

- **Costs.** Many government contracts are based on reimbursements for contractor expenses instead of a fixed price for goods and services. The complex nature of government programs means that many things simply can't be bought off the shelf. But contracting without established prices makes it much harder to control the costs of a public-private partnership.

  The reimbursement model creates incentives for providers to prescribe extra medical treatment. Researchers have found that billions of dollars every year go to unnecessary medical procedures, and that nearly half of all Medicare patients undergo procedures that have little or no benefit.[17] One survey showed that even about a fifth of doctors believe there's a large amount of overtreatment in medical care. They cite reasons like the fear of malpractice, patient requests for special tests and drugs, and difficulties in accessing past medical records.[18] In a system where medical providers make the key decisions on health care—and health-care spending—the incentives for decisions that drive up the cost of care are inescapable.

- **Fraud.** These challenges cascade into increased risks of fraud in Medicare. GAO has noted that "There are no reliable estimates of the extent of fraud in the Medicare program, or in the health care industry as a whole." GAO continued, "By its very nature, fraud is difficult to detect, as those involved are engaged in intentional deception."[19] But the Department of Health and Human Services' Office of Inspector General has found numerous instances of fraud in the program. These include a Florida doctor charged in a

$681 million substance abuse treatment scheme; a Philadelphia-area doctor sentenced to prison for illegal distribution of oxycodone; two owners of telemedicine companies indicted for a nationwide scheme of kickbacks and bribes involving medically unnecessary braces for Medicare recipients; and four Detroit physicians found guilty of fraud for prescribing more than 6.6 million doses of opioids that were medically unnecessary. In this case, some of the prescriptions were resold by drug dealers on the street.[20]

- *The departure of private partners.* One of the biggest risks in public-private partnerships is that a private partner can simply walk away from the arrangement. The more the government depends on private partners, the bigger that risk becomes. Many private organizations have come to depend on government revenue and have strong incentives to continue their partnerships. But the government has likewise become more dependent on these partnerships to deliver the goods and services on which people depend.

- *Accountability.* As noted earlier, the complexity of many government programs makes accountability hugely challenging. In the case of Medicare, government can suffer from what economists call information asymmetry—where the service providers and insurance companies know far more about the program's operations than does the government. Accountability *requires* information, and the government shouldn't be at an information disadvantage for the programs it funds.

   The government deals with this in part by writing regulations and auditing the program to ensure compliance. But no matter how many controls are put into place, government agencies often still find it extremely difficult to hold their partners fully accountable. According to GAO, a significant share of Medicare spending—$43 billion in 2020, or more than 6 percent of all federal spending—represents "improper payments" such as duplicate payments and those made to ineligible recipients.[21]

A New System of Accountability

Controlling these risks traditionally has depended on the legislative delegation of power to the bureaucracy and the hierarchical control of operations by its leaders. As public-private partnerships increase in number, size, and scope, the scale of the problem has grown. Moreover, in many of these partnerships, applying the traditional hierarchical approach is simply impossible. The collection of complex partnerships means that there *is* no hierarchy—and frequently, no real control. Again, who's in charge when *no one* is fully in charge?

Escaping Traditional Traps

The question is no longer whether a service should be delivered by a private or public player, but instead how all the sectors—public, private, and nonprofit—should be arrayed and managed to produce the best societal outcomes. Governments must determine the kinds of systems, platforms, organizational structures, and bridgebuilding needed to operate a government that mostly orchestrates resources rather than owning them, and funds services rather than directly providing them.

Toward Systems Thinking

The simple fact is this: public bureaucracies today only rarely are instruments of direct government action. Instead, they've become holding companies for expertise, which are often employed to shape the roles of their private and nonprofit partners. Their main purpose is more and more to maintain and deploy that expertise and to connect it with partners in other organizations.

The purpose of public policy is to produce public value. In some cases, government is at the center of the ecosystem and ultimately responsible for outcomes such as child welfare. In such cases, government *must* be hands on. In other cases, such as the effort to make consumer goods more environmentally sustainable, the prime responsibility lies in private hands. Government's role in such cases is to guide and *accelerate* action.

Most fundamentally, we need *systems thinking.* We need bridge-builders who understand the full scope of the organization's work, including governing laws, policies, and regulations as well as the patterns, interdependencies, and governance structures of complex and interrelated systems. And to make all this work, we need to move away from the traditional traps and toward an approach that supports bridgebuilders.

This challenge plays out constantly in real-life examples, including the important story of the stunningly successful effort to save the world from computer collapse at the dawn of the 2000s.

Saving the World from Y2K

In the late 1990s, information technology experts began to worry that flipping the calendar to year 2000 would cause serious problems. Much of the computer systems governing everything from banking systems to streetlights had been assembled with lines of code using two digits for years—66 for the year 1966, for example. The convention originated at a time when economy in the lines of computer code was very important, but the programmers never stopped to consider what would happen when the programs reached the end of the 1900s. When the calendar flipped from 1999 to 2000, the program wouldn't be able to tell whether the date was 1900 or 2000. That, in turn, risked chaos in computer systems around the world. Experts labeled this the "Year 2000"—or Y2K—problem. The more they looked, the more problems they found. The Social Security Administration's computers *alone* contained 50 million lines of code, all of which had to be checked and fixed as necessary if the recipients were to continue getting their checks on time.

These warnings caught the ear of the White House, and President Bill Clinton created a Council on Y2K Conversion. To head it, he turned to John Koskinen, a seasoned problem solver who had brought organizations as diverse as the Penn Central railroad company and the Teamsters Pension Fund back from financial ruin. That experience brought him to Washington, DC, first as the capital's deputy mayor and then as OMB's deputy director for management.

The job was truly enormous. Programmers had to evaluate every computer system to see if it was vulnerable to collapse on New Year's Day in 2000. The problem was global. Airlines and air traffic control relied on computers, as did financial systems and satellite communications, and all of them were vulnerable to the Y2K problem. So too, it turned out, were traffic lights and water treatment plants and nuclear reactors. Koskinen later quipped, "I seemed to be a logical choice. It's possible that I was also the only one willing to take the job."

Koskinen set up shop not far from the White House and immediately made an important strategic decision. He had a blank check from the president to assemble the resources he needed, but rather than build up a large staff, he collected fewer than two dozen people to help him. His philosophy was simple—the project was immense, complex—and the federal government couldn't accomplish it on its own. Instead, he aimed to coordinate the efforts of the private companies that by necessity *had* to do most of the work. His basic strategy was to serve as a bridgebuilder.

Koskinen put together partnerships in twenty-five different areas, including pharmaceutical firms, chemical companies, utilities, finance, and many more. He worked with national trade organizations to overcome their concerns, saying "that we were from the federal government and really *were* there to help them, not tell them what to do."

Stimulating partnerships among private companies required sharing information, and in many organizations, attorneys said that doing so could open them to lawsuits and violations of antitrust laws.[22] The trial lawyers opposed the limitation on litigation. Collaboration between potential litigants helped fuel cooperation that was so badly needed.

At the state and local levels, the problem was very different. Elected officials didn't know much about the problem and it was easy for subordinates to sweep the problem away. Koskinen urged governors and mayors to regularly ask their senior leadership, "How are we doing on Y2K?" That, they discovered, signaled a high level of commitment to the problem—and told staff that they needed to have some answers the next time the senior staff met.

The problem didn't stop at the nation's borders. Koskinen attempted to focus the UN's attention on the issue but found little enthusiasm for it. So, he put together a working group of one hundred countries, and each nation began developing its own response to the pending crisis.

Koskinen clearly understood the complexity of the job and the risk he was taking leading an effort that depended so much on private action. He explained later, "I had said at my initial press interview that being the Y2K czar was the greatest bag-holder job in the world. If things went well, everyone would ask 'What was that all about?' And, if there were major failings, they would want to know 'What was the name of that guy who was supposed to be in charge?'"

When the morning of January 1, 2000, arrived, everyone breathed a sigh of relief. The predicted global shutdowns never materialized. In fact, some cynics wondered if the whole effort was a big fuss over nothing. There were enough breakthrough cases, however, to illustrate what might have happened without Koskinen's efforts. Satellites for the Defense Department's intelligence network went down. Around the United States, airports lost their windshear detectors. Japanese engineers found they couldn't monitor nuclear power plants' safety systems. And one of this book's authors went to the garage to start a car only to trigger its theft detection system. The only way to turn off the alarm was to shut down the car, only after annoying neighbors trying to sleep off their New Year's Eve hangovers.

Y2K was a *very* real crisis that was averted by Koskinen's tiny office—and by the coordinated networks they built around the world.

It was truly a remarkable effort in which private organizations created significant public value under the government's leadership. The key, Koskinen found, was "organizing a working group of people affected by a common problem and listening to what they have to say." He concluded, "With luck, we'll get through each crisis we face, but we can't rely on luck to make it happen."[23]

Within such blended systems, accountability becomes defined not by the processes created by overseers but by the players' focus on results—

and by ensuring transparency in the results achieved. It's success in creating public value, not in checking procedural boxes, that becomes the foundation of accountability and performance.

And this underlines the importance of bridgebuilders like John Koskinen, who must weave together the systems on which complex systems depend.

The New Steps to Accountability

This leads us to new steps for accountability.

- *Step away from the "how" and focus on the "what."* Instead of relying on processes, bridgebuilding brings a fresh focus on *outcomes*—on *what* policymakers need to accomplish.

- *Concentrate on connecting with partners.* Instead of concentrating on structure, bridgebuilding focuses on organizing bureaucracies to ensure strong connections—and minimal friction—with partners in outcomes.

- *Put tools at the center.* Instead of attempting to jam the entire collection of indirect tools—contracts, grants, and tax incentives, among others—into traditional bureaucracy, bridgebuilding puts the tools at the center and organizes action around them to make them as effective as possible.

- *Surround the effort with equity.* Instead of concentrating on compliance, bridgebuilding focuses on establishing rules to ensure fair and equitable treatment of individuals and providing frontline administrators with the flexibility needed to make that happen.

- *Create reservoirs of information.* Instead of organizing by hierarchy, bridgebuilding focuses on creating reservoirs of knowledge and expertise.

- *Make people a key asset.* Instead of seeing employees as cogs in a machine, bridgebuilding sees them as repositories of expertise and the organization's most valuable assets.

- *Focus on citizens.* Bridgebuilding puts citizens at the center, with a direct focus on customer service and a reminder to all that organizations exist to serve citizens, not to focus on the games bureaucracies play.

- *Make conversations transparent.* Instead of an internal process of accountability, bridgebuilders make information about outcomes clear and readily available to everyone.

- *Redefine accountability through these steps.* Accountability remains the basic building block of the rule of law, but bridgebuilding transforms accountability according to these principles.

Ten Ways Bridgebuilders Can Create a New System of Accountability

Inside the Organization

- **Become better buyers: no blind marriage—instead, deep courting.** The current methods traditionally used for many procurements is essentially a very expensive blind wedding. Winners are often chosen not necessarily because they will do the best job, or even a good job, but because they are the cheapest, or have the right mix of small business set-asides, or they know how to navigate byzantine procurement requirements. Bridgebuilders instead get up close and personal with contractors. They shorten request-for-proposal (RFP) time periods, asking vendors to focus instead on creating working prototypes so evaluators can try them out. Unlike traditional procurement, this system is more show than tell—the better to see which contractor best meets their needs.[24]

- **Identify a dedicated person or group to solve the problem.** Bridgebuilders create positions or teams that are singularly focused on solving the problem at hand. "If you can't identify that person, you're unlikely to make much progress, and it's amazing how many big issues you can identify that literally don't have a person waking up every day saying I'm responsible for the whole thing," says one senior US federal government executive we spoke to.

- **Broaden your concept of accountability.** Bridgebuilders look at the bigger picture. They move beyond a narrow description of accountability that focuses mostly on timelines and achieving near-term targets to one that is laser-focused on the end goal.

- **Employ systems thinking.** Bridgebuilders need to understand the full scope of their organization's work, including the governing laws, policies, and regulations, as well as the patterns, interdependencies, and governance structures of the multiple, interrelated, complex systems operating internally necessary to deliver on a given outcome.

- **Adopt shared funding models.** Blended government often means working across both sectors and government agencies. Shared funding models can facilitate cross-agency initiatives. The New South Wales government in Australia invested $1.6 billion into its Digital Restart Fund in 2021 to accelerate whole of government digital transformation and make the state the digital capital of the southern hemisphere.

Across the Network

- **Set clearly defined boundaries.** Bridgebuilders should ensure that they communicate and clarify stakeholder responsibilities, obligations, or commitments, so they know what they are accountable for. "They have to be accountable for commitments that they make, just the same way as we want to have governments accountable," says Simona Petrova-Vassileva, Secretary, UN Chief Executives Board (CEB).

- **Create outcome-focused partnerships with flexible, informal hierarchies.** Formal organizational structures may not always be the most enabling for cross-boundary networks. "When partnerships are focused on outcomes, the structure of those partnerships will take different forms based on the intended outcomes, aligned incentives, and the relationship managers," says NASA's Jenn Gustetic. "You want to focus on concrete outcomes first, and build a team of the right people, resources, and incentives around those outcomes. That's why not every partnership looks alike."[25]

- **Develop accountability by design.** Helsinki's Carbon-Neutral 2035 action plan, which is highly collaborative in nature, assigns clear responsibilities to specific persons and organizations. Though the city takes overall responsibility for the plan, it has delegated a specific contact person who monitors the implementation of a specific action. By clearly defining the responsibility of each stakeholder, bridgebuilders can ensure orderly implementation of cross-sector projects.[26]

- **Strengthen shared accountability.** Ensure shared accountability between stakeholders to achieve goals. Transparent processes and clear rules of engagement are necessary. So too are shared decision-making and mutual learning to grow the partnership. "There needs to be accountability for outcomes and interests that go beyond the participants," says David Warm, the executive director of the Mid-America Regional Council. "Make sure that what you do is transparent, open, and accountable to not only the partners but to the public interests that go beyond the partners."[27]

Chapter 9

Cultivate Cross-Boundary Leaders

All Partners in the Governance Process Have a Responsibility to Lead—Jointly

On the awful morning of September 11, 2001, New York City's first responders suddenly found themselves scrambling into action at the biggest crisis scene they'd ever faced. Fire Department Battalion Chief Joe Pfeiffer was blocks away when he looked up to see American Airlines Flight 11 hit the North Tower. The department's dispatcher urgently told units around the city, "Send every available ambulance, everything you got to the World Trade Center now!"[1]

In Washington, the FBI's Special Agent Christopher Combs was teaching a class at the District of Columbia Fire Academy when his pager went off. As soon as he checked, he knew two things: that the nation was under attack, and that he'd soon be on his way to New York City to support the investigation into the attacks on the towers. Combs rushed home and put in a load of laundry to get ready for what he expected would be a lengthy deployment to New York. But as he headed back to the office, listening to police radio, he heard that a plane had just hit the Pentagon. He turned on his emergency lights and sped across the bridge into Virginia, just before gridlock shut down Washington's roads.[2]

Combs arrived at the crash site just eleven minutes after American Airlines Flight 77 crashed into the side of the Pentagon. He knew immediately that first responders were facing a partial building collapse and a fire fed by aviation fuel. It was a monumental—and monumentally complex—disaster scene.

Who's in Charge?

Of everything that happened that morning, one of the more important yet least-known events was Combs's decision, as senior federal law enforcement official on the scene, to turn control of the response over to the Arlington County fire chief. Anyone who watches television or movies knows that FBI agents are take-charge types who rarely cede control to local officials—but this one did.

Combs, a former New York City firefighter, had worked as an FBI agent to develop response plans with local officials. For years, they'd drilled on what they'd do at the scene of a major event. Their basic strategy was simple: the agency with the most-needed expertise would take command. The Pentagon site was a truly enormous fire, so Arlington County Fire Department (ACFD) Chief Edward Plaugher took control of the scene. It worked remarkably smoothly, not only because of this policy, but also because a full range of agencies, including the FBI, the National Park Service, and Arlington County police and fire officials, had drilled together regularly and knew how to support each other.

Lessons from a Decade Before

The most recent drill, in fact, had been conducted just a few days before September 11. These drills had been a regular part of the Washington area's emergency response system since the 1982 crash of Air Florida Flight 90 at the 14th Street bridge. Flight 90, headed from Washington to Fort Lauderdale, barely made it into the air before crashing into the Potomac River, killing seventy passengers, four crew members, and four persons on the bridge. Four passengers and one crew member survived the accident, thanks in part to the heroic work of one passenger, Arland D. Williams Jr., who helped others to safety before drowning in the river. The bridge later was renamed to honor Williams's lifesaving work.[3]

Snowy weather complicated the emergency response, as did the crash location. The boundary between Virginia and the District of Columbia lies along the Virginia shoreline, so the crash occurred in DC waters—even though some responders swam the short distance from Virginia to rescue survivors. Due to heavy snow, access to the crash scene from the river's Washington side was almost impossible. Rescuers who reached the site found they didn't have the equipment they needed to attempt a rescue. Even assembling lifelines to reach survivors in the tail of the plane proved impossible. A US Park Police helicopter made its way from its base to pull a few survivors from the water before the plane sank.

Two days later, a *Washington Post* story lauded the work of the rescuers, but also made a telling point: "There also were some inexplicable delays in response, missed signals, occasional squabbles and too few helicopters to fly survivors to the sixty-eight doctors waiting at the area's largest shock trauma unit at the Washington Hospital Center."[4]

Given the horrific conditions, the rescue of *any* survivors was a significant accomplishment. Behind the scenes, however, emergency preparedness planners in the capital region began conferring about the struggle to coordinate the response at the scene. They soon created a joint emergency response strategy involving area local governments, the Maryland and Virginia state governments, and federal teams from agencies including the Park Police and the FBI.

Three elements anchored this strategy. First, the participants agreed to work together as a team, each agency offering its best experts to plan in common for emergencies. Secondly, they agreed to conduct regular drills to test their preparedness and response. And finally, they agreed that the unit with the expertise most needed at the scene would be put in command.

And that's why Chris Combs, the lead agent on the scene from the federal government's chief law enforcement agency, ceded control of the scene to a local fire department. It might not happen in a movie, but it was a major reason for the success of the firefighting and rescue operation at the Pentagon on September 11. It was even more remarkable because, as the after-action report described, "the physical effects of the September 11 terrorist attack on the Pentagon by far exceeded what anyone might possibly have imagined."[5]

The team quickly reached the Pentagon, set up a command center and got to work. The fire department first extinguished the flames and stabilized the building. Other team members dealt with the grim task of collecting human remains. Cadaver dogs helped search the wreckage and experts sifted it for classified documents that had been strewn everywhere. FBI agents carefully gathered evidence to help investigators probe the attack later, while Arlington County police officers handled security at the scene. An after-action report concluded: "Relations between the FBI, the ACFD, and the entire Washington Metropolitan Area fire and rescue community were outstanding, thanks largely to the work of Special Agent Combs . . . the fire community knew what to expect from the FBI."[6] In the end, it was an exceptionally difficult day for Combs. He lost two cousins in the response to the World Trade Center attacks.

Coordination was superb except in one respect: the Pentagon's own security and emergency response team hadn't been part of the post–Air Florida coordination project. Few firefighters had drilled in the vast Pentagon complex and knew little about its water lines or emergency equipment. The building's security team understandably was frantic and struggled to secure a scene with hundreds of emergency response personnel swarming through top-secret rooms amid fears of more attacks.

This nearly led to tragedy. When ACFD Captain Chuck Gibbs noticed that parts of the building were near collapse, he convinced the Pentagon team of the urgency of the problem and followed up with an order to evacuate the area. But liaising with them took valuable minutes, and the delay could have cost some first responders their lives. Even so, in the words of the after-action report, "One can only marvel" at what was accomplished.[7]

Building Cross-Boundary Leadership

The Washington-area emergency response team dealt amazingly well with a disaster that went beyond anything it had anticipated. But its experience also offers a series of lessons for the future.

First, it's often impossible to predict what problems government partners will face. Every new event carries its own requirements, and while the past can offer important lessons, it rarely repeats itself. The capital region's response to the attack on the Pentagon was based largely on the team members' experiences with the Air Florida crash. *Continuous learning*, then, is an essential element.

Responses to complex problems require a *network* of organizations with differing expertise. No one organization has the capacity to respond to most complex problems. And again, it's impossible to know in advance what expertise will be needed to deal with new problems as they arise.

Effective networks are bound together by *preexisting relationships*. What made the response at the Pentagon work was the fact that the team members knew each other, had drilled together, and trusted one another. Nothing makes that point more strongly than the fact that the Pentagon team, which had *not* been part of the drills, struggled to integrate itself with the first responders, especially in the critical first hours of the disaster. Fortunately, connections among the rest of the team were superb.

Finally, such networks aren't self-organizing. Networks need *leaders*— and deciding who will lead raises its own challenges. The capital-area emergency responders already had decided that the organization with the competence most needed at the site would lead the team.

In an important footnote to this case, the team held a small ceremony ten days after the terrorist attack. With the fire department's response and recovery operation completed, the chief turned control of the scene over to the FBI for a detailed criminal investigation. The team took the relationships among its members very seriously, and those relationships were built on respect for each other's work. As the crisis at the Pentagon evolved, so too did the network involved and the people leading it.

In fighting a crisis they'd never anticipated, the Pentagon responders proved effective due to preexisting relationships of trust, which provided a foundation for the entire effort.

Who Leads across Boundaries?

Interorganizational networks have become essential to modern administration. Multiple organizations must participate to make anything that matters work. As a 2014 report published by the IBM Center for the Business of Government noted, "Networks have been established in the public and nonprofit sector to create collective solutions to complex problems through cross-boundary action."[8]

Cross-boundary leadership doesn't necessarily entail a chain of command, formal roles, or hierarchies. Instead, it often depends on *informal* relationships among network members. A 2004 *Public Administration Review* study says that "informal power based on interpersonal relations can be more important than formal power. This means that new modes of leadership that rely on the role of the facilitator or broker are needed." Network structures depend on mutual trust among members and the recognition that they *need* each other to accomplish what each member wants.[9]

Effective networks require a long list of other factors, such as conflict management.[10] Previous studies have tended to pay far more attention to the functions networks must perform than to *who* should perform them. But concentrating on the "what" without identifying the "who" is a prescription for conflict.

In New York City, for instance, any significant emergency scene requires close coordination between the fire and police departments. But guaranteeing that cooperation can be tough in the face of existing interservice rivalries. In April 2014, for example, the city's fire and police departments agreed to play a charity hockey game. Partway through the game, a brawl between players broke out that took referees twenty minutes to quell.

Their rivalry dates from the 1980s, when fire prevention strategies cut down on the number of calls for the fire department and the NYFD was dispatched to more alarms, such as car crashes, that previously had been NYPD turf. Before this era, as retired NYPD detective Robert Louden told the *New York Times*, there was a sense that "the police department was always in charge of everything." When responsibilities for emergencies shifted, turf wars inevitably followed. At various times, the two departments fought over who had the best scuba divers and, in one case, who was in charge of dealing with a burglar stuck in a restaurant chimney, a disagreement that ended up in a fight.[11]

Such tensions usually were a source of wry jokes and embarrassing news stories. On the morning of September 11, however, the tensions got in the way of collaboration.

Coordination between firefighters and police officers on the scene was crippled by their long-standing conflicts. When an NYPD helicopter pilot indicated that the towers were likely to collapse, police commanders ordered their people out of the buildings. Along the way, police officers said they passed along word to firefighters in the stairwells, and that "some of these firefighters essentially refused to take orders from cops." At least one firefighter backed up that statement, but another said that police officers "ran past him without advising him to evacuate," according to the 9/11 Commission report.[12]

The tale of the tensions between these two departments is colorful and occasionally tragic, but it's scarcely unusual. Frictions among parts of a network can be difficult, costly, and dangerous, but they're inevitable in a world in which every part of a network has its own goals as well as common goals it shares with others. These problems can be solved by an

FIGURE 9-1

Ecosystem integrator brings together multisector partners

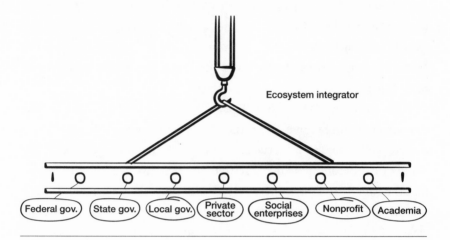

unquestioned leader who can synchronize team actions (figure 9-1). But in the real world, no organization wants to surrender its autonomy, and most feel *they* ought to lead.

This is the central problem of cross-boundary leadership. That's why the case of the Pentagon on 9/11 provides such important lessons—they put the players with key expertise in charge of the network and built trust among the players well in advance. And it's a lesson that carries forward into Maryland's job training program.

Maryland EARN: Industry-Led Partnerships

In April 2015, the city of Baltimore garnered national headlines and wall-to-wall cable news coverage for weeks on end. Protests and riots engulfed the city throughout the spring in response to the tragic death of Freddie Gray, a twenty-five-year-old black man who died of a spinal cord injury while in police custody.

On the heels of the unrest, another important—but little noticed—development also occurred in Baltimore. Jane Addams Resource Corporation (JARC), a Chicago-based nonprofit focused on reskilling manufacturing workers in the metal trades, opened its doors in a former elementary school in Park Heights, a distressed neighborhood not far from the epicenter of the protests. "We launched our training program the same day as the uprising started," recalls Regan Brewer, the executive director of JARC. "It was a challenging time to be in the city to say the least."[13] Despite the turmoil all around them, hundreds of applicants from the neighborhood lined up to apply for the program.

Founded more than three decades earlier, JARC's secret sauce was its deep understanding of the metal trades and the evolving skills needed by companies in this sector. "We live in the metalworking space," said Brewer. JARC applied this knowledge to reskill existing workers seeking to update their skill sets as well as job seekers interested in starting a new career in the metal trades. A major focus of JARC was providing second chances: more than 60 percent of the workers in their training programs have a criminal background. JARC's track record of placing job seekers in metalworking jobs is exemplary: 85 percent of trainees are placed in jobs; 89 percent of them are still employed in those jobs after 180 days.[14]

Brewer says one factor making Baltimore an attractive place for JARC to open a center was the presence of EARN Maryland (Employment Advancement Right Now), the state's unique approach to workforce development. In contrast to most other state workforce development programs, the EARN program was industry led: the employers themselves design the curriculum based on the skills they need. Industry forms "strategic industry partnerships," which could include nonprofits, workforce development boards, institutions of higher education, and local governments, to deliver the training and provide support services.

EARN brought together employers with similar talent needs and had them collaborate on grant proposals to the state. Those proposals described the skills the companies were looking for and suggested programs to train potential employees in those skills. A program could combine a variety of training methods, including classroom and online instruction, on-the-job training, internships, and certification programs as well as providing a host of support services. "We might provide a 30-hour class on blueprint reading," said Brewer. "Or it could be mapping out an entire career pathway for all the welders or machine operators. Or financial education, which is a huge component of what we do."

The EARN model contrasted sharply with how Maryland previously delivered workforce development. Mary Keller, EARN's director, dubbed the traditional model "train and pray." Training providers would provide more generalized skills training and "hope" the trainees could find a job. "A really important stakeholder was completely missing from the equation—the employers," said Keller. "The result was that training wasn't nearly as relevant as it should be."[15]

The most promising proposals received grants from EARN to design and deliver the training. To ensure a high success rate, EARN conducted a rigorous grant review and followed up to make sure the training program was creating successful job placements. "If in a program with forty people, only twenty-five get hired, the team goes back to the partnership to reassess their needs," explained Kelly M. Schulz, Maryland's former Commerce Secretary. As a state legislator, Schulz had sponsored and then helped pass the bill to create EARN. "We thought it was a really ingenious way to look at workforce development by bringing in industry so we could supply them with the exact type of workforce they needed with the exact type of skills most in demand," said Schulz. Little did she know at the time that just months later, as the newly appointed Maryland Secretary of Labor, she would be the person charged with implementing her bill.

EARN opened its doors in 2014. Since then, it has supported hundreds of strategic industry partnerships. Of the approximately 4,500 unemployed or underemployed individuals who completed EARN training for entry-level jobs, more than 84 percent secured employment.[16]

Funding for EARN came entirely from state sources. Each dollar invested in EARN generated $18.97 in economic activity. By way of comparison, the average nationwide return on a dollar invested in federally funded workforce development programs yielded just $3.41.[17]

Because EARN designed training around the actual needs of companies and job seekers, it could satisfy a wide variety of labor needs. While JARC focused on metal trades, other partnerships trained workers in areas such as information technology. For example, the employers in the

Advanced Cyber Training Consortium helped workers find employment in the field of cybersecurity. Participants got the chance to earn industry-recognized credentials and receive internships and on-the-job training to meet the requirements for entry-level positions.

Even hard-to-place job seekers found success with EARN. Civic Works, another EARN grantee, helped candidates, including those with criminal backgrounds, find employment in environmental sustainability. Of the 269 people who completed training through Civic Works, 246 secured jobs.[18] They key to its success? Close relationships with employers with real labor market needs. "We build our curriculum and partnership around really committed employers that are able to invest time in co-developing the curriculum with us as well as partnering with us around hiring for job openings," said Eli Allen, Civic Work's senior program director.

One key to EARN's success was its high degree of flexibility. "Other government workforce development initiatives have very high reporting and documentation burdens and little flexibility for us to make pivots as we implement a program," explained Allen. "In contrast, EARN is incredibly flexible. When we need to make a pivot and change our training plan or there is a change in the labor market and we need to shift some of our outcomes or funding between different training modules, they are really flexible in working with us to make those changes."

EARN demonstrated that deciding who should lead cross-sector partnerships can be one of the most critical design decisions made by bridgebuilders. In this case, the policy decision by Maryland leaders to support the cross-sector collaboration, rather than push itself to the lead, led to the program's success.

Government often needs to take the lead in creating such partnerships. However, no agency can address on its own most of the daunting and urgent challenges that society faces, from unemployment and public health to poverty and climate change. In 1997, Tony Blair, then prime minister of the United Kingdom, coined the phrase *joined-up government*, both to underline the importance of coordination across government entities and government's essential role in focusing that coordination on government's outcomes. This approach became popular across the globe. Turning the concept into effective results, however, proved elusive, because in many cases funding remained trapped in agency silos and the information technology needed to weave the connections together often fell short.[19]

Government leaders are still working to join up government—and they are making progress. A notable success story is the US federal government's multiyear initiative to create cross-agency priorities.

Federal Cross-Agency Priority Goals

In 1993, Congress passed the Government Performance and Results Act (GPRA) to support the Clinton administration's "reinventing government" initiative, inspired by the bestseller by David Osborne and Ted Gaebler.[20] The initiative promised "a government that works better and costs less," and one major goal was to create performance measures for government programs so that top officials and citizens alike could hold federal agencies accountable for their work.

For the first time in the nation's history, federal managers had to set performance goals for their programs and define measures for assessing the results. The US Government Accountability Office (GAO) applauded the law "for adding greatly to government performance—a particularly vital goal at a time when resources are limited and public demands are high."[21] A decade after its passage, GAO produced an unusually glowing report card on GPRA. The law, it concluded, "established a solid foundation of results-oriented performance planning, measurement, and reporting in the federal government," although GAO noted that agency support for the process was inconsistent.[22]

When Obama administration officials assessed GPRA, they noted a few big issues. First, they were aware the act didn't have universal support from top officials throughout the government. Furthermore, the act didn't give the administration effective leverage over activities involving multiple federal agencies. In essence, they were grappling with the major theme of this book: the growing gap between government's organizational structure and the demands placed upon it. Too many national problems stretch across the missions of different agencies, and GPRA's agency-based performance goals, while laudable, didn't provide the leverage needed to nudge the government in the direction the administration wanted.

Bridgebuilding

The search for this leverage led to the 2010 Government Performance and Results Modernization Act. A provision of the act gives the White House the power to define performance goals reaching across agency boundaries, and to maintain a focus on them for the four-year life of a presidential administration.[23]

These cross-agency priority (CAP) goals gave the Obama administration a powerful vehicle for defining major priorities across the federal government as well as tools to ensure that government managers would put their energy behind the effort. But who would lead the effort—and how could they ensure that CAP goals didn't become just one more item on already overburdened to-do lists?

The Office of Management and Budget took the lead and, in 2014, rolled out a set of goals the administration wanted to apply to all agencies. Highlights on the list included "delivering world-class customer service," "delivering smarter IT," "opening data to spark innovation," and "strengthening federal cybersecurity." GAO gave the effort a strong endorsement, concluding in 2016 that OMB had "improved implementation" of the CAP goals.[24]

Big Wins

The CAP goals produced truly significant improvements in federal management, in areas including:

- *Employee engagement.* Measures of federal employees' engagement with their jobs had fallen for three straight years, creating problems for all government programs. An effort launched in 2014 by OMB, the Office of Personnel Management, and the

White House attempted to improve employee morale by strengthening agency leadership, yielding significant results. Employee engagement scores rose from 64 to 72 percent.[25]

- *Infrastructure permitting process.* Few things frustrated persons both inside and outside government more than the long delays involved in permitting infrastructure projects. An OMB-led effort to work with agencies to shrink those delays reduced the average time needed for obtaining a permit from 4.5 years to 2.5 years, a 45 percent reduction that saved billions of dollars.[26]

- *Category management.* Federal agencies often conducted their own purchasing instead of taking advantage of the vast economies of scale that could result from bundling multiple agencies' purchases of key items ranging from security services to information technology. This bundling strategy, coordinated by teams of government procurement managers, saved $27.3 billion over three years and reduced the number of duplicative federal contracts by 43 percent.[27]

- *Security clearances.* Many important government programs require employee security clearances but processing them often led to frustratingly long delays. One CAP goal led to the creation of a "Trusted Workforce" program, aimed at both speeding clearance reviews and putting clearance holders in a continuous vetting process that prevented big backlogs when new reviews came due every five or ten years. Ninety-five percent of federal clearance holders were moved into the Trusted Workforce program, which reduced the security clearance backlog from 700,000 to 175,000 persons.[28]

The Key to Bridgebuilding

The CAP goals led to truly impressive successes as well as what GAO calls "important tools that can help decision makers address challenges facing the federal government."[29] At the core of the effort was a collection of key strategic decisions designed to ensure continuity during the life of a presidential administration as well as strong support from the very top, with tight collaboration among the White House, OMB, and federal agency managers.

The effort couldn't have succeeded without strong leadership from a small but effective group at the OMB. They worked hard to coordinate the efforts across the federal government, especially to get federal officials on board. The CAP process was designed to solve the ongoing problem of savvy, sometimes crafty federal managers who knew how to sidestep White House initiatives. These managers often had no incentive to align themselves with the latest ideas coming from the White House, regardless of which party was in power. At the same time, the OMB team knew that nothing could work without agency buy-in.

After the passage of GPRAMA, the OMB team faced the challenge of finding leverage across the government—and steering the effort with a small staff. The team's first step was to identify key players in agencies across the federal government who wake up every day thinking about and feeling responsible for a CAP goal. Then, to beef up the small OMB team, senior officials created the White House Leadership Development Program that brought in fifteen to twenty senior career officials every year who could be dispatched to work on parts of the cross-agency projects. After a decade, the program boasted more than two hundred alumni across fifty agencies. The program focused on building diversity into the selection of fellows, which program director Rebeca Lamadrid called "the secret sauce of innovation."[30]

The OMB team of thirteen eventually was supplemented by employees temporarily assigned from other federal agencies; the White House Leadership Development fellows; and then about 120 more people from across the federal government who were responsible for various elements of the CAP goals. From this base, over time the OMB team talked with more than a thousand federal employees. Without these teams and their outreach efforts to federal agencies, it would not have been possible for the CAP goals to have any impact. At the core of the bridgebuilding strategy was the remarkable skill of the OMB career officials in expanding their baker's dozen team to a hundred and then a thousand employees throughout the federal government. The small size of the central team made it nimble. The large size of its government-wide contacts gave it reach. And rather than waiting for an organization to be formally created or a network to emerge, they consciously built the network they needed to advance the CAP goals.

And that points to the core of the team's conscious bridgebuilding strategy. They made a virtue of the small size of the team, knowing they must find allies throughout government if they were going to get anything done. The core team's engagement started with the larger group of fellows and assigned employees, then key partners in agencies throughout the government, and then a thousand or more other federal partners.

The team didn't wait for a network to materialize. They consciously built the network needed to advance the CAP goals, step by step.

Ten Ways Bridgebuilders Can Lead across Boundaries

Inside the Organization

- **Create a common vision.** Bridgebuilders begin by establishing goals important to all stakeholders and building the team around them. After the 1982 crash of Air Florida Flight 90, Washington-area first responders joined in a cross-boundary strategy involving local governments, the Maryland and Virginia state governments, the federal Park Police, and the FBI to meet the common purpose of improving emergency response.

- **Identify a cross-sector "translator" to lead the effort.** It's important for bridgebuilders to identify someone to lead the effort who is adept at working across sectors. "The new disruptor in urban problem-solving is the cross-sector translator," write Elwood Hopkins and

James Ferris in "Philanthropy and the City." "The leaders who are creating transformative efforts in cities today are increasingly 'translators' who can find points of intersection between the government, business, philanthropy, and nonprofits."[31]

- **Shift to collaborative leadership.** Bridgebuilders must be able to influence persons outside their own hierarchies to achieve shared goals. The OMB team influenced a wide range of federal employees outside their formal purview, including employees temporarily assigned from other agencies, White House Leadership Development fellows, and 120 people from across the federal government who were responsible for elements of the CAP goals.

- **Empower team members.** Bridgebuilders should be comfortable with not being the smartest person in the room. They need to hire the right people, empower them, and allow them to drive performance. "Hire people who are much smarter than you—give them your vision, give them direction, and get out of the way," explained Michael A. Nutter, former mayor of Philadelphia. "Let them do their job, and more often than not, when they tell you that you're wrong or going down the wrong path, they're going to be right."[32]

- **Demonstrate empathy and understanding.** "One trait bridgebuilders have in common is a penchant for empathy, because you really have to understand different stakeholder perspectives to a degree that most don't," said Josh Marcuse, the former director of the Defense Innovation Board, now at Google. "You really have to be able to imagine all the different stakeholders coming to the table and be able to sit in every seat at the table to figure out how to structure these partnerships."[33]

Across the Network

- **Understand and leverage individual strengths.** Bridgebuilders must understand the relative strengths of each network member and provide them with appropriate roles. Special Agent Combs ensured clarity for the roles assigned to the FBI, the Arlington County Fire Department, and the Washington-area fire and rescue community.

- **Build capabilities around skills rather than authority.** Effective cross-sector leadership requires a skill set built around team building, problem solving, and impact. "It's important to understand how to build skill sets around influence rather than authority," said David B. Smith, CEO of X Sector Labs and former managing director of the Presidio Institute, "because you're working with people in organizations that often have no formal accountability to you."[34]

- **Equip partners to tell powerful stories.** "To be able to tell our stories, we created ambassadors around different community members and businesses and groups of individuals that were hugely successful," said Kelly M. Schulz, former secretary of the Maryland Department of Commerce. "We gave them little pins and certificates to talk positively about the programs that they're trying to create that are impacting real people's lives. It can be challenging, but you have to make it a mission. It has to be intentional."[35]

- **Pay attention to social relationships.** It can be easy to think of the different players simply as boxes on an organizational chart. But they're real people with real relationships. Understanding and mapping those relationships can help build trust and pinpoint where new connections need to be made, or where novel ideas may be hiding.

- **Cultivate flexible, adaptable networks.** Bridgebuilders encourage the development of networks that are dynamic, responsive to challenges, and receptive to other stakeholders. "We let our partnerships define what their outcomes are and how they view their success," said Mary Keller, EARN Maryland's program administrator. "They tell us what they think they'll be able to achieve with the funding. We really value their input . . . we've been flexible in making sure outcomes are achieved."[36]

Chapter 10

Make the Exceptional Routine

The New Era of Public Management Requires Scaling Bridgebuilding across Government

As a businessman, Michael Bloomberg was a lone wolf, making his own name a prestigious brand for his company, its famous financial data terminal, and its news outlet. His second career, as a philanthropist and public official, was *very* different, as he pivoted to building bridges to work across boundaries. In three terms as mayor of New York, Bloomberg engaged government, business, and philanthropy in myriad partnerships aimed at solving complex problems, nurturing innovation, and delivering value to the city's residents.

However singular and personal his business achievements, his legacy of a dozen years in office is largely one of collaboration.[1] That collaboration, in turn, demonstrates how tremendously useful bridgebuilding can be, even for routine government programs.

Bridgebuilding in the Big Apple

Effective bridgebuilding relies on nonpartisan credibility. Bloomberg signaled his independence early in his political career, a rare feat in a city with a long history of machine politics. Though a lifelong Democrat, he ran for mayor as a Republican and avoided fundraising and public financing, using his own fortune to outspend his general election opponent five to one. When he won, he owed few favors to the donors, unions, industry lobbies, interest groups, and party functionaries who traditionally wield power.

Bloomberg set the stage for his blended government approach from his first day in office, not long after the September 11 attacks. "Rebuilding our city," he told his inauguration crowd, "will not be easy in the current economic climate. It will require tough decisions and hard choices by all of us, in government, the nonprofit sector, business and labor."[2] Just as John Hickenlooper's approach to the job as Denver's mayor, Bloomberg's governing approach quickly centered on public-private partnerships.[3] When tackling major challenges, from climate change to domestic violence to educational reform, the mayor and his team worked to engage every sector's full capacity and capabilities.

Trees as Building Blocks

Realizing that trees could be an effective and affordable mechanism to pull carbon from the atmosphere, Bloomberg launched the Million-TreesNYC program in 2007. Led by the city's Department of Parks and Recreation and the nonprofit New York Restoration Project, it aimed to slash the city's carbon footprint by planting a million trees. Most of those trees would go in public spaces, while private partners—both individual citizens as well as businesses and nonprofits—would plant the other 30 percent on privately owned but publicly accessible land.[4]

"The big innovation for us was being able to take on the whole landscape beyond the traditional jurisdiction of the Parks Department," said Amy Freitag, executive director of the New York Restoration Project. "We had to figure out how to partner with private property holders."[5] Freitag and her colleagues ultimately secured $25 million in private contributions for MillionTreesNYC. To plant trees in low-income neighborhoods, leaders worked with community-based development organizations that encouraged property owners to request trees. The program also formed ties with a wide variety of local environmental organizations, assembling representatives from those groups into a large advisory board that provided ideas, resources, and skills.[6]

In 2015, the year after Bloomberg's third term ended, MillionTreesNYC finally reached the million mark. In the dozen years before the program launched, only 120,000 trees had been planted in the city.[7] The effort removed about 2,200 tons of air pollution a year in the city.[8]

Tackling Education through Innovative Partnerships

With climate change, Bloomberg tackled an issue about which city residents cared, but didn't necessarily experience directly. Millions of New Yorkers, though, had personal, daily experience with the city's sprawling public school system. High spending, low test scores, racial segregation, overcrowding, violence, and crumbling facilities—all were long-standing and seemingly intractable problems, even with the city's immense resources.[9] After decades of efforts, few New Yorkers put much stock in "reforms" anymore.

Bloomberg made education his signature issue and signaled a willingness to shake things up by appointing as schools chancellor Joel Klein, a prominent prosecutor with no background in education and a willingness to implement disruptive change.[10] One of Klein's big early moves was to ask charter school corporations to open city schools, giving parents new alternatives and pushing public schools to improve their performance to retain students.[11] Like many US mayors, Bloomberg had little direct authority over the city's school system, so he pressed the state legislature to grant him control. Eighteen months after he took office, a state law granted him power over the city's $12 billion education budget, 80,000 teachers, and 1.1 million students—and responsibility for their success or failure.[12]

Funding reform would be a problem no matter who held the purse strings, so the mayor and Klein ramped up efforts to attract foundation and private-sector money.[13] In Bloomberg's first five years in office, philanthropists contributed some $311 million for a wide range of education initiatives, including an academy for principal training, renovations to school libraries and playgrounds, and new funding for arts education.

The campaign raised funds from donors who had never seen themselves as having a stake in public education. Bloomberg and Klein, plugged into the corporate world, were able to make personal appeals for public service in business language. To provide vehicles for public-private collaboration, they relaunched the city's moribund Fund for Public Schools and launched an Office of Strategic Partnerships, run by the well-connected Caroline Kennedy.

The effort paid off not only in high-dollar donations but in prominent business leaders' direct engagement. *New York Daily News* publisher Mortimer Zuckerman, for instance, agreed to serve as vice chairman of the Fund for Public Schools and personally donated $1.5 million to create an academically selective high school. "I [had] made financial grants to both NYU and Columbia," said Zuckerman, "but never to the public school system."[14]

Unusual partnerships flourished. In 2004, a group of city retailers approached Kennedy and asked how they could support public education. Together, they developed Shop for Public Schools, an annual week-long event in which New York City merchants, local and national, donate a portion of sales to the program.[15] In 2008, New Line Cinemas lent glamour to the cause when the Radio City Music Hall's red-carpet premiere of *Sex and the City: The Movie* became the charitable partner for the Fund for Public Schools.[16]

Bloomberg's lessons

Few administrations have ever invested as much time, money, and focus as Michael Bloomberg's did into embedding public-private collaboration across multiple sectors. It offers a valuable study of how to make blended government work at scale. One big takeaway is similar to what we saw with Denver: the importance of dedicating staff to build relationships with private-sector partners. "Every mayor needs a team or a person whose job it is to foster partnerships with businesses and other organizations," said Patti Harris, CEO of Bloomberg Philanthropies and former first deputy mayor of New York City.[17]

Harris and her colleagues outlined a collection of key steps:[18]

- **Create an independent organization** to channel private support for public programs and maintain accountability.

- **Define opportunities** and address how partners can play a role.

- **Engage the private sector** not simply as funders but as real allies.

- **Ensure that constituents and private partners understand** the benefits of collaborative programs, the roles partners play, and how outcomes will be measured.

- **Create a robust system of performance data.** To make public-private partnerships work to everyone's satisfaction, deliverables and reporting requirements must be established and monitored. Under Bloomberg, the Fund for Public Schools watched for missed milestones and wayward initiatives, working with the city's Department of Education and funders to get programs back on track.[19]

- **Manage expectations and keep supporters on board.** Organizations should begin a broad campaign by implementing programs that are easy to replicate and that give smaller donors the sense that their support makes a real impact.[20]

Not every reform initiative succeeded and some of them were controversial, but Bloomberg's efforts nevertheless pointed toward a new model for civic governance.[21] Corporate and philanthropic funding enabled the city to experiment with approaches that would have been difficult to support with taxpayer dollars. And a focus on data—not only student testing but new school report cards—brought greater accountability to teachers, schools, and the school system.[22]

Conducting the Orchestra

As we near the end of our exploration of bridgebuilding, a fundamental question comes into focus. Is bridgebuilding a special art suited for extraordinary people facing extraordinary problems? Or is it an approach that all leaders, facing the full range of problems, can and indeed *should* use all the time?

Our path through the issues of this book points clearly toward the answer. Bridgebuilding isn't just a way to accomplish *some* things; it's how we should do *everything*. It's a set of skills that managers at all levels of all agencies, and at all levels of government, vitally need. There are three reasons for this.

First, as we've seen, bridgebuilding has proven remarkably effective in addressing a vast range of very different problems, from issues of truly global importance like Y2K to improvements in government's basic functions. It's impossible to ignore the enormous power bridgebuilders brought to the cases we've explored.

Second, as we discussed at the beginning of this book, it's nearly impossible to identify *any* important public issue that lies within the control of a single government agency. Networks of closely linked players are more than just one way of doing government. They've become the way nearly *all* parts of government work.

A fire scene, for instance, attracts emergency responders including fire and police departments and emergency medical technicians. Water quality is the responsibility of the local sewage district and its giant treatment equipment, the sanitation department that manages landfills, private as well as public trash haulers, and farmers who work to prevent stormwater runoff, among others. State road construction and snowplowing involve partnerships with private contractors. The federal government distributes foreign aid through a large network of private and nonprofit contractors. As with a conductor and his orchestra, such complex partnerships require bridgebuilders to tie the interrelated parts together (figure 10-1).

Third, the "vending-machine" approach to public policy, in which policymakers insert money and wait expectantly for goods and services to pop out, might capture the imagination of the media and ordinary citizens. But it *doesn't* capture the realities of implementation. Leaders have found that getting the results they want depends on their skill in managing across boundaries. The increasing complexity of modern public policy *demands* competent bridgebuilders.

Bridgebuilding therefore is essential even in government's most routine functions. It is even more important when it comes to solving the most daunting and wicked problems it faces.

Wicked Problems

Government increasingly faces "wicked" problems, a term describing big issues that involve huge amounts of information and *enormous* potential for unintended consequences—problems that seem to go beyond the usual strategies of problem-solving and policy analysis, and whose solutions inevitably will cross many organizational boundaries.

Wicked problems, in short, are challenges that defy traditional approaches, pose big risks, and yet demand solutions. Analysts once made a distinction between ordinary public policy problems and wicked problems, and indeed it's tempting to think of them in this way.[23] But today, few public policy problems are "ordinary," in the sense that they can be fixed with already established solutions. It's hard to find problems that don't fit the wicked-policy rubric. And it's hard, therefore, to find problems that don't need bridgebuilders.

FIGURE 10-1

Conducting the orchestra

Grand Challenges

In 2013, President Barack Obama announced a plan to "give scientists the tools they need to get a dynamic picture of the brain in action."[24] Brain-related issues, from Parkinson's to PTSD, had become a frontier of modern medicine. Understanding the mechanics of the brain might reveal how a person's complex electrochemical network reacts to shocks, and that, in turn, could lead to new treatments.

But Obama's vision—the Brain Research through Advancing Innovative Neurotechnologies (BRAIN) Initiative—would be difficult to realize. PET scans require an injection of radioactive isotopes and show activity only in broad regions of the brain. Functional magnetic resonance imaging (fMRI) shows cross-sections of the brain at work but with too little detail to be useful for much research. The BRAIN Initiative had seven goals that were specific, incredibly ambitious, and yet possible.

Obama had issued a *grand challenge*, a time-honored way of catalyzing a problem, uniting disciplines and sectors to create inventions without an existing development pipeline. Advocates characterize grand challenges as open-ended missions that are "ambitious yet achievable."[25] They challenge the world's brightest and most resourceful to coalesce around a problem, in competition or collaboration, and solve it. They draw attention from deep pockets and curious minds, directing their energy to important work.

Such challenges, ambitious in scale and scope, have long attracted hungry, ambitious minds. In 1900, German mathematician David Hilbert presented his international colleagues with twenty-three unsolved mathematical puzzles, spurring innovation in mathematics for decades to follow.[26] In 1990, the US National Institutes of Health (NIH) launched the Human Genome Project to decipher the human genetic inheritance—an effort that paid off in 2020, when researchers around the globe used the information to swiftly develop COVID-19 vaccines.[27]

Obama's neuroscience challenge attracted wide support from private entities, philanthropies, and nonprofits. A range of federal agencies became involved, acting as catalysts. The Food and Drug Administration facilitated transparency and regulatory predictability for neurological devices, while DARPA supported the initiative through neurotechnological programs, and the National Science Foundation assembled scientific and engineering resources from national and international communities.[28]

What followed was a revolution in neuroscience research. Additional funding of more than $400 million in 2017 quadrupled the initial investment and massively expanded the BRAIN Initiative's scope.[29] General Electric and the US Department of Energy joined the collaborative. Google came on board with software and infrastructure to handle the expected data deluge.[30] Academics and organizations outside neuroscience broadened the range of solutions by offering expertise in engineering, biochemistry, and other fields.[31] Japan and Australia launched parallel efforts based on international collaboration and knowledge-sharing.[32]

A grand challenge is a great way for an agency—or a president—to catalyze change without being overly prescriptive about the steps involved, and without having to fully shoulder the responsibility for managing either entries or results. In the 1980s, organizations launched several widely publicized grand challenges focused on artificial intelligence, sparking research that continues today.[33] But even more notable are grand challenges devoted to global health and development issues.[34]

In 2003, for instance, the Gates Foundation's Global Health Initiative engaged scientists across disciplines to work toward breakthrough advances for health challenges in the developing world.[35] Five years later, a committee of subject-matter experts launched Grand Challenges for Engineering, identifying goals—including lowering the cost of solar energy, ensuring access to clean water, securing cyberspace, and preventing nuclear terror—to inspire engineers to improve the quality of human life.[36]

Some grand challenges attract attention, participants, funding, and results. Others fail to create much impact. What makes challenges successful? Some factors include:

- *Clearly articulated goals.* The NIH Human Genome Project, launched in 1990, clearly stated its mission as "analyzing the structure of human DNA and determining the location of the estimated 100,000 human genes."[37] In 2011, the US Department of Energy defined its SunShot Initiative's goal as to "drive down the cost of solar electricity to $0.06 per kilowatt-hour or lower than $1 per watt."[38] This led to a reduction in the cost of average solar PV panels by 60 percent and solar electric systems by more than 70 percent. Along with that, in 2015 alone, US solar energy systems displaced more than 28 million metric tons of carbon emissions.[39]

- *A diverse set of actors to elicit innovative perspectives.* The Cancer Grand Challenge, launched in 2015 by Cancer Research UK and the US National Cancer Institute, supports seven multi-disciplinary teams and more than six hundred "investigators and collaborators" in nine countries.[40] In 2021, four teams were selected. Each received approximately $25 million over five years, giving the teams of scientists the flexibility and scale to innovate and carry out cutting-edge research.[41]

- *Identification of specific bottlenecks behind the problem.* It's important to channel resources effectively without constraining participants. During World War II, the Office of Scientific Research and Development pulled together laboratories and factories to create a scalable production process for penicillin, which previously was a major bottleneck in the treatment of malaria.[42]

- *Permit seamless collaboration.* Allow for easy exchange of knowledge and information among participating entities. Early in the COVID-19 pandemic, the NIH announced the Accelerating COVID-19 Therapeutic Interventions and Vaccines partnership, a public-private alliance to create a coordinated research strategy for vaccines and therapeutics.[43]

Grand challenges don't always generate grand results. But initiatives using a multidisciplinary approach can spur innovation by encouraging and rewarding promising ideas.

Climate Change as the Wickedest Problem of Them All

There's a strong case for the use of truly blended strategies such as grand challenges to deal with wicked problems. But the wickedest problem of all is climate change. That our climate is changing and that the pace of change is accelerating are measurable, scientific facts. Research shows us that those changes are already significant to human life and the global economy. Efforts to date to address the causes and impacts of climate change leads us to the conclusion that no individual, community, country, or continent can solve this problem alone.

As Australian political scientists Joshua Newman and Brian W. Head have noted, all climate challenges "display wicked tendencies." They have become urgent to the point that "trial and error is not politically possible," and that problems flowing from them "are far-reaching and cascading." There's been a large and unresolved struggle about the appropriate scale of action—local, national, or international—and "abundant and rigorous generation of knowledge has failed to turn the wicked social problem of climate change into a technical problem to be resolved through science."[44] And any solution will require intense and effective cross-boundary action.

The challenge is enormous. In 2021, the UN's Intergovernmental Panel on Climate Change warned of a steady, increasing parade of extreme weather events. UN Secretary-General António Guterres called it "a code red for humanity. The alarm bells are deafening, and the evidence is irrefutable."[45] But, as Deloitte's Michael Raynor and Derek Pankratz warned in their analysis on business's role in climate action:

> Averting calamitous levels of global warming is almost certain to demand action of such breadth, depth, and urgency that company- or industry-level actions alone (even aggregated and accelerated) are likely to fall short. And to realize the most ambitious impacts at a planetary scale requires the mobilization of a host of actors at the scale of entire business ecosystems, cutting across

traditional industry boundaries and often including governments, nonprofits, academia, and others.[46]

To the collection of wicked problems posed by climate change, we
can add one more. Unlike all the other cases in this book, which showed
how bridgebuilders have produced effective results, we can't report
any major progress on climate change. For climate activists, the frus-
tration has been that increasingly powerful evidence hasn't produced
effective joint action.

There have been important steps, to be sure. Car manufacturers have
announced plans to electrify their fleets, including Chrysler (by 2028)
and General Motors (by 2035). Ford plans to electrify at least 40 percent
of its cars by 2030, and the announcement of an all-electric F-150 pickup
truck, the anchor of its best-selling F-series line, generated an enormous
amount of excitement. Electricity generation through renewable energy,
through the plummeting cost of wind and solar, has been a revolution.
But so far, it's simply not enough.

Accountability in the System of Systems

Success will depend not only on the individual actions of governments
and corporations. It also requires the creation of a "system of systems,"
because "The transition to a low-carbon economy demands the synchro-
nized transformation of multiple, interdependent systems," as one
Deloitte analysis pointed out (see figure 10-2). That report continued,
"What's needed is a more holistic system of systems approach that unlocks
critical opportunities in the transition to a low-carbon economy by working at the intersection of emerging low-carbon initiatives."[47]

The prime example is the automobile industry's electric car programs.
These companies won't be able to sell large numbers of electric cars unless
the cars have enough range to get drivers to where they want to go—and
unless they can recharge them easily once they arrive. A robust network
of rapid-charging stations, however, will be difficult to develop unless
designers and those operating charging stops are convinced there's a

FIGURE 10-2

Shifting to net-zero emissions will require transforming complex and interconnected systems across sectors

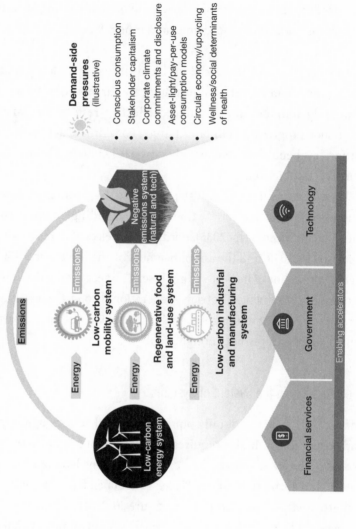

Demand-side pressures
(illustrative)

- Conscious consumption
- Stakeholder capitalism
- Corporate climate commitments and disclosure
- Asset-light/pay-per-use consumption models
- Circular economy/upcycling
- Wellness/social determinants of health

Negative emissions system (natural and tech)

Emissions

Emissions Low-carbon mobility system

Emissions Regenerative food and land-use system

Emissions Low-carbon industrial and manufacturing system

Energy

Energy

Energy

Low-carbon energy system

Financial services   Government   Technology

Enabling accelerators

Systems-level transformation

The net-zero economy will be composed of **complex and interconnected systems.**

Achieving shifts of the requisite speed and scale is only possible through **nonlinear, disruptive shifts within and across each of these systems.**

That, in turn, requires finding points of leverage that can **engender positive feedback loops or create tipping points.**

Urgently catalyzing these exponential systems changes is perhaps our last, best hope for averting the most devastating impacts of climate change.

Source: Deloitte analysis.

market for their services. Moreover, there's a fundamental problem of creating enough generating capacity to produce all the electrons that are needed and to get them to the charging stations. Success, again, will require an effective system of systems.

Simona Petrova-Vassileva, secretary of the UN's Chief Executives Board, has said that all of the players in the complex ecosystem have to move from being participants in the debate to responsible parties in action. "They have to be accountable for commitments that they make, just the same way as we want to have the governments accountable," she says.[48] Multilateralism is a building-block concept here; it's built into the definition of the action network. And even more fundamentally, it's a framework for holding all the players accountable.

Private companies can and will act on the basis of the profit motive. Consumer demand will push them toward cars that reduce the carbon footprint. Private companies also need to act more broadly to develop a systematic way of contributing to public value. And they need to be held accountable for producing what they promise.

Government's Role as System Architect

Although private companies have begun to move aggressively on climate change, the world is unlikely to grapple successfully with the problem without governments. And governments, in turn, are unlikely to play this role without fresh new strategies to deal with an increasingly complex and blended world. Climate action requires the creation of new climate ecosystems. Successful management of these ecosystems will lead governments to create new roles for leaders equipped with the skills and tools needed to produce results. These five roles are most important (figure 10-3):[49]

- *Integrators,* to build the ecosystem so that all participants can work together effectively.

- *Problem solvers,* to work out solutions for particular problems.

FIGURE 10-3

Government roles in the climate-action ecosystem

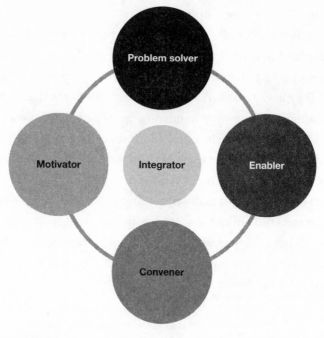

Source: Deloitte analysis.

- *Enablers,* to eliminate barriers with human capital development, data management, and tactical funding.

- *Motivators,* to provide incentives ranging from public recognition to financial support through grants, contracts, and tax incentives.

- *Conveners,* to assemble a wide range of players and foster effective collaboration on everything from conferences and hackathons to crowdsourcing and citizen engagement.

With climate change, as with all wicked problems—and, indeed, almost any public problem—effective action is inevitably *blended* action. Blended action, in turn, requires building the diverse partnerships needed to surround and act on a problem; driving work toward results; fueling the work with the necessary human, financial, and data resources; and holding the entire system accountable. Government can't act alone. Neither can private companies.

But government isn't just one more player in a complex network. Its primary role is as system architect, to catalyze action. The other players provide what each is best at. That's the way great orchestras work, and it's the key to bridgebuilding for the mid-twenty-first century and beyond.

Ten Ways Bridgebuilders Can Scale Bridgebuilder Know-How across Government

Inside the Organization

- **Spur innovative solutions to wicked problems.** Bridgebuilders can create opportunities for stakeholders to find breakthrough solutions for wicked societal problems through prizes, grand challenges, and pay-for-success approaches. More than a hundred pay-for-success arrangements have connected "buyers" of social outcomes— including governments, foundations, and philanthropists—with solvers of problems around the world.[50]

- **Build government careers around bridgebuilding.** As governments cultivate their expertise in bridgebuilding, they'll need more employees skilled in motivating, enabling, convening, and integrating players across the sectors. This could entail creating positions for public-private bridgebuilders and defining a competency model for them. "Governments need to build the internal capacities to identify leverage points outside government and a stronger ability to collaborate across sectors," said Jennifer Park of Results for America.[51]

- **Make it easier to move in and out of government.** With workers often choosing careers that span multiple roles and employers, government agencies should make it easier—and more rewarding for workers who choose to return to public service—to move in and out of the public sector. Bridgebuilders can do this by strengthening alumni programs to encourage "boomerang" employees by using special hiring authorities and creating opportunities for short-term public service assignments through secondments or programs such as the US Presidential Innovation Fellows and White House Fellows. "It's the idea that we have a workforce in the future who have been developed in part by being at NASA and in part by being in other organizations, so that we really are learning and giving people experiences that add up to a really meaningful career," said Jane Datta, chief human capital officer at NASA.[52]

- **Break down internal silos.** Wicked problems are innately multisectoral and require a whole-of-government response. Bridgebuilders support seamless linkages among various entities by developing nimble structures that transcend organizational boundaries and jurisdictions. Climate innovation, for example, calls for collaboration among government domains including transportation, health, agriculture, and energy.

- **Channel resources toward intentional relationship building.** Bridgebuilders should create internal structures and dedicated staff to reach out and engage consistently across the different sectors. "Every mayor needs a team or a person whose job is to foster partnerships with businesses and other organizations," says Patricia Harris, CEO of Bloomberg Philanthropies and former first deputy mayor of New York City.[53]

Across the Network

- **Tackle wicked problems as a team sport.** You can't tackle wicked problems without partners. Bridgebuilders need "a really high tolerance for ambiguity. You have to believe that your [organization] can contribute vitally to the mission—and that you're incapable of solving them on your own," said Josh Marcuse, the former executive director of the Defense Innovation Board who now leads Google's federal strategy.[54]

- **Understand the system you're trying to change.** Bridgebuilders need to deeply understand any system they want to change. "Many nonprofits and funders take on an issue they care about without fully understanding the larger system in which they are operating: the underlying causes of the problem, the levers needed to effect change or the other players in the space," wrote Heather McLeod Grant, CEO and founder of Open Impact. "As a consequence, many programs end up only tackling one small piece of a larger puzzle, in isolation."[55]

- **Identify the highest-impact leverage points to drive change.** Catalyze collective impact by identifying the greatest leverage points and using them to design the most effective network structure.[56] In addressing climate change, this means finding points of leverage that can stimulate positive feedback loops across industries and create tipping points to get to net zero. Governments can help shape such incentives through policies such as emissions caps and carbon pricing.[57]

- **Identify a portfolio of interventions.** Working in concert on wicked opportunities doesn't have to mean converging on one solution. More than "moon shots," this is about buckshot. A full portfolio of strategic interventions has the best chance of hitting the goal.

- **Tap into each partner's "superpower."** Bridgebuilders should ensure all partners join forces and attack the problem with a portfolio of interventions from each partner's arsenal. To tackle the opioid crisis, for example, in 2016 the CDC issued new guidelines for prescribing such drugs for chronic pain. State and federal agencies, physicians, and medical colleges updated their educational materials to better warn physicians about opioid abuse and addiction risks. As a result, prescriptions of opioids to high-risk patients fell by 29 percent.[58]

The Urgency of Bridgebuilding

n this book, we've taken aim at the fundamental challenges of modern governance and offered a holistic approach to address them:

- *Urgency.* The pace of change is accelerating and, too often, citizens are disappointed with government's results. *But smart, agile bridgebuilders can improve government's service to citizens and rebuild democracy's promise.*

- *Complexity.* Governments are facing increasingly interrelated problems. COVID-19, for example, demonstrated that health problems are also economic problems. *It is tempting to pick off individual pieces of complex problems, but solutions to these problems require engaging all their intricate and interrelated parts.*

- *Mismatch.* Despite the accelerating pace of change, governance remains trapped in the vending-machine model, where policymakers put money in the top and wait impatiently for programs to come out the bottom. That doesn't work anymore. *Blended government, with bridgebuilders at the helm, provides an alternative model of governance that matches the challenges we face today.*

- *Blending.* With the rise of blended government, there has been a massive growth in the range of actors in the public, private, and nonprofit sectors involved in governance. That, in turn, has blurred the boundaries between the sectors of society. *Instead of*

lamenting this, policymakers should embrace it—blended govern-
ment creates a host of new ways of engaging the public and new
ways of collaborating across sectors to create greater public value.

- **Data.** The increase of information provides much greater
  capability to integrate action across the sectors. Too often,
  however, the links remain unconnected. *Data can create the*
  language that bridgebuilders need to make those connections.

- **Trust.** The public's trust in government to deliver on its promises
  has dropped to historically low levels. In fact, distrust has become
  the central problem of democracy in the twenty-first century, not
  just in the United States but around the world. The core of the
  problem is that the people too often simply do not believe that
  governments can deliver on their promises. *From Police Chief*
  McFee's work in Edmonton to Audrey Tang's COVID-19 response in
  Taiwan, the bridgebuilders in this book demonstrate how trust-
  centered leaders can improve the performance of public programs.

These challenges are large. They're accelerating. If governments don't
find more effective solutions, the consequences are likely to get worse.

But, as we explore in this book, we are optimistic. We have described
more than one hundred specific strategies and tips, proven by some of
the world's best managers, to crack these problems. Even more, the book
builds a new model of public administration, a model that pushes far
beyond the creaky vending-machine approach.

The vending machine is an obsolete approach to governance. It is a
model based on hierarchies, authority, structures, and processes.
What we lay out, instead, is a model that reaches across boundaries to
connect the players who share the capacity and responsibility for producing results. It focuses on building shared commitment to important outcomes, instead of giving orders through authority. It focuses
on connecting the links that contribute to public value, instead of concentrating on reorganizing to solve every new problem. It focuses on
bridgebuilders, the key players who make connections across boundaries,
instead of management-by-process. It is a model that is horizontal, weaving

together results-oriented networks, instead of vertical, working from the top down.

What people want most is an effective way to create public value—to attack the problems they care most about. They do not care who does the job—they just want the job to get done. Our approach focuses squarely on how leaders, both inside and outside government, can produce the best outcomes. It focuses on how they can synchronize the massive investments that all sectors—public, private, and nonprofit—are making to maximize the results that citizens want. And most of all, it focuses on managing solutions to problems, not managing the agencies that, inevitably, have only one part of the answer.

Our approach is ambitious and hopeful. It is also realistic. It comes not from our own wish list for governance but from the steps that the most effective leaders have proven. These bridgebuilders have demonstrated the model can work.

We know the individual principles work. What we most need now is for leaders everywhere to weave the principles together into a new strategy of governance—and then to bring them to scale. That will elevate citizens' trust in our governance institutions. Citizens, in turn, will receive the value they want and pay for.

The Challenges of Bridgebuilding

The ten bridgebuilding principles outline the steps that governments need to improve outcomes and strengthen trust. The risks of *not* taking them are huge. But there are also substantial challenges in moving down the road we must take.

- *The broken chain of accountability.* The political system, especially legislators and reporters, often seek a target of responsibility for every program, especially when a program experiences a hiccup (and in complex programs, hiccups are inevitable). In blended government, however, no single person or organization is ever in full charge of the effort. The collision of traditional norms (which operate vertically) and operating realities (which operate horizontally) can play havoc with accountability. The more governments move into a world of blended government, the bigger the accountability problem will be.

How can governments manage this risk? Accountability in blended government requires focusing on outcomes. The more governments switch to performance (what governments do) from process (how governments do it), the more they will enhance accountability. Achieving outcomes, such as in Houston's strategy to address the crisis of homelessness profiled earlier in the book, defines accountability.

- *Defining the private contributions to public value.* Blended government brings private and nonprofit players into important partnerships for creating public value. Sometimes it is through contracts. Sometimes it's through the ways that public goals fuel business expansion. But, at any point, a private organization could decide to change its focus or withdraw from the blended network. On the other hand, to the degree that private organizations embrace public policy goals—in the environmental, social, and governance (ESG) movement, for example—they risk becoming embroiled in public-sector political battles, just in a different setting.

  Bridgebuilding depends heavily on partnerships between the public, private, and nonprofit sectors. If partners can withdraw at any point, the stability of the holistic system can be undermined. Government's private and nonprofit partners respond to incentives, and smart bridgebuilders seek strong outcomes by building effective and stable incentives. That was the core of Charlie Bolden's effort to transform NASA's strategy to buying space on private launch vehicles, and it is the foundation for the Center for Medicare and Medicaid Service's long-term strategy for its private partners in health care. The more complex the partnerships among the organizations pursuing core objectives, the riskier the partnerships can be. Effective bridgebuilders focus

their leadership on building strategies to create stable partnerships, not by issuing orders or relying on arm's-length
engagement.

- *Building political support for bridgebuilding.* The era of blended
  government means, at the least, that more private organizations
  will be involved in public policy and that public policy will draw
  in more private partners. That worries some analysts. *The Economist,* for example, has expressed concern about what it calls "the
  new interventionism," a growing instinct for exercising the power
  of government over the private sector. That could lead to growing
  mistrust not only of government but also of the private companies that collaborate with it.[1]

  That means, in part, that private businesses might "shift from
  satisfying consumers towards currying favour with political
  leaders," *The Economist* worried. That, in turn, might favor some
  private-sector companies over others, with "flagging dynamism"
  and reduced innovation in the private sector and a government
  with a bigger reach into private organizations.

  It is a valid concern, but in most of the world, we have passed
  the point where it's possible to push government's role back.
  Citizens expect more things, they expect government to do harder
  things, and that inevitably means that government must work
  more closely with its private-sector partners. When private-sector
  companies encounter speed bumps, on the other hand, citizens
  expect government will step in to solve the problem.

  When mothers complained in early 2022 that infant formula
  produced by a private company was making their babies sick, the
  company closed a plant for months. President Biden launched a
  series of aggressive steps to get formula back on the shelves, from
  speeding up regulatory review of the factory to flying formula in
  from abroad. FDA Commissioner Robert Califf told CNN that
  the administration is "doing everything we can" to resolve the
  shortage.[2] The irony, of course, was that the administration had not
  caused the problem. It was, rather, the product of a private-sector

manufacturing problem (although analysts debated whether the regulators should have done a more effective job in overseeing the plant). But that did not insulate the White House from calls to fix the problem.

Public policies require private partners. Private problems often demand public solutions. How can bridgebuilders manage the risk? The blended strategy requires high levels of transparency, especially about who does what, and a laser-like focus on results, which is all anyone really cares about.

- *Bridgebuilder burnout.* Bridgebuilding, by its very nature, is very hard and risky work. It creates great stress on bridgebuilders, to the extent that some managers may shy away from its stresses and tensions. Collaborative leadership is difficult, and the incentives inside the structure of most organizations often do not support leaders who take chances.

  Management consultant Eric Garton has pointed to what he called "excessive collaboration" in "organizations with too many decision makers and too many decision nodes." There can be "endless rounds of meetings and conference calls to ensure that every stakeholder is aligned," with "collaboration far beyond what is needed to get the job done." The result, he says, is "collaboration overload" that burns out some managers and discourages others.[3] This carries a double risk: bridgebuilders who become overloaded and burnt out; and other managers who take one look at the consequences and decide to dig deeper foxholes in which to hide. Especially because bridgebuilding is relatively new in its scope and scale, it still has not worked into the standard operating procedures of most agencies. Because it is such a large step from the traditional vending-machine model, bridgebuilding takes an extra measure of courage, and in many agencies, that can bring substantial additional risk.

  How can governments manage the bridgebuilder burnout risk? They can recognize that while every government employee increasingly is part of an organization pursuing a blended strategy, not every employee needs to be a bridgebuilder-in-chief. As the classic *Strengthsfinder* reminds its readers, not everyone is good at everything, and trying to force everyone to do the same job is certain to make for unhappy employees and unproductive organizations.[4] All employees need a clear sense—and a supportive culture—for their own role in the bridgebuilding enterprise. And the key bridgebuilders themselves need to be released from the tyranny of inboxes and calendars to develop the energetic focus on outcomes that leading in a collaborative environment requires. Not everyone needs to be a bridgebuilder, but everyone needs to support the bridgebuilding mission.

As Joellen Jarrett, chief learning officer for the Small Business Administration, told us, "We have moved out of the time when people operate within a position description."[5] The new world of blended government requires a new world of blended government managers within government—a government full of bridgebuilders. That, in turn, requires a fresh look at matching people to mission, in government and in its partners.[6] There are signs of such movement across the world, but it needs to come to scale for bridgebuilding to be successful—and, of course, for government itself to thrive in the blended government age.

Rising to the Challenge

The problems governments face and the solutions governments need, inevitably, build on blended government. Governing this blended system requires bridgebuilders.

This is not to say that bridgebuilders wipe away the myriad challenges societies face. But it is to say that, without bridgebuilders, our fate will inevitably be much worse.

Our future, however, is not one of wallowing in the complexities governments encounter. The underlying theme of the ten principles in this book is one of both enthusiasm and success. The bridgebuilders we feature each approached very tough problems with energy and a commitment to improving the lives of the people around them. By developing bridge-building strategies, they achieved success. That's why our message is a powerful and hopeful one.

So we know we've got this. We face some tough steps: building capacity to master the ten principles, weaving them together in a concerted whole, taking them to scale, and building trust in our institutions to support them as a strategy for twenty-first-century governance. That's not an easy road. But it's far better than the alternative of a government with performance and trust racing each other downhill, and it offers a different, better road forward for the decades to come.

It offers the best opportunities for improving government's results and trust in public institutions. And that, in turn, provides the best foundation for strengthening democratic governance in the twenty-first century.

A 100-Day Plan for Bridgebuilding in Your New Government Job

1. ***Decide on the five most important things you want to accomplish.*** It's tempting to move into a new leadership role with grand ambitions about what to do and what to stop. Sliding into that position, however, always takes time—more time than you might expect—which leaves less time to get things done. There's always time to expand the portfolio later, and it's much easier to do so with a foundation of initial successes. Successes come easier when the focus is sharper.

2. ***Recognize that, most of the time, you'll be running to catch a moving train, because you'll rarely be able to launch new programs.*** The organization you're leading will have an existing mission and ongoing programs, and they'll be around long after you leave. Your leadership can make a big difference not only by nudging existing programs in better directions, but also by determining where and how you can make the most of new possibilities as they arise.

3. ***Define in advance what success will look like, so you'll know you're making progress and can describe it to everyone.*** It's one

thing to announce an initiative. It's another to announce success in a way that convinces everyone that your initiative represents real progress. Leaders are most successful when they can forge their own path through political crosswinds, and they're most successful in building support for that path if they can demonstrate progress to others.

4. *Understand that you can accomplish a lot—but not on your own.* Serving the public well is among the most rewarding things anyone can accomplish. Smart leaders can make enormous progress. But no organization can *ever* control every problem that matters. Your job is to *constantly* build alliances with the partners you need to get things done.

5. *Map the system you're trying to steer so that you understand the players and their roles in the network.* A systematic map of partnerships is just as important as an analysis of a proposed policy's economics. Many of these networks are highly complex but navigating them is far easier when you understand the connections among players.

6. *Understand that the main challenge of collaborative leadership is to encourage all the players to row in the same direction—and that requires knowing what drives everyone's oars.* Good leaders know to "steer, not row," but it's a challenge to make sure your rowers are working together. There's nothing more frustrating than watching the boat you captain go in circles. In the world of public affairs, this means carefully considering the best incentives for every single player and building a system that offers them support—and you may need different incentives for each.

7. *Sometimes, private partners will contribute the most to public value, so you must find the right balance among public and private players.* Public leaders often are uncomfortable with the idea of private or nonprofit partners playing the lead role in an important public program, but that's often how things work.

Leadership sometimes means getting out of their way—or smoothing their path toward the higher public value everyone wants.

8. ***Reshape internal incentives.*** Reimagine incentives such as performance evaluations and bonuses to encourage team members to make external connections and try new things. Too many governmental processes are inward-looking and take on lives of their own. This can discourage innovation by blinding you to potentially valuable connections with partners outside your organization. Just as managing incentives for partners is important, so too is transforming the incentives provided for your own team.

9. ***Don't be surprised by the unpredictable—it's the one thing you can predict.*** It's a constant source of surprise for us that leaders are surprised by surprises. The unexpected is something every leader *should* expect. Smart leaders anticipate where surprises may arise and prepare for them. A crisis can be a positive turning point for an important program—or can end in fear, confusion, and failure. Manage the former to avoid the latter.

10. ***Build the partnerships you'll need to manage surprise, because success depends on preexisting relationships.*** Smart leaders prepare for surprises by developing nimble networks that allow them to respond quickly and effectively. You can lead effectively by pointing to the results the network can produce and organizing it to produce them.

11. ***Information is the language of results.*** Create shared data links among all members of the network. Connections among organizations often break down, both because of technical problems and because the players don't fully understand what the other players are saying. Data, especially when focused on results and expressed in easily understood language such as powerful graphs and charts, can provide the glue that holds organizations together and focuses them on common goals.

12. ***Avoid obsessing about processes—it's results that matter most for
    everyone.*** The biggest trap for members of a complex network,
    after "it's not my problem," is the deadly phrase, "That's not the
    way we do it here." Leaders and their organizational members can
    obsess about processes. These matter, of course, but they have no
    larger meaning unless they lead to the results you seek. When
    organizations work together to solve tough problems, they can
    trip over one another if their internal processes get more atten-
    tion than their shared goals. *Outcomes* matter most, and in
    effective networks they trump processes.

How to Teach This

T he core idea of this book is that today's managers need new skills to meet the new challenges they—and all of us—face in the world of public affairs. The most important corollary is that the next generation of managers should be trained in the skills they'll need to do this well.

Our book is, in part, an argument for a new approach to delivering public value to people. But it's *also* an outline that can be used to teach students and executives alike to become bridgebuilders.

Each element of the following syllabus outline features a key takeaway; a classic reading that can supplement the new approaches outlined in the book; a case example of how to put those approaches to work; and a discussion question for classroom conversation or written assignment.

1: Knock Down Barriers

- *Takeaway:* The traditional approach to management, founded on hierarchy and authority, is a poor fit for most problems modern managers face.

- *Reading:* Luther Gulick, "Notes on the Theory of Organization," in Luther Gulick and L. Urwick, eds., *Papers on the Science of Administration* (New York: Routledge, 1936; republished 2003 as well as a 2017 reprinting from Forgotten Books).

- *Case:* Katherine Barrett, Richard Greene, and Donald F. Kettl, *Managing the Next Crisis: Twelve Principles for Dealing with Viral Uncertainty* (Washington, DC: IBM Center for the Business of Government, 2021), https://www.businessofgovernment.org /report/managing-next-crisis.

- *Discussion question:* If governance is blended, how should we determine who is responsible for what, so we can hold them—and the system as a whole—accountable for results?

2: Seek Mutual Advantage

- *Takeaway:* Shared governance builds on mutual pursuit of shared strategies.

- *Classic:* Mark H. Moore, *Creating Public Value: Strategic Management in Government* (Cambridge, MA: Harvard University Press, 1995).

- *Case:* Manuela Andreoni, Hiroko Tabuchi, and Albert Sun, "How America's Appetite for Leather in Luxury SUVs Worsens Amazon Deforestation," *New York Times*, November 17, 2021, https://www.nytimes.com/2021/11/17/climate/leather-seats-cars -rainforest.html?searchResultPosition=10.

- *Discussion question:* Does the private sector's growing role in producing public value damage democracy's pursuit of accountability?

3: Nurture Private Partners

- *Takeaway:* Accountability is central to the role of government, and *effective* accountability requires building the public spirit into private operations.

- *Classic:* Harold Seidman, *Politics, Position, and Power: The Dynamics of Federal Organization* (New York: Oxford University Press, 1970).

- *Case:* Bill Gates, "We Can Eradicate Malaria—Within a Generation," November 2, 2014, https://www.gatesnotes.com/Health /Eradicating-Malaria-in-a-Generation.

- *Discussion question:* To what degree can—and should—we enlist the private and nonprofit sectors in the effort to advance public value?

4: Build Trustworthy Networks

- *Takeaway:* Shared governance builds on mutual pursuit of shared strategies.

- *Classic:* Francis Fukuyama, *Trust: The Social Virtues and the Creation of Prosperity* (New York: Free Press, 1995).

- *Case:* Gerry McNeilly, *Broken Trust: Indigenous People and the Thunder Bay Police Service* (Kenora, ON: Office of the Independent Policy Director, December 2018), http://gct3.ca/broken-trust -indigenous-people-and-the-thunder-bay-police-service/.

- *Discussion question:* Can government earn our trust if it has to rely on outside partners to implement public policies?

5: Grow Catalytic Government

- *Takeaway:* Government often doesn't so much manage or deliver as it shapes and integrates solutions.

- *Classic:* Lester M. Salamon, ed., *The Tools of Government: A Guide to the New Governance* (New York: Oxford University Press, 2002).

- *Case:* Julia Belluz, "The Media Loves the Gates Foundation. These Experts Are More Skeptical," *Vox*, June 10, 2015, https:// www.vox.com/2015/6/10/8760199/gates-foundation-criticism.

- *Discussion question:* How has government's role changed from steering—directing the players about what to do—to catalyzing—weaving the different players together in a common effort to produce common goals?

6: Focus on Outcomes

- *Takeaway:* Internal rules can't impede the search for multisectoral success.

- *Classic:* Herbert Kaufman, *Red Tape: Its Origins, Uses, and Abuses* (Washington, DC: Brookings Institution, 1977).

- *Case:* Nicholas Bagley, "The Procedure Fetish," Niskanen Center, December 7, 2021, https://www.niskanencenter.org/the-procedure-fetish/.

- *Discussion question:* As implementation relationships become more complex, it becomes easier for everyone to resort to accountability through processes—so how can we make sure that the pursuit of *outcomes* rises to the top?

7: Make Data the Language

- *Takeaway:* Data creates a shared language and grammar for discussions.

- *Classic:* Charles E. Lindblom, "The Science of 'Muddling Through,'" *Public Administration Review* 19, no. 2 (1959): 79–88.

- *Case:* Louis Vasquez, "Houston's Unhoused Population Decreased Due to a $200 Million Investment, a New Report Says," *Houston Public Media*, March 16, 2022, https://www.houstonpublicmedia.org/articles/news/houston/2022/03/16/421190/houstons-unhoused-population-dropped-due-to-a-200-million-investment-a-new-report-says/#:~:text=Housing-,Houston's%20unhoused%20population%20decreased%20due%20to%20a%20%24200%20million%20investment,a%2064%25%20decrease%20since%202011; and Houston Coalition for the Homeless, https://www.homelesshouston.org/.

- *Discussion question:* We know we're in the midst of the information age, but how can we use data to produce better results?

8: Redefine Accountability

- *Takeaway:* Accountability is essential—and *effective* accountability depends on redefining the foundations of the public interest.

- *Classic:* Jody Freeman, "Extending Public Law Norms through Privatization," *Harvard Law Review* 116 (March 2003): 1285–1352.

- *Case:* Paul C. Light, "The True Size of Government Is Nearing a Record High," Brookings Institution, October 7, 2020, https://www.brookings.edu/blog/fixgov/2020/10/07/the-true-size-of-government-is-nearing-a-record-high/.

- *Discussion question:* The existing rule of law, focused on top-down accountability, is rapidly becoming obsolete—but how should we replace it?

9: Cultivate Cross-Boundary Leaders

- *Takeaway:* All partners in the governance process, public and private, have a responsibility to share in leadership.

- *Classic:* Stephen Goldsmith and William D. Eggers, *Governing by Network: The New Shape of the Public Sector* (Washington, DC: Brookings Institution Press, 2004).

- *Case:* "Arlington County After-Action Report on the Response to the September 11 Terrorist Attack on the Pentagon," 2002, http://www.policefoundation.org/wp-content/uploads/2018/07/pentagonafteractionreport.pdf.

- *Discussion question:* If governance increasingly occurs through integrated networks, who should lead—and who ought to decide the answer to that question?

10: Make the Exceptional Routine

- *Takeaway:* Learning how to attack complex problems in complex settings can also provide a useful guide for improving the day-to-day implementation of government programs.

- *Classic:* H. W. Rittel and M. M. Webber, "Dilemmas in a General Theory of Planning," *Policy Sciences* 4, no. 2 (1973) 155–169, https://www.cc.gatech.edu/fac/ellendo/rittel/rittel-dilemma.pdf.

- *Case:* Peter Meyer, "New York City's Education Battles," EducationNext, November 2, 2009, https://www.educationnext.org/new-york-citys-education-battles/.

- *Discussion question:* Should we be depressed—or excited—about the growing complexity of public problems and the systems we've created to attack them?

Notes

Introduction

1. National Fire Protection Association, "Fire Department Calls," September 2022, https://www.nfpa.org/News-and-Research/Data-research-and-tools/Emergency-Responders /Fire-department-calls.

2. Pew Research Center, "Public Trust in Government: 1958–2022," June 6, 2022, https://www.pewresearch.org/politics/2022/06/06/public-trust-in-government-1958-2022/.

3. Kenneth Finegold, Laura Wherry, and Stephanie Schardin, "Block Grants: Historical Overview and Lessons Learned," Urban Institute, April 21, 2004, http://webarchive.urban.org /publications/310991.html.

4. Reagan Presidential Library, "President's Private Sector Survey on Cost Control," March 29, 2021, https://www.reaganlibrary.gov/archives/topic-guide/presidents-private-sector -survey-cost-control-grace-commission.

5. David Osborne and Ted Gaebler, *Reinventing Government: Creating a Government That Works Better and Costs Less* (Reading, MA: Addison-Wesley, 1992).

6. John Kamensky, "National Partnership for Reinventing Government: A Brief History," January 1999, https://govinfo.library.unt.edu/npr/whoweare/history2.html#5years.

7. Thomas B. Rosenstiel, "Gore on 'Letterman'? It's No Joke," *Los Angeles Times*, September 10, 1993, https://www.latimes.com/archives/la-xpm-1993-09-10-ca-33466-story.html.

8. White House, "President's Management Agenda," 2001, https://georgewbush-whitehouse .archives.gov/omb/budintegration/pma_index.html; US State Department, "President's Management Agenda," 2009, https://2009-2017.state.gov/documents/organization/79674.pdf; White House, "President's Management Agenda," 2018, https://trumpadministration.archives .performance.gov/PMA/PMA.html; Jason Miller, "Updates on the Presidential Management Agenda," February 17, 2022, https://www.whitehouse.gov/omb/briefing-room/2022/02/17 /updates-on-the-presidents-management-agenda/. In addition, the *Analytical Perspectives* volume in each year's collection of budget documents released by the Office of Management and Budget contains updated summaries of each administration's progress.

9. Commission on Evidence-Based Policymaking, "The Promise of Evidence-Based Policymaking," September 2017, https://bipartisanpolicy.org/wp-content/uploads/2017/10/CEP -Final-Report.pdf.

10. Chief Information Officers Council, "Foundations for Evidence-Based Policymaking Act of 2018," https://www.cio.gov/policies-and-priorities/evidence-based-policymaking/.

Chapter 1

1. See, for instance, Donald F. Kettl, *System under Stress: Homeland Security and American Politics*, 3rd ed. (Washington, DC: Congressional Quarterly Press, 2014).

2. Thad Allen, "15 Years Later, Adm. Thad Allen Recalls the Journey to Katrina," *The Day*, August 30, 2020, https://www.theday.com/article/20200830/OP03/200839981.

3. Scott Berinato, "You Have to Lead from Everywhere," *Harvard Business Review*, November 2010, https://hbr.org/2010/11/you-have-to-lead-from-everywhere.

4. FEMA, "A Whole Community Approach to Emergency Management: Principles, Themes, and Pathways for Action," FDOC 104-008-1, December 2011, https://www.fema.gov /sites/default/files/2020-07/whole_community_dec2011__2.pdf.

5. Amanda Penn, "Walmart's Hurricane Katrina Response: How They Saved the Day," *Shortform*, December 12, 2019, https://www.shortform.com/blog/walmart-hurricane-katrina/.

6. Home Depot, "Behind the Scenes: Home Depot's Hurricane Headquarters," September 5, 2019, https://corporate.homedepot.com/news/company/behind-scenes-home-depots -hurricane-headquarters.

7. Steve Vogel, "Officials and Experts Praising FEMA for Its Response to Hurricane Sandy," *Washington Post*, November 1, 2012, https://www.washingtonpost.com/politics /decision2012/officials-and-experts-praising-fema-for-its-response-to-hurricane-sandy/2012/11 /01/7a6629d8-2447-11e2-ac85-e669876c6a24_story.html.

8. Shelly Banjo, "Big-Box Retailers Spring into Action," *Wall Street Journal*, October 31, 2012, https://www.wsj.com/articles/SB10001424052970204707104578091141759708804.

9. Jennifer Steinhauer and Michael S. Schmidt, "Man behind FEMA's Makeover Built Philosophy on Preparation," *New York Times*, November 3, 2012, https://www.nytimes.com /2012/11/04/us/the-man-behind-femas-post-katrina-makeover.html.

10. Homeland Security Digital Library, "FEMA: Public-Private Partnerships," https://www .hsdl.org/?abstract&did=17554.

11. US Department of State, "U.S. Refugee Admissions Program Priority Designation for Afghan Nationals," August 2, 2021, https://www.state.gov/u-s-refugee-admissions-program -priority-2-designation-for-afghan-nationals/.

12. Frances Kai-Hwa Wang, Cresencio Rodriguez-Delgado, and Adam Kemp, "Tens of Thousands of Afghans Have Resettled across the U.S. Now, the Challenge Is Making a Home," *PBS NewsHour*, February 3, 2022, https://www.pbs.org/newshour/nation/tens-of-thousands-of -afghans-have-resettled-across-the-u-s-now-the-challenge-is-making-a-home.

13. Airbnb, "Housing for 10,000 Afghan Refugees," December 15, 2021, https://news.airbnb .com/housing-for-10000-afghan-refugees/.

14. Dan Bartlett, "Supporting Our Neighbors: An Update on Walmart's Work to Welcome Afghan Refugees," November 30, 2021, https://corporate.walmart.com/newsroom/2021/11/30 /supporting-our-neighbors-an-update-on-walmarts-work-to-welcome-afghan-refugees.

15. Tent Partnership for Refugees, "30+ Major Companies Join the Tent Coalition of Afghan Refugees," September 21, 2021, https://www.prnewswire.com/news-releases/30-major -companies-join-the-tent-coalition-for-afghan-refugees-301381375.html.

16. Historically, the United States—"a nation of immigrants," as John F. Kennedy put it—has taken in more refugees than any other country. But the Trump administration dramatically lowered the annual cap even as drought and war forced millions in Syria, Haiti, and elsewhere from their homes—hence Canada stepping in to fill the gap. Jynnah Radford and Phillip Connor, "Canada Now Leads the World in Refugee Resettlement, Surpassing the U.S.," Pew Research Center, June 19, 2019, https://www.pewresearch.org/fact-tank/2019/06/19/canada -now-leads-the-world-in-refugee-resettlement-surpassing-the-u-s/.

17. Canadian Press, "Canada Resettled More Refugees Than Any Other Country in 2018, UN Says," *CBC*, June 20, 2019, https://www.cbc.ca/news/politics/canada-resettled-most-refugees -un-1.5182621.

18. Deborah Amos, "'New Era in Resettlement': U.S. Refugee Advocates Count on More Community-Based Help," NPR, May 6, 2021, https://www.npr.org/2021/05/06/993153650/new -era-in-resettlement-u-s-refugee-advocates-count-on-more-community-based-help.

19. Centers for Medicare and Medicaid Services, "Justification of Estimates for Appropriations Committees, Fiscal Year 2022," 2021, https://www.cms.gov/files/document/fy2022-cms -congressional-justification-estimates-appropriations-committees.pdf.

20. Katherine Barrett, Richard Greene, and Donald F. Kettl, *Managing the Next Crisis: Twelve Principles for Dealing with Viral Uncertainty* (Washington, DC: IBM Center for the

Business of Government, 2022), https://www.businessofgovernment.org/report/managing
-next-crisis.

21. Courtney Buble, "Dr. Anthony Fauci: Preparing for Pandemics Takes an 'All-of-
Government Approach,'" *Government Executive*, February 9, 2022, https://www.govexec.com
/management/2022/02/dr-anthony-fauci-preparing-pandemics-takes-all-government
-approach/361792/.

22. Thomas H. Kean et al., *9/11 Commission Report*, 2002, 336, https://www.9-11commission
.gov/report/911Report.pdf.

23. Kean et al., *9/11 Commission Report*, 408.

24. President's Committee on Administrative Management, "Report of the Committee,"
1937, http://onlinebooks.library.upenn.edu/webbin/book/lookupname?key=United%20
States%2E%20President%27s%20Committee%20on%20Administrative%20Management.

25. First Commission on Organization of the Executive Branch of the Government,
"Concluding Report: Report to Congress," 1949, https://www.archives.gov/research/guide-fed
-records/groups/264.html.

26. Amitai Etzioni, *Comparative Analysis of Complex Organizations*, rev. ed. (New York:
Free Press, 1975).

27. Craig W. Thomas, "Reorganizing Public Organizations: Alternatives, Objectives, and
Evidence," *Journal of Public Administration and Theory* 3 (1993): 457–486.

28. US Senate, "Clara Barton's Benefactor," accessed August 12, 2022, http://www.senate.gov
/artandhistory/history/minute/Clara_Bartons_Benefactor.htm.

29. American Red Cross, "Founder Clara Barton," accessed August 12, 2022, http://www
.redcross.org/content/dam/redcross/enterprise-assets/about-us/history/history-clara-barton-v5
.pdf.

30. Clara Barton Missing Soldiers Office Museum, "Clara Barton's Missing Soldiers Office,"
accessed August 12, 2022, http://www.clarabartonmuseum.org/mso-short/.

31. Brookings Institution, "The Cost of the Manhattan Project," accessed April 18, 2022,
https://www.brookings.edu/the-costs-of-the-manhattan-project/.

32. W. Henry Lambright, *Powering Apollo: James E. Webb of NASA* (Baltimore, MD: Johns
Hopkins University Press, 1995), 2.

33. Interview with Mariam Mansury, a former senior staffer for Swanee Hunt, August 12,
2022.

34. Synergos, "Women Waging Peace: Swanee Hunt's Vision for Inclusive Security,"
accessed August 12, 2022, http://www.synergos.org/news-and-insights/2008/women-waging
-peace-swanee-hunts-vision-inclusive-security.

35. Inclusive Security, "About Us," https://www.inclusivesecurity.org/about-us/.

36. The Institute of Politics at Harvard University, "Five Questions for Swanee Hunt,"
accessed November 30, 2022, https://iop.harvard.edu/iop-now/5-questions-swanee-hunt.

37. Luther Gulick, "Notes on the Theory of Organization," in *Papers on the Science of
Administration*, edited by Luther Gulick and Lyndall Urwick (Concord, NH: Rumford, 1937),
3–45; Max Weber, *Economy and Society: An Outline of Interpretative Sociology*, edited by
Guenther Roth and Claus Wittich (Berkeley: University of California Press, 1978 [1922]).

38. Garrett M. Graff, "Escape from New York: The Great Maritime Rescue of Lower
Manhattan on 9/11," *New York Magazine*, September 11, 2021, https://nymag.com/intelligencer
/2021/09/the-great-maritime-rescue-of-lower-manhattan-on-9-11.html.

39. Graff, "Escape from New York"; John Hanc, "On 9/11, a Flotilla of Ferries, Yachts and
Tugboats Evacuated 500,000 People away from Ground Zero," *Smithsonian Magazine*,
September 9, 2021, https://www.smithsonianmag.com/history/911-flotilla-boats-evacuated
-500000-new-yorkers-safety-180978614/.

40. Graff, "Escape from New York."

41. Interview with Joshua Marcuse, head of federal strategy at Google, November 8, 2021.

42. William D. Eggers et al., "Linked-Up Government," *Deloitte Insights*, March 24, 2022,
https://www2.deloitte.com/us/en/insights/industry/public-sector/government-trends/2022
/joined-up-connected-government.html.

43. Interview with Anne-Marie Slaughter, May 17, 2022.

44. Eggers et al., "Linked-Up Government."

Chapter 2

1. World Health Organization, "Malaria," April 6, 2022, https://www.who.int/news-room/fact-sheets/detail/malaria.

2. Centers for Disease Control and Prevention, "Malaria's Impact Worldwide," https://www.cdc.gov/malaria/malaria_worldwide/impact.html; World Health Organization, "Malaria," December 8, 2022, https://www.who.int/news-room/fact-sheets/detail/malaria#:~:text=The%20estimated%20number%20of%20malaria,malaria%20deaths%20in%20the%20Region.

3. Natasha Bach, "Bill Gates Is Pouring Another $1 Billion into the Fight against Malaria," *Fortune*, April 18, 2018, https://fortune.com/2018/04/18/bill-gates-foundation-malaria/; Bill Gates, "We Can Eradicate Malaria—Within a Generation," *GatesNotes*, November 2, 2014, https://www.gatesnotes.com/Health/Eradicating-Malaria-in-a-Generation.

4. World Malaria Report 2020, November 26, 2020, https://reliefweb.int/attachments/5adfc2b9-0e73-3c8b-97cd-c197b6864385/WMR-2020-v5-double-embargoed.pdf.

5. The Global Fund, "Global Fund Overview," https://www.theglobalfund.org/en/overview/; CDC, "Malaria Vaccine Recommended for Broader Use by WHO: 'Best Thing Since Bed Nets,'" accessed April 19, 2022, https://www.cdc.gov/parasites/features/malaria_vaccine_who.html.

6. Gates, "We Can Eradicate Malaria."

7. RBM Partnership to End Malaria, "Coordinated Action towards Ending Malaria," accessed April 19, 2022, https://endmalaria.org/about-us.

8. William Eggers and Anna Muoio, "Wicked Opportunities," Deloitte, 2015, https://www2.deloitte.com/us/en/insights/focus/business-trends/2015/wicked-problems-wicked-opportunities-business-trends.html.

9. Robert T. Jones et al., "The Role of the Private Sector in Supporting Malaria Control in Resource Development Settings," *The Journal of Infectious Diseases* 222, no. 8 (Suppl., October 29, 2020), https://www.ncbi.nlm.nih.gov/pmc/articles/PMC7594257/.

10. ExxonMobil, "Our Partners Are Dedicated to Reducing Malaria's Threat," June 21, 2021, https://corporate.exxonmobil.com/Sustainability/Community-engagement/The-fight-against-malaria/Our-partners-are-dedicated-to-reducing-malarias-threat.

11. Malaka Gharib, "Why the U.S. Is Pledging $4.3 Billion to the Global Fund," NPR, September 15, 2016, https://www.npr.org/sections/goatsandsoda/2016/09/15/493760787/why-the-u-s-is-pledging-4-3-billion-to-the-global-fund.

12. The Global Fund, "Global Fund Overview," accessed April 19, 2022, https://www.theglobalfund.org/en/overview/.

13. World Health Organization, "WHO Recommends Groundbreaking Malaria Vaccine for Children at Risk," October 6, 2021, https://www.who.int/news/item/06-10-2021-who-recommends-groundbreaking-malaria-vaccine-for-children-at-risk.

14. Apoorva Mandavilli, "First Malaria Vaccine Approved by W.H.O.," *New York Times*, October 6, 2021, https://www.nytimes.com/2021/10/06/health/malaria-vaccine-who.html.

15. Roger Schwarz, "Is Your Team Coordinating Too Much, or Not Enough?" *Harvard Business Review*, March 23, 2017, https://hbr.org/2017/03/is-your-team-coordinating-too-much-or-not-enough.

16. Julian De Freitas et al., "Common Knowledge, Coordination, and Strategy Mentalizing in Human Social Life," *Proceedings of the National Academy of Sciences* 116, no. 28 (June 28, 2019), https://www.pnas.org/doi/10.1073/pnas.1905518116.

17. Centre for Public Impact, "By the People, for the People: Colorado Governor John Hickenlooper," September 17, 2015, https://www.centreforpublicimpact.org/insights/by-the-people-for-the-people.

18. John Hickenlooper, *Real Change: Leveraging Community Partnerships to Solve Real-World Problems*, unpublished manuscript, 51.

19. Interview with Jamie Van Leeuwen, director of youth and community engagement with the Emerson Collective and former senior adviser to Denver Mayor John Hickenlooper, September 16, 2021.

20. Hickenlooper, *Real Change*, 63–67.

21. Hickenlooper, *Real Change*, 30.

22. Denver Rescue Mission, "Chris Conner on Why Denver Rescue Mission Matters," accessed April 18, 2022, https://denverrescuemission.org/chris-conner-on-why-denver-rescue-mission-matters/.

23. Michael Kimmelman, "How Houston Moved 25,000 People from the Streets into Homes of Their Own," *New York Times*, June 14, 2022, https://www.nytimes.com/2022/06/14/headway/houston-homeless-people.html.

24. Houston Coalition for the Homeless, "How Are We Doing? Homelessness 101," accessed April 18, 2022, https://www.homelesshouston.org/houston-facts-info#Homelessness101.

25. Federal Communications Commission, Fourteenth Broadband Deployment Report, January 19, 2021, 2, https://docs.fcc.gov/public/attachments/FCC-21-18A1.pdf; and John Busby, Julia Tanberk, and Tyler Cooper, "BroadbandNow Estimates Availability for All 50 States; Confirms That More Than 42 Million Americans Do Not Have Access to Broadband," *BroadbandNow Research*, May 5, 2021, https://broadbandnow.com/research/fcc-broadband-overreporting-by-state.

26. Emily A. Vogels, "Some Digital Divides Persist between Rural, Urban and Suburban America," Pew Research Center, August 19, 2021, https://www.pewresearch.org/fact-tank/2021/08/19/some-digital-divides-persist-between-rural-urban-and-suburban-america/.

27. Eve Stotland, "One-Third of New Yorkers Don't Have Internet Access: That Is an Issue for Funders," Philanthropy New York, May 26, 2021, https://philanthropynewyork.org/news/one-third-new-yorkers-don-t-have-internet-access-issue-funders.

28. Editorial Board, "Doing Schoolwork in the Parking Lot Is Not a Solution," *New York Times*, July 18, 2020, https://www.nytimes.com/2020/07/18/opinion/sunday/broadband-internet-access-civil-rights.html.

29. Sindya Bhanoo, "How the Digital Divide Is Failing Texas Students—And Why That Might Be About to Change," *Texas Monthly,* August 8, 2021, https://www.texasmonthly.com/news-politics/how-the-digital-divide-is-failing-texas-students/.

30. Katie Kienbaum et al., "How Local Providers Built the Nation's Best Internet Access in Rural North Dakota," Institute for Local Self-Reliance, May 2020, 6, https://ilsr.org/wp-content/uploads/2020/05/2020-05-North-Dakota-Internet-Access-Case-Study.pdf.

31. U.S. News, 2019 Best States Ranking, "Overview of North Dakota," accessed April 18, 2022, https://www.usnews.com/news/best-states/north-dakota#state-rankings.

32. Institute for Local Self-Reliance, "Local Providers," 6.

33. Marisa Jackels, "North Dakota Leads the Nation in Fiber Optic Access," Emerging Prairie, 2021, https://www.emergingprairie.com/north-dakota-leads-the-nation-in-fiber-optic-access/.

34. Center for American Progress, "Anchor Tenants for Broadband Networks," April 8, 2009, https://www.americanprogress.org/article/idea-of-the-day-anchor-tenants-for-broadband-networks/.

35. Fred Pace, "Facebook's Fiber Infrastructure Project Route Going through Milton, Barboursville, Huntington," *The Herald-Dispatch*, August 23, 2020, https://www.herald-dispatch.com/news/facebook-s-fiber-infrastructure-project-route-going-through-milton-barboursville-huntington/article_2f481e25-3123-5a7b-825a-7e4d94d95bbb.html; and Linda Hardesty, "Facebook Lays Fiber across the Entire State of Indiana," Fierce Telecom, March 26, 2021, https://www.fiercetelecom.com/operators/facebook-lays-fiber-across-entire-state-indiana.

36. New River Gorge Regional Development Authority, "Facebook Fiber Network Project Groundbreaking in West Virginia," November 22, 2019, https://nrgrda.org/facebook-fiber-network-project-groundbreaking-in-west-virginia/.

37. "New Public-Private Partnership to Boost Broadband in Southeastern New Mexico," *BroadbandCommunities*, February 12, 2020, https://www.bbcmag.com/breaking-news/new -public-private-partnership-to-boost-broadband-in-southeastern-new-mexico.

38. Sally Aman, "Dig Once: A Solution for Rural Broadband," *USTelecom*, April 12, 2017, https://www.ustelecom.org/dig-once-a-solution-for-rural-broadband/.

39. Aaron C. Boley and Michael Byers, "Satellite Mega-Constellations Create Risks in Low Earth Orbit, the Atmosphere and on Earth," *Nature*, May 20, 2021, https://www.nature.com /articles/s41598-021-89909-7.

40. Brian Greenberg et al., "5G in Government: The Future of Hyperconnected Public Services," *Deloitte Insights*, August 28, 2020, https://www2.deloitte.com/us/en/insights/industry /public-sector/future-of-5g-government.html.

41. Jason Murdock, "SpaceX Starlink Internet 'Catapulted Us into the 21st Century,' Native American Tribe Says," *Newsweek*, September 10, 2020, https://www.newsweek.com/spacex -starlink-internet-hoh-tribe-washington-state-elon-musk-1537783.

42. Michael Kan, "Native American Tribe Gets Early Access to SpaceX's Starlink and Says It's Fast," *PCMag*, October 8, 2020, https://in.pcmag.com/networking/138454/native-american -tribe-gets-early-access-to-spacexs-starlink-and-says-its-fast.

43. Tweet from the Hoh Tribe, October 7, 2020, https://twitter.com/tribehoh/status /1313901793261187073?lang=en.

44. National Aeronautics and Space Administration, *The State of NASA Procurement—2019: A Year in Review*, 8, https://www.nasa.gov/sites/default/files/atoms/files/state-of-procurment -2019-year-in-review.pdf.

45. James Oberg, "7 Myths about the Challenger Shuttle Disaster," *NBC News*, January 26, 2006, https://www.nbcnews.com/id/wbna11031097. Analysts are now saying it didn't explode, in the traditional sense.

46. Doug Adler, "Why Did NASA Retire the Space Shuttle?" *Astronomy*, November 12, 2020, https://astronomy.com/news/2020/11/why-did-nasa-retire-the-space-shuttle.

47. Adler, "NASA."

48. National Aeronautics and Space Administration, "New NASA Partnerships to Mature Commercial Space Technologies, Capabilities," November 9, 2020, https://www.nasa.gov/press -release/new-nasa-partnerships-to-mature-commercial-space-technologies-capabilities.

49. Interview with former NASA administrator Charles Bolden Jr., June 15, 2020.

50. Frederick Winslow Taylor, *The Principles of Scientific Management* (New York: Harper and Brothers, 1911).

51. Danny Buerkli, "A Tale of Two Paradigms—Meet the Ideas Which Are Quietly Changing Public Administrations around the World," August 23, 2019, https://medium.com /centre-for-public-impact/a-tale-of-two-paradigms-meet-the-idea-which-is-quietly-changing -public-administrations-around-e2e57171f451.

52. Mark Foden, "Episode 1: About the Clock and the Cat," December 1, 2018, https:// markfoden.com/clockcat/2018/12/episode-1-introduction.

53. Syon P. Bhanot and Elizabeth Linos, "Behavioral Public Administration: Past, Present, and Future," *Public Administration Review* 80, no. 1 (January 2020): 168–171; Erik-Hans Klijn, "Complexity Theory and Public Administration: What's New?" *Public Management Review* 10, no. 3 (2008): 299–317; Jack Wayne Meek, "Complexity Theory for Public Administration and Policy," *Emergence: Complexity & Organization* 12, no. 1 (January 2010): 1–4; Elizabeth Anne Eppel and Mary Lee Rhodes, *Complexity Theory in Public Administration* (London: Routledge, 2019); and Centre for Public Impact, *The Shared Power Principle: How Governments Are Changing to Achieve Better Outcomes* (London: Centre for Public Impact, July 2019).

54. Mahesh Kelkar et al., "Addressing Homelessness with Data Analytics," *Deloitte Insights*, September 25, 2019, https://www2.deloitte.com/us/en/insights/industry/public-sector/home lessness-data.html; and William D. Eggers, "A 'Whole of Government' Approach to Social Problems," *Governing*, January 12, 2017, https://www.governing.com/archive/col-whole-of -government-approach-social-problems-veterans-homelessness.html.

55. Interview with Charles Bolden Jr., June 15, 2020.

56. David B. Smith and Jeanine Becker, "The Essential Skills of Cross Sector Leadership," *Stanford Social Innovation Review*, Winter 2018, Federal Reserve Bank of San Francisco, https://ssir.org/articles/entry/the_essential_skills_of_cross_sector_leadership; and Beth Siegel et al., "Pathways to System Change: The Design of Multisite, Cross-Sector Initiatives," July 21, 2015, https://www.frbsf.org/community-development/publications/working-papers/2015/july/pathways-to-system-change-multisite-cross-sector-initiatives/.

57. US Federal Emergency Management Agency, "COVID-19 Pandemic: Supply Chain Expansion Line of Effort," May 18, 2020, https://www.fema.gov/news-release/2020/05/18/COVID-19-pandemic-supply-chain-expansion-line-effort.

58. William Eggers and Anna Muoio, "Wicked Opportunities," Deloitte, 2015, 8, https://www2.deloitte.com/content/dam/Deloitte/za/Documents/strategy/za_Wicked_Opportunities_3.pdf.

59. Interview with Jamie Van Leeuwen, September 16, 2021.

60. Interview with David Warm, September 30, 2021.

Chapter 3

1. (1.5°C warming, expected by 2030.) Oliver Milman, Andrew Witherspoon, Rita Liu, and Alvin Chang, "The Climate Disaster Is Here," *Guardian*, October 15, 2021, https://www.theguardian.com/environment/ng-interactive/2021/oct/14/climate-change-happening-now-stats-graphs-maps-cop26.

2. Matthew R. Sanderson, Burke Griggs, and Jacob A. Miller, "Farmers Are Depleting the Ogallala Aquifer Because the Government Pays Them to Do It," The Conversation, November 9, 2020, https://theconversation.com/farmers-are-depleting-the-ogallala-aquifer-because-the-government-pays-them-to-do-it-145501.

3. Tom DiLiberto, "Climate.gov Tweet Chat: Talk with a Sea Level Rise Expert about Past and Future Risk of High-Tide Flooding on U.S. Coasts," NOAA Climate.gov, updated March 15, 2022, https://www.climate.gov/news-features/features/climategov-tweet-chat-talk-sea-level-rise-expert-about-past-and-future-risk.

4. "Global Forest Watch Dashboard," Global Forest Watch, accessed April 18, 2022, https://www.globalforestwatch.org/dashboards/global/.

5. Brendan Borrell, "Saving the Maya Rainforest," The Nature Conservancy, November 10, 2021, https://www.nature.org/en-us/magazine/magazine-articles/saving-the-maya-rainforest/.

6. Borrell, "Saving the Maya Rainforest."

7. Borrell, "Saving the Maya Rainforest."

8. "Impact Investment Catalyst Program," Asociacion Costa Rica Por Siempre, accessed April 18, 2022, https://costaricaporsiempre.org/en/programas/programa-catalizador-de-inversiones-de-impacto/.

9. "II Debt-for-Nature Swap U.S.–C.R," Asociacion Costa Rica Por Siempre, accessed April 18, 2022, https://costaricaporsiempre.org/en/programas/ii-canje-de-deuda-por-naturaleza-ee-uu-c-r/.

10. US Agency for International Development, "Financing Forest Conservation: An Overview of the Tropical Forest and Coral Reef Conservation Act," July 12, 2021, https://www.usaid.gov/tropical-forest-conservation-act.

11. US Agency for International Development, "Financing Forest Conservation."

12. "Blue Bonds: An Audacious Plan to Save the World's Ocean," The Nature Conservancy, updated March 4, 2021, https://www.nature.org/en-us/what-we-do/our-insights/perspectives/an-audacious-plan-to-save-the-worlds-oceans/.

13. "Global Investments for Conservation," The Nature Conservancy, accessed April 18, 2022, https://www.nature.org/en-us/about-us/where-we-work/latin-america/belize/rio-bravo-conservation-area/.

14. "Global Investments for Conservation."

15. Interview with Andrew Deutz, January 20, 2022.

16. "A Post-Storm Response and Reef Insurance Primer," The Nature Conservancy, accessed April 18, 2022, https://www.nature.org/content/dam/tnc/nature/en/documents/A_POST _STORM_RESPONSE_REEF_INSURANCE_PRIMER_2021_final.pdf.

17. Norul Mohamed Rashid, "Land and Property," United Nations and the Rule of Law, blog, accessed April 18, 2022, https://www.un.org/ruleoflaw/thematic-areas/land-property -environment/land-and-property/.

18. Business Roundtable, "Business Roundtable Redefines the Purpose of a Corporation to Promote 'An Economy That Serves All Americans,'" August 19, 2019, https://www .businessroundtable.org/business-roundtable-redefines-the-purpose-of-a-corporation-to -promote-an-economy-that-serves-all-americans.

19. Sara Fischer, "Businesses under More Pressure to Save Society," Axios, May 20, 2021, https://www.axios.com/trust-corporations-business-government-65e2d1f3-93e4-4eba-906f -4f435af3bf84.html.

20. "Understanding Generation Z in the Workplace," Deloitte, https://www2.deloitte.com /us/en/pages/consumer-business/articles/understanding-generation-z-in-the-workplace.html.

21. "The Rise of the Socially Responsible Business: Deloitte Global Societal Impact Survey," *Deloitte*, January 2019, deloitte-global-societal-impact-survey-jan-2019.

22. "The Rise of the Socially Responsible Business."

23. "Announcing the 2021 Rankings of America's Most JUST Companies," *JUST Capital*, accessed April 18, 2022, https://justcapital.com/reports/announcing-the-2021-rankings-of -americas-most-just-companies/.

24. "Do Sustainable Banks Outperform? Driving Value Creation through ESG Practices," Deloitte, accessed April 18, 2022, https://www2.deloitte.com/global/en/pages/financial-services /articles/gx-driving-value-creation-through-esg-practices.html.

25. "Do Sustainable Banks Outperform?"

26. Sean Collins, "Advancing Environmental, Social, and Governance Investing: A Holistic Approach for Investment Management Firms," *Deloitte Insights,* February 20, 2020, https://www2.deloitte.com/us/en/insights/industry/financial-services/esg-investing -performance.html.

27. Porter Novelli, "Employee Perspectives on Responsible Leadership during Crisis," January 2, 2021, https://www.porternovelli.com/wp-content/uploads/2021/01/02_Porter-Novelli-Tracker -Wave-X-Employee-Perspectives-on-Responsible-Leadership-During-Crisis.pdf.

28. William Eggers, "The Purpose-Driven Professional," *Deloitte Insights*, September 8, 2015, https://www2.deloitte.com/us/en/insights/topics/corporate-responsibility/harnessing -impact-of-corporate-social-responsibility-on-talent.html.

29. Tom Schoenwaelder et al., "The Purpose Premium: Why a Purpose-Driven Strategy Is Good for Business," *Monitor Deloitte*, accessed April 18, 2022, https://www2.deloitte.com /content/dam/Deloitte/us/Documents/process-and-operations/purpose-premium-pov.pdf.

30. Schoenwaelder et al., "The Purpose Premium."

31. "2018 Cone/Porter Novelli Purpose Study: How to Build Deeper Bonds, Amplify Your Message and Expand the Consumer Base," *Cone Communications,* accessed April 18, 2022, https://www.conecomm.com/research-blog/2018-purpose-study.

32. "2018 Cone/Porter Novelli Purpose Study."

33. Max Meyers and William D. Eggers, "What Government Can Learn from Venture Capital," *Deloitte Insights,* accessed April 18, 2022, https://www2.deloitte.com/us/en/insights /industry/public-sector/government-venture-capital.html.

34. Alex Keown, "Pharma Industry Comes Together to Support Manufacture of COVID-19 Vaccines," BioSpace, January 29, 2021, https://www.biospace.com/article/sanofi-gsk-to-support -pfizer-and-biontech-vaccine-manufacturing/#:~:text=Both%20Sanofi%20and%20Novartis%20 entered,the%20United%20Kingdom%20and%20elsewhere.

35. Anne-Marie Slaughter, *The Chessboard and the Web: Strategies of Connection in a Networked World* (New Haven, CT: Yale University Press, 2017).

36. G. John Ikenberry, review of *The Chessboard and the Web: Strategies of Connection in a Networked World*, by Anne-Marie Slaughter, *Foreign Affairs*, May/June 2017, https://www.foreignaffairs.com/reviews/capsule-review/2017-04-14/chessboard-and-web-strategies-connection-networked-world.

37. "Giving Pledge Adds 14 Billionaires to Philanthropist List," *U.S. News*, December 14, 2021, https://www.usnews.com/news/business/articles/2021-12-14/giving-pledge-adds-14-billionaires-to-philanthropist-list#:~:text=The%20Giving%20Pledge%20announced%20Tuesday,231%20philanthropists%20from%2028%20countries.

38. Mark Hrywna, "Giving in 2020 Hit Record $471 Billion, Up 5.1%," *The NonProfit Times*, June 15, 2021, https://www.thenonprofittimes.com/npt_articles/giving-in-2020-hits-record-471-billion-up-5-1/.

39. European Commission, "Commission Presents Action Plan to Boost the Social Economy and Create Jobs," September 12, 2021, https://ec.europa.eu/social/main.jsp?langId=en&catId=89&furtherNews=yes&newsId=10117.

40. "Business for Good: The Size and Economic Contribution of Social Enterprise in Australia," December 2021, https://socialenterpriseaustralia.org.au/business-for-good/.

41. World Youth Report: Youth Social Entrepreneurship and the 2030 Agenda, "Chapter 1: Social Entrepreneurship," *United Nations*, https://www.un.org/development/desa/youth/wp-content/uploads/sites/21/2020/10/WYR2020-Chapter1.pdf.

42. Mark H. Moore, "Creating Public Value: Strategic Management in Government," *Harvard University Press*, March 25, 1997, https://www.hup.harvard.edu/catalog.php?isbn=9780674175587.

43. KVUE Profiles, "Alan Graham, President, CEO and Founder of Mobile Loaves & Fishes," Facebook post, November 9, 2017, https://www.facebook.com/51638951177/posts/10215210059430671.

44. Alan Graham, "Gospel con Carne," podcast, accessed April 18, 2022, https://mlf.org/gospel-con-carne-podcast/.

45. Graham, "Gospel con Carne."

46. Mobile Loaves and Fishes, "Truck Ministry," accessed April 18, 2022. https://mlf.org/truck-ministry/.

47. Amy Costello and Frederica Boswell, "What Does a Community-Based Approach to Chronic Homelessness Look Like?" *Nonprofit Quarterly*, November 3, 2021, https://nonprofitquarterly.org/what-does-a-community-based-approach-to-chronic-homelessness-look-like/.

48. Eva Ruth Moravec, "In Austin, A Community Offers Tiny Houses for the Chronically Homeless," *Washington Post*, October 26, 2018, https://www.washingtonpost.com/graphics/2018/national/tiny-houses/#austin.

49. Tiffany Fishman, et al., "Transportation Trends 2020: What Are the Most Transformational Trends in Mobility Today?" *Deloitte Insights*, April 13, 2020, https://www2.deloitte.com/us/en/insights/industry/public-sector/transportation-trends.html.

50. Tiffany Dovey Fishman and Michael Flynn, "Using Public-Private Partnerships to Advance Smart Cities," Deloitte Center for Government Insights, 2018, https://www2.deloitte.com/content/dam/Deloitte/global/Documents/Public-Sector/gx-ps-public-private-partnerships-smart-cities-funding-finance.pdf.

51. Joseph Chun, Joseph Tay, and Tan Wei Shyan, "A Closer Look at Singapore's Mandatory Corporate ESG Disclosures and Associated Legal Risks," *International Financial Law Review*, June 29, 2021, https://www.iflr.com/article/b1sgmvnqlndxc8/a-closer-look-at-singapores-mandatory-corporate-esg-disclosures-and-associated-legal-risks.

52. Sean Collins, "Advancing Environmental, Social, and Governance Investing: A Holistic Approach for Investment Management Firms," *Deloitte Insights*, February 20, 2020, https://www2.deloitte.com/us/en/insights/industry/financial-services/esg-investing-performance.html.

53. We Robotics, "How Delivery Drones Are Being Used to Tackle COVID-19," April 25, 2020, https://blog.werobotics.org/2020/04/25/cargo-drones-COVID-19/.

54. Syed Fasiuddin, "COVID-19 Outbreak Provides Test-Bed for Need-Based Insurance in India," *Economic Times*, March 17, 2020, https://bfsi.economictimes.indiatimes.com/news

/insurance/COVID-19-outbreak-provides-test-bed-for-need-based-insurance-in-india/74672696; Claire Woffenden, "FCA's Launches Digital Sandbox Pilot," *Fintech Times*, May 11, 2020, https://thefintechtimes.com/fcas-launches-digital-sandbox-pilot/.

55. For instance, David Jones and Mark Potter, "Unilever Names Nestle's Polman as CEO, Shares Leap," Reuters, September 4, 2008, https://www.reuters.com/article/us-unilever/unilever-names-nestles-polman-as-ceo-shares-leap-idUSL44874120080904; Sudeshna Sen, "Unilever Poaches Nestle's Paul Polman as CEO," *Economic Times*, September 4, 2008, https://economictimes.indiatimes.com/news/international/unilever-poaches-nestles-paul-polman-as-ceo/articleshow/3445305.cms?from=mdr.

56. David Jones, "Unilever Shares Tumble after Scraps Targets," Reuters, February 5, 2009, https://www.reuters.com/article/uk-unilever/unilever-shares-tumble-after-scraps-targets-idUKTRE51415Q20090205.

57. Andy Boynton and Margareta Barchan, "Unilever's Paul Polman: CEOs Can't Be 'Slaves' to Shareholders," *Forbes*, July 20, 2015, https://www.forbes.com/sites/andyboynton/2015/07/20/unilevers-paul-polman-ceos-cant-be-slaves-to-shareholders/?sh=11862de1561e; Geoffrey James, "Why Unilever Stopped Issuing Quarterly Reports," *Inc.*, January 23, 2018, https://www.inc.com/geoffrey-james/why-unilever-stopped-issuing-quarterly-reports.html.

58. Unilever, "Unilever Sustainable Living Plan," November 2010, https://assets.unilever.com/files/92ui5egz/production/9752ff2d82b8afabb507eb92c47b5dad795801d5.pdf/unilever-sustainable-living-plan.pdf; Marc Gunther, "Inside Unilever's Big, Broad, Bold Sustainability Plan," *GreenBiz*, November 16, 2010, https://www.greenbiz.com/article/inside-unilevers-big-broad-bold-sustainability-plan.

59. C.K. Prahalad and Stuart Hart introduced the concept in 2002, partly based on the example set by Unilever and its subsidiaries in India and Brazil. C.K. Prahalad and Stuart Hart, "The Fortune at the Bottom of the Pyramid," Booz & Co., January 10, 2002, https://www.strategy-business.com/article/11518.

60. Julia Finch, "Unilever Unveils Ambitious Long Term Sustainability Programme," *Guardian*, November 14, 2010, https://www.theguardian.com/business/2010/nov/15/unilever-sustainable-living-plan.

61. Unilever, "Unilever Sustainable Living Plan," November 2010, https://assets.unilever.com/files/92ui5egz/production/9752ff2d82b8afabb507eb92c47b5dad795801d5.pdf/unilever-sustainable-living-plan.pdf

62. Unilever, "Sustainability Performance Data," accessed April 18, 2022, https://www.unilever.com/planet-and-society/sustainability-reporting-centre/sustainability-performance-data/; "Sustainability Reporting Centre," Unilever, accessed April 18, 2022, https://www.unilever.com/planet-and-society/sustainability-reporting-centre/

63. "Lessons Learnt: New Ways of Measuring Social Impact," Unilever, May 14, 2020, https://www.unilever.com/news/news-search/2020/lessons-learnt-new-ways-of-measuring-social-impact/.

64. Paul Polman and Andrew Winston, *Net Positive: How Courageous Companies Thrive by Giving More Than They Take* (Boston: Harvard Business Review Press, 2021).

65. Daphné Dupont-Nivet, "Inside Unilever's Sustainability Myth," *New Internationalist*, April 13, 2017, https://newint.org/features/web-exclusive/2017/04/13/inside-unilever-sustainability-myth.

66. Interview with Paul Polman, August 18, 2022.

67. Polman and Winston, *Net Positive*.

68. Elizabeth Matsangou, "Unilever CEO Paul Polman Is Redefining Sustainable Business," *European CEO*, April 15, 2016, https://www.europeanceo.com/business-and-management/unilever-ceo-paul-polman-is-redefining-sustainable-business/.

69. Paul Polman and Eva Zabey, "Building a Nature-Positive Economy," *Project Syndicate*, April 28, 2021, https://www.project-syndicate.org/commentary/three-ways-to-boost-environmental-social-governance-performance-by-paul-polman-and-eva-zabey-2021-04. "Unilever has been around for 100-plus years," Polman told investors in late 2010. "We want to be around for several hundred more years. So if you buy into this long-term value-creation model—which is

equitable, which is shared, which is sustainable—then come and invest with us. If you don't buy into this, I respect you as a human being, but don't put your money in our company." Michael Skapinker, "Corporate Plans May Be Lost in Translation: What Will Investors Make of Unilever's Sustainability Programme?" *Financial Times*, November 22, 2010, https://www.ft.com/content /78cf6070-f66e-11df-846a-00144feab49a.

70. "The Rise of the Socially Responsible Business: Deloitte Global Societal Impact Survey," Deloitte, January 2019, 3, https://www2.deloitte.com/global/en/pages/about-deloitte/articles /societal-impact-survey-deloitte-global.html.

71. Interview with Josh Marcuse, former director of the Defense Innovation Board, November 5, 2021.

72. Ikenberry, review of *The Chessboard and the Web*.

73. Meyers and Eggers, "What Government Can Learn from Venture Capital"; and "UN Agency Partners with Mastercard to Help Improve Food Delivery around the World," *UN News*, September 13, 2012, https://news.un.org/en/story/2012/09/419482.

74. US Agency for International Development, "Financing Forest Conservation."

75. Interview with Andrew Deutz, director of Global Policy, Institutions and Conservation Finance, The Nature Conservancy, January 20, 2022.

76. "World's First Coral Reef Insurance Policy Triggered by Hurricane Delta," The Nature Conservancy, December 7, 2020, https://www.nature.org/en-us/newsroom/coral-reef-insurance -policy-triggered/.

77. As described in Ghana Mining Health Initiative, "A Mining Health Initiative Case Study: Newmont Ghana's Akyem Mine: Lessons in Partnership and Process," January 2013, https://assets.publishing.service.gov.uk/government/uploads/system/uploads/attachment_data /file/210176/Newmont-Ghana-MHI-case-study.pdf

78. William D. Eggers and Paul Macmillan, *The Solution Revolution: How Business, Government, and Social Enterprises Are Teaming Up to Solve Society's Toughest Problems* (Boston: Harvard Business Review Press, 2013).

79. Interview with Andrew Deutz, director of Global Policy, Institutions and Conservation Finance, The Nature Conservancy, January 20, 2022.

Chapter 4

1. See, for instance, Gerry McNeilly, "Broken Trust: Indigenous People and the Thunder Bay Police Service," Office of the Independent Policy Director, December 2018, http://oiprd.on .ca/wp-content/uploads/OIPRD-BrokenTrust-Final-Accessible-E.pdf.

2. Office of the Independent Police Review Director, "EPS Review of Broken Trust Report," April 2019, https://edmontonpolicecommission.com/wp-content/uploads/2019/04/5.4-EPS -Review-of-Broken-Trust-Report-3.pdf; and Emily Mertz, "'Our Actions Caused Pain': Edmonton Police Chief Apologizes to LGBTQ2 Community on Behalf of EPS," *Global News*, May 3, 2019, https://globalnews.ca/news/5232164/edmonton-police-chief-lgbtq-apology-eps/.

3. Michael Bussière, "Is It Time to Reinvent Policing? Edmonton Chief of Police Dale McFee Thinks So," *Ottawa Life*, March 25, 2021, https://www.ottawalife.com/article/is-it-time -to-reinvent-policing-edmonton-chief-of-police-dale-mcfee-thinks-so.

4. Edmonton Police Service, "Evidence-Based Policing (EBP)," https://www.edmonton police.ca/AboutEPS/Vision2020/EvidenceBasedPolicing; and Edmonton Police Service, "Vision 2020," https://www.edmontonpolice.ca/AboutEPS/Vision2020.

5. Interview with Dale McFee, chief of Edmonton Police, December 14, 2021.

6. Edmonton Police Service, "2SLGBTQ+ Allies Consultation and Reconciliation Portal," https://www.epsinput.ca/lgbtq2s.

7. Bussière, "Is It Time to Reinvent Policing?"

8. Anna Junker, "Edmonton Police Launch Community Solutions Accelerator, Using Data to Reduce Crime," *Edmonton Journal*, February 11, 2020, https://edmontonjournal.com/news/local -news/edmonton-police-launch-community-solutions-accelerator-using-data-to-reduce-crime.

9. Motorola Solutions, "Partnering with Technology to Fight Crime and Improve Public Safety," February 11, 2020, https://newsroom.motorolasolutions.com/news/partnering-with -technology-to-fight-crime-and-improve-public-safety.htm.

10. Lee Berthiaume, "Canadians' Trust in Police Drops amid Anti-Racism Protests, Poll Suggests," *Canadian Press*, June 16, 2020, https://www.thestar.com/news/canada/2020/06/16 /canadians-trust-in-police-drops-amid-anti-racism-protests-poll-suggests.html; CBC News, "Thousands Attend Anti-Racism Protest at Alberta Legislature," June 6, 2020, https://www.cbc .ca/news/canada/edmonton/edmontonians-join-the-wave-of-voices-protesting-the-death-of -george-floyd-1.5600180; and Edmonton Police Service, "Our Commitment to Action," accessed April 19, 2022, https://commitmenttoaction.ca/commitment-to-action.

11. Janice Johnston, "'No Apologies Needed': Edmonton Police Chief Reflects on Year of Change," CBC News, December 30, 2019, https://www.cbc.ca/news/canada/edmonton/police -chief-mcfee-edmonton-year-end-1.5409663.

12. Interview with Dale McFee, chief of Edmonton Police, December 14, 2021.

13. Organisation for Economic Cooperation and Development, "Trust in Government," accessed April 19, 2022, https://www.oecd.org/gov/trust-in-government.htm.

14. See, for instance, Donald F. Kettl, *Can Governments Earn Our Trust?* (Cambridge: Polity Press, 2017).

15. Francis Fukuyama, *Trust: The Social Virtues and the Creation of Prosperity* (New York: Free Press, 1995), 27–28.

16. Pew Research Center, "Public Trust in Government: 1958–2021," May 17, 2021, https:// www.pewresearch.org/politics/2021/05/17/public-trust-in-government-1958-2021/.

17. Organisation for Economic Co-operation and Development, *OECD Trust Survey Report* (Paris: OECD, 2021), https://www.oecd.org/governance/trust-in-government/.

18. Donald F. Kettl, "Can Governments Earn Our Trust?" Centre for Public Impact, August 3, 2017, https://www.centreforpublicimpact.org/insights/can-governments-earn-trust.

19. Asif Dhar et al., "Can More US Consumers Be Swayed to Take the COVID-19 Vaccine? Overcoming Access, Trust, Hesitancy, and Other Barriers," *Deloitte Insights*, November 10, 2021, https://www2.deloitte.com/us/en/insights/industry/health-care/vaccine-access-trust-barriers -to-vaccination.html.

20. Jake Blumgart, "The Persistent Belief That Government Doesn't Work," *Governing*, August 18, 2021, https://www.governing.com/now/the-persistent-belief-that-government-doesnt -work.

21. Tony D'Emidio et al., "The Global Case for Customer Experience in Government," McKinsey & Company, September 10, 2019, https://www.mckinsey.com/industries/public-and -social-sector/our-insights/the-global-case-for-customer-experience-in-government.

22. Organisation for Economic Co-operation and Development, "Trust in Government."

23. Organisation for Economic Co-operation and Development, *Building Trust to Reinforce Democracy: Main Findings from the 2021 OECD Survey on Drivers of Trust in Public Institutions* (Paris: OECD, 2021), https://www.oecd-ilibrary.org/sites/b407f99c-en/index.html?itemId= /content/publication/b407f99c-en.

24. John O'Leary, Angela Welle, and Sushumna Agarwal, "Improving Trust in State and Local Government: Insights from Data," *Deloitte Insights*, September 22, 2021, https://www2 .deloitte.com/us/en/insights/industry/public-sector/trust-in-state-local-government.html.

25. Leslie K. John, Tami Kim, and Kate Barasz, "Ads That Don't Overstep," *Harvard Business Review*, January–February 2018, https://hbr.org/2018/01/ads-that-dont-overstep.

26. Interview with Siim Sikkut, chief information officer for Estonia, April 15, 2021.

27. Kyle Kucharski, "31 Percent of People Don't Trust Facial-Recognition Tech," *PCMag*, May 28, 2019, https://www.pcmag.com/news/31-percent-of-people-dont-trust-facial-recognition -tech; and Suzanne Rowan Kelleher, "Most Americans Trust Facial Recognition Technology— But Not at the Airport," *Forbes*, June 13, 2019, https://www.forbes.com/sites/suzannerowankelleher /2019/06/13/most-americans-trust-facial-recognition-technology--but-not-at-the-airport/?sh =902115e5c029.

28. See, for instance, Don Norman, "Human-Centered Design: How to Focus on People When You Solve Complex Global Challenges," Interaction Design Foundation, May 27, 2021, https://www.interaction-design.org/literature/article/human-centered-design-how-to-focus-on -people-when-you-solve-complex-global-challenges.

29. US General Accounting Office, "VA Health Care: More National Action Needed to Reduce Waiting Times, but Some Clinics Have Made Progress," August 2001, https://www.gao .gov/assets/240/232610.pdf.

30. Scott Bronstein, Nelli Black, and Drew Griffin, "Veterans Dying Because of Health Care Delays," CNN, January 30, 2014, https://www.cnn.com/2014/01/30/health/veterans -dying-health-care-delays/; and Anthony Zurcher, "VA Hospital Cover-Up: An 'Authentic Scandal,'" *BBC Echo Chambers*, blog, May 20, 2014, https://www.bbc.com/news/blogs -echochambers-27480206.

31. US Department of Veterans Affairs, "Veteran Trust in VA Health Care Rises above 90 Percent for the First Time," April 30, 2020, https://www.va.gov/opa/pressrel/pressrelease.cfm?id=5435.

32. Partnership for Public Service, "2020 Winner: Management Excellence," accessed April 19, 2022, https://servicetoamericamedals.org/honorees/neil-c-evans-m-d-kathleen-l -frisbee-ph-d-and-kevin-galpin-m-d/.

33. Performance.gov, "Improving Customer Experience with Federal Services," accessed April 19, 2022, https://www.performance.gov/CAP/cx/; and US Department of Veterans Affairs, "VA Customer Profile and Veterans Signals Programs Recognized by FedHealthIT," *Vantage Point*, blog, June 18, 2019, https://www.blogs.va.gov/VAntage/61703/va-customer-profile -veterans-signals-programs-recognized-fedhealth/.

34. US Department of Veterans Affairs, "Veterans Health Administration Outpatient Services Surveys," April 23, 2020, https://www.blogs.va.gov/VAntage/wp-content/uploads/2020 /04/VHAOutpatientServices_Trust_23APR2020.pdf.

35. US Department of Veterans Affairs, "VA Customer Profile and Veterans Signals Programs Recognized."

36. Interview with Tom Allin, former chief veterans experience officer at the US Department of Veterans Affairs, February 24, 2021.

37. US Census Bureau, "About the Decennial Census of Population and Housing," accessed April 19, 2022, https://www.census.gov/programs-surveys/decennial-census/about.html.

38. Pew Research Center, "Public Trust in Government: 1958–2021."

39. Diane Elliott et al., "Assessing Miscounts in the 2020 Census," Urban Institute, June 2019, 8–9, https://www.urban.org/sites/default/files/publication/100324/assessing _miscounts_in_the_2020_census_1.pdf.

40. Naomi Schalit, "Why Some Americans Don't Trust the Census," The Conversation, March 9, 2020, https://theconversation.com/why-some-americans-dont-trust-the-census-130109.

41. Wired Insider, "Counting through Chaos," accessed April 19, 2022, https://www.wired .com/sponsored/story/deloittedigital-counting-through-chaos/?utm_source=onsite-share&utm _medium=email&utm_campaign=onsite-share&utm_brand=wired; and interview with Deloitte team working with Census Bureau, June 24, 2021.

42. Interview with Zackary Schwartz, division chief, Communications Directorate, US Census Bureau, January 27, 2022.

43. As quoted in Tom Temin, "How the Census Bureau Knocked Down Stupid and Potentially Harmful Internet Rumors," Federal News Network, June 3, 2021, https://federalnewsnetwork.com /people/2021/06/how-the-census-bureau-knocked-down-stupid-and-potentially-harmful-internet -rumors/.

44. Wired Insider, "Counting through Chaos."

45. Adelle M. Banks, "Black Church Leaders Push for Census Participation Despite Coronavirus," Religion News Service, March 27, 2020, https://religionnews.com/2020/03/27 /black-church-leaders-push-for-census-participation-despite-coronavirus/.

46. "Census 2020," https://www.skinnerleaders.org/census2020?blm_aid=28141.

47. Banks, "Black Church Leaders."

48. US Census Bureau, "2020 Census Response Rate Update: 99.98% Complete Nationwide," October 19, 2020, https://www.census.gov/newsroom/press-releases/2020/2020-census-all-states -top-99-percent.html.

49. For example, many of the most significant leaks of classified information in recent years have come from contractors. The fallout of those leaks does not appear to have significantly damaged those companies' stock performance, but it *has* had measurable impacts on trust in intelligence agencies. See, for instance, Chicago Council on Global Affairs, "2020 Public Attitudes on US Intelligence," by Stephen Slick and Joshua Busby, May 20, 2021, https://www.thechicago council.org/research/public-opinion-survey/public-attitudes-us-intelligence-2020.

50. Laura Hautala, "Facial Recognition Can Speed You through Airport Security, but There's a Cost," CNET, March 21, 2019, https://www.cnet.com/news/facial-recognition-can -speed-you-through-airport-security-but-theres-a-cost/.

51. Sushumna Agarwal et al., "Focusing Inward: How Improving Employee Engagement Can Help Rebuild Trust in Government," *Deloitte Insights*, October 8, 2021, https://www2 .deloitte.com/us/en/insights/industry/public-sector/trust-in-government-employee -engagement.html; and John Taft et al., "SOF Culture Is the Mission: Culture Is Key to Special Operations' Transition to Great Power Competition," *Deloitte Insights*, July 15, 2020, https://www2.deloitte.com/content/dam/insights/us/articles/6539_SOF-Culture/DI_SOF -Culture.pdf.

52. Interview with Exeter, New Hampshire, resident, June 18, 2021.

53. International Civil Aviation Organization, "Safety," https://www.icao.int/safety/Pages /default.aspx.

54. "2023 Edelman Trust Barometer: Navigating a Polarized World," https://www.edelman. com/trust/2023/trust-barometer?utm_source=newsletter&utm_medium=email&utm_campaign =newsletter_axiosam&stream=top.

55. US Department of Veterans Affairs, "VA Customer Profile and Veterans Signals Programs Recognized by FedHealthIT," June 18, 2019, https://www.blogs.va.gov/VAntage/61703 /va-customer-profile-veterans-signals-programs-recognized-fedhealth/.

56. Tom Christensen and Per Laegreid, "Trust in Government: The Relative Importance of Service Satisfaction, Political Factors, and Demography," *Public Performance & Management Review* 28, no. 4 (November 2002): 679–690, https://www.researchgate.net/publication /259369331_Trust_in_Government_The_Relative_Importance_of_Service_Satisfaction _Political_Factors_and_Demography.

57. Interview with Michael A. Nutter, former mayor of Philadelphia, January 6, 2022.

58. Interview with Dale McFee, chief of Edmonton Police, December 14, 2021.

59. Interview with Zackary Schwartz, division chief, Communications Directorate, US Census Bureau, January 27, 2022.

60. City of Portland Office of Equity and Human Rights, "Promising Practices in Government to Advance Racial Equity," accessed April 19, 2022, https://www.portlandoregon.gov/oehr /article/564991.

Chapter 5

1. The Aviation History Online Museum, "Pratt and Whitney J57 Engine," http://www .aviation-history.com/engines/j57.htm.

2. US Army Signal Corps Officer Candidate School Association, "Mission Statement," October 2013, https://web.archive.org/web/20131110173944/http:/www.armysignalocs.com /index_oct_13.html.

3. Brookings Institution, "The Costs of the Manhattan Project," August 1998, https://www .brookings.edu/the-costs-of-the-manhattan-project/.

4. US Department of Energy, "The Manhattan Project: An Interactive History," https:// www.osti.gov/opennet/manhattan-project-history/index.htm.

5. Frederick C. Mosher, "The Changing Responsibilities and Tactics of the Federal Government," *Public Administration Review* 40, no. 6 (November-December 1980): 541, https://www.jstor.org/stable/3110305?origin=crossref. See also Donald F. Kettl, *Government by Proxy: (Mis?)Managing Federal Programs* (Washington, DC: Congressional Quarterly Press, 1988); and Lester M. Salamon, ed., *The Tools of Government: A Guide to the New Governance* (New York: Oxford University Press, 2002).

6. Frederick C. Mosher, "The Changing Responsibilities and Tactics of the Federal Government," *Public Administration Review* 40, no. 6 (November-December 1980): 541, https://www.jstor.org/stable/3110305?origin=crossref. See also Donald F. Kettl, *Government by Proxy: (Mis?)Managing Federal Programs* (Washington, DC: Congressional Quarterly Press, 1988); and Lester M. Salamon, ed., *The Tools of Government: A Guide to the New Governance* (New York: Oxford University Press, 2002).

7. David Osborne and Ted Gaebler, *Reinventing Government: How the Entrepreneurial Spirit Is Transforming the Public Sector, from the Schoolhouse to Statehouse, City Hall to the Pentagon* (Reading, MA: Addison-Wesley, 1992), 32.

8. Travis A. Whetsell et al., "Government as Network Catalyst: Accelerating Self-Organization in a Strategic Industry," *Journal of Public Administration Research and Theory* 30, no. 3 (July 2020), https://academic.oup.com/jpart/article/30/3/448/5722026. See also Robert Agranoff, "Inside Collaborative Networks: Ten Lessons for Public Managers," *Public Administration Review* 66 (December 2006): 56–65, https://www.jstor.org/stable/4096570; Chris Ansell and Alison Gash, "Collaborative Governance in Theory and Practice," *Journal of Public Administration Research and Theory* 18, no. 4 (2008): 543–571, https://academic.oup.com/jpart/article/18/4/543/1090370; Kirk Emerson and Tina Nabatchi, *Collaborative Governance Regimes* (Washington, DC: Georgetown University Press, 2015); and Keith G. Provan and Patrick Kenis, "Modes of Network Governance: Structure, Management, and Effectiveness," *Journal of Public Administration Research and Theory* 18, no. 2 (April 2008): 229–252, https://academic.oup.com/jpart/article/18/2/229/935895.

9. Organisation for Economic Co-operation and Development, "The COVID-19 Crisis: A Catalyst for Government Transformation," November 10, 2020, https://www.oecd.org/coronavirus/policy-responses/the-COVID-19-crisis-a-catalyst-for-government-transformation-1d0c0788/.

10. Samuel Johnson quoted at Goodreads, https://www.goodreads.com/quotes/192643-depend-upon-it-sir-when-a-man-knows-he-is.

11. See, for example, General Leslie M. Groves, *Now It Can Be Told: The Story of the Manhattan Project* (New York: Da Capo Press, 1962), chs. 4–7.

12. US Department of Energy, "The Atomic Energy Commission and Postwar Biomedical Radiation Research," https://ehss.energy.gov/ohre/roadmap/achre/intro_4.html.

13. US Environmental Protection Agency, "Summary of the Atomic Energy Act," March 21, 2022, https://www.epa.gov/laws-regulations/summary-atomic-energy-act.

14. US Department of Energy Office of the General Counsel, "Price-Anderson Act," https://www.energy.gov/gc/price-anderson-act.

15. Center for Nuclear Science and Technology Information, "The Price-Anderson Act," November 2005, https://cdn.ans.org/policy/statements/docs/ps54-bi.pdf.

16. US Energy Information Administration, "Nuclear Explained: U.S. Nuclear Industry," April 18, 2022, https://www.eia.gov/energyexplained/nuclear/us-nuclear-industry.php.

17. Joel Primack and Frank von Hippel, *Advice and Dissent: Scientists in the Political Arena* (New York: Basic Books, 1974), ch. 2.

18. "Here's a Peek at Tomorrow's Huge Planes," *Popular Mechanics,* April 1960, https://books.google.com/books?id=99sDAAAAMBAJ&pg=PA86&dq=true#v=onepage&q=true&f=true.

19. Congressional Research Service, *U.S. Research and Development Funding and Performance: Fact Sheet,* September 13, 2022, https://sgp.fas.org/crs/misc/R44307.pdf

20. Max Meyers and William D. Eggers, "What Government Can Learn from Venture Capital," *Deloitte Insights,* May 23, 2019, https://www2.deloitte.com/us/en/insights/industry/public-sector/government-venture-capital.html.

21. "America's Top Givers 2022: The 25 Most Philanthropic Billionaires," *Forbes*, January 19, 2022, https://www.forbes.com/sites/forbeswealthteam/2022/01/19/americas-top-givers-2022-the-25-most-philanthropic-billionaires/?sh=bc90a133a6cc.

22. Mark Hrywna, "Giving in 2020 Hit Record $471 Billion, Up 5.1%," *The NonProfit Times*, June 15, 2021, https://www.thenonprofittimes.com/npt_articles/giving-in-2020-hits-record-471-billion-up-5-1/.

23. Julia Belluz, "The Media Loves the Gates Foundation: These Experts Are More Skeptical," *Vox*, June 10, 2015, https://www.vox.com/2015/6/10/8760199/gates-foundation-criticism.

24. Jeffrey Rissman and Hallie Kennan, "Low-Emissivity Windows," American Energy Innovation Council, March 2013, https://bipartisanpolicy.org/download/?file=/wp-content/uploads/2013/03/Case-Low-e-Windows.pdf.

25. Research and Markets, "Low-E Glass: Global Market Trajectory & Analytics," April 2021, https://www.researchandmarkets.com/reports/5140383/low-e-glass-global-market-trajectory-and.

26. Paul Sisson, "Nine Days in, Cyberattack Continues at Scripps Health," *San Diego Union-Tribune*, May 10, 2021, ww.sandiegouniontribune.com/news/health/story/2021-05-10/nine-days-in-cyber-attack-continues-at-scripps-health.

27. Randy Dotinga, "San Diego EDs Deluged with Patients after Cyberattack," *MedPage Today*, October 30, 2021, https://www.medpagetoday.com/meetingcoverage/acep/95357; Christian Dameff, "Stopping Digital Thieves: The Growing Threat of Ransomware," testimony before the Subcommittee on Oversight and Investigations, US House of Representatives Committee on Energy and Commerce, July 20, 2021, https://energycommerce.house.gov/sites/democrats.energycommerce.house.gov/files/documents/Witness%20Testimony_Dameff_OI_2021.07.20.pdf.

28. Andy Greenberg, "The Colonial Pipeline Hack Is a New Extreme for Ransomware," *Wired*, May 8, 2021, https://www.wired.com/story/colonial-pipeline-ransomware-attack/.

29. Christina Wilkie, "Colonial Pipeline Paid $5 Million in Ransom One Day after Cyberattack, CEO Tells Senate," *CNBC*, June 9, 2021, https://www.cnbc.com/2021/06/08/colonial-pipeline-ceo-testifies-on-first-hours-of-ransomware-attack.html; and Will Englund and Ellen Nakashima, "Panic Buying Strikes Southeastern United States as Shuttered Pipeline Resumes Operations," *Washington Post*, May 12, 2021, https://www.washingtonpost.com/business/2021/05/12/gas-shortage-colonial-pipeline-live-updates/.

30. US Department of Homeland Security, "Ransomware Guide," September 2020, https://www.cisa.gov/stopransomware/ransomware-guide; and William C. Barker et al., *Cybersecurity Framework Profile for Ransomware Risk Management* (Gaithersburg, MD: US National Institute of Standards and Technology), June 2021, https://csrc.nist.gov/CSRC/media/Publications/nistir/draft/documents/NIST.IR.8374-preliminary-draft.pdf.

31. Sean Lyngaas, "US Officials Believe Russia Arrested Hacker Responsible for Colonial Pipeline Attack," *CNN*, January 14, 2022, https://www.cnn.com/2022/01/14/politics/us-russia-colonial-pipeline-hack-arrest/index.html.

32. National Institute of Standards and Technology, "Success Story: Israel National Cyber Directorate Version 1.0," March 1, 2022, https://www.nist.gov/cyberframework/success-stories/israel-national-cyber-directorate-version-10.

33. Daniel Estrin, "In Israel, Teaching Kids Cyber Skills Is a National Mission," *Times of Israel*, February 4, 2017, https://www.timesofisrael.com/in-israel-teaching-kids-cyber-skills-is-a-national-mission/; Matthew Kalman, "Israeli Military Intelligence Unit Drives Country's Hi-Tech Boom," *Guardian*, August 12, 2013, https://www.theguardian.com/world/2013/aug/12/israel-military-intelligence-unit-tech-boom; and Gil Press, "6 Reasons Israel Became a Cybersecurity Powerhouse Leading the $82 Billion Industry," *Forbes*, July 18, 2017, https://www.theguardian.com/world/2013/aug/12/israel-military-intelligence-unit-tech-boom.

34. Yonit Wiseman, "Israel's Cybersecurity Startups Post Another Record Year in 2021," *TechCrunch*, January 4, 2022, chcrunch.com/2022/01/04/israels-cybersecurity-startups-post

-another-record-year-in-2021/; and Israeli National Cyber Directorate, "Israeli Cyber Security Continued to Grow in 2021: Record of $8.8 Billion Raised," January 20, 2022, https://www.gov.il /en/departments/news/2021cyber_industry.

35. As interviewed by Melissa Kate Griffith in 2018 for her dissertation, *The Mice That Roar: What Small Countries Can Teach Great Powers about National Cyber-Defense*, University of California at Berkeley, summer 2020, 82, https://escholarship.org/content/qt5335q7d9 /qt5335q7d9_noSplash_362876fdeb18fcbe55a61c4d6a070a90.pdf.

36. Idan Tendler, "From the Israeli Army Unit 8200 to Silicon Valley," *TechCrunch*, March 20, 2015, https://techcrunch.com/2015/03/20/from-the-8200-to-silicon-valley/; and Richard Behar, "Inside Israel's Secret Startup Machine," *Forbes*, May 11, 2016, https://www .forbes.com/sites/richardbehar/2016/05/11/inside-israels-secret-startup-machine/?sh =27f325381a51.

37. Robert Lakin, "The Secretive Israeli Army Unit That Recruits Like Harvard—and Churns Out High-Profile Startups," *Battery*, blog, August 31, 2015, https://www.battery.com /blog/secretive-israeli-army-unit-that-recruits-like-harvard/; and Corin Degani, "An Elite Israeli Intelligence Unit's Soldiers Are Sworn to Secrecy—but Tell All on LinkedIn," *Haaretz*, November 18, 2021, https://www.haaretz.com/israel-news/tech-news/2021-11-18/ty-article/ .premium/an-israeli-intell-units-soldiers-are-sworn-to-secrecy-but-tell-all-on-linkedin /0000017f-e0e5-d568-ad7f-f3ef63350000.

38. Martin Chulov, "Israel Appears to Confirm It Carried Out Cyberattack on Iran Nuclear Facility," *Guardian*, April 11, 2021, https://www.theguardian.com/world/2021/apr/11/israel -appears-confirm-cyberattack-iran-nuclear-facility.

39. Deloitte, "The Israeli Technological Eco-system: A Powerhouse of Innovation," https:// www2.deloitte.com/il/en/pages/innovation/article/the_israeli_technological_eco-system.html.

40. Government of Estonia, "This Is the Story of the World's Most Advanced Digital Society," https://digiexpo.e-estonia.com/history/.

41. Victor Yasmann, "Russia: Monument Dispute with Estonia Gets Dirty," *Radio Free Europe/Radio Liberty*, May 4, 2007, https://www.rferl.org/a/1076297.html; and Ian Traynor, "Russia Accused of Unleashing Cyberwar to Disable Estonia," *Guardian*, May 16, 2007, https://www.theguardian.com/world/2007/may/17/topstories3.russia.

42. Joshua Davis, "Hackers Take Down the Most Wired Country in Europe," *Wired*, August 21, 2007, https://www.wired.com/2007/08/ff-estonia/.

43. Mark Landler and John Markoff, "Digital Fears Emerge After Data Siege in Estonia," *New York Times*, May 29, 2007, https://www.nytimes.com/2007/05/29/technology/29estonia .html; and Patrick Jackson, "The Cyber Raiders Hitting Estonia," *BBC*, May 17, 2007, http://news .bbc.co.uk/1/hi/world/europe/6665195.stm.

44. Republic of Estonia, "Cybersecurity Strategy 2019–2022," July 2019, https://dea.digar.ee /cgi-bin/dea?a=d&d=JVestinformsyst201907.2.7.3&e=-------et-25--1--txt-txIN%7ctxTI%7ctx AU%7ctxTA------------.

45. See, for instance, Federal Bureau of Investigation, "GameOver Zeus Botnet Disrupted," June 2, 2014, https://www.fbi.gov/news/stories/gameover-zeus-botnet-disrupted.

46. Limor Kessem, "The Necurs Botnet: A Pandora's Box of Malicious Spam," *SecurityIntelligence*, April 24, 2017, https://securityintelligence.com/the-necurs-botnet-a-pandoras-box-of -malicious-spam/.

47. Brian Barrett, "How Microsoft Dismantled the Infamous Necurs Botnet," *Wired*, March 18, 2020, https://www.wired.com/story/microsoft-necurs-botnet-takedown/.

48. Interview with Jenn Gustetic, director of Early Stage Innovations and Partnerships at NASA, November 8, 2021.

49. Tanya Filer, "How Governments Can Turn Procurement into a Climate Innovation Tool," *Brookings TechStream*, September 16, 2021, https://www.brookings.edu/techstream/how -governments-can-turn-procurement-into-a-climate-innovation-tool/.

50. Morgan Stanley, "Space: Investing in the Final Frontier," July 24, 2020, https://www .morganstanley.com/ideas/investing-in-space.

51. Benjamin Reinhardt, "Why Does DARPA Work?" June 2020, https://benjaminreinhardt.com/wddw#distillation.

52. Paul Sonne, "How a Secretive Pentagon Agency Seeded the Ground for a Rapid COVID Cure," *Washington Post*, July 30, 2020, https://www.washingtonpost.com/national-security/how-a-secretive-pentagon-agency-seeded-the-ground-for-a-rapid-coronavirus-cure/2020/07/30/ad1853c4-c778-11ea-a9d3-74640f25b953_story.html.

53. William B. Bonnvillian, Richard Van Atta, and Patrick Windham, eds., *The DARPA Model for Transformative Technologies: Perspectives on the U.S. Advanced Research Projects Agency* (Cambridge: OpenBook Publishers, 2019), 216.

54. William D. Eggers et al., "Government as Catalyst: Driving Innovation Ecosystems," *Deloitte Insights*, March 24, 2022, https://www2.deloitte.com/za/en/insights/industry/public-sector/government-trends/2022/government-transformation.html.

55. Reinhardt, "Why Does DARPA Work?"

56. For a comprehensive analysis of government's role in innovation, see Mariana Mazzucato, *Mission Economy: A Moonshot Guide to Changing Capitalism* (New York: Harper Business, 2021).

57. Interview with Jenn Gustetic, November 8, 2021.

58. BRAIN Initiative, "Food and Drug Administration and the BRAIN Initiative," https://www.braininitiative.org/alliance/food-and-drug-administration/; and "National Science Foundation & The BRAIN Initiative," https://www.braininitiative.org/alliance/national-science-foundation/; and Defense Advanced Research Projects Agency, "DARPA and the Brain Initiative," https://www.darpa.mil/program/our-research/darpa-and-the-brain-initiative.

59. Interview with Jenn Gustetic, November 8, 2021.

60. John Dillard and Steve Stark, "Understanding Acquisition: The Valley of Death," *Army AL&T Magazine*, Spring 2022, https://asc.army.mil/web/news-understanding-acquisition-the-valley-of-death/.

Chapter 6

1. Stuart A. Thompson, "How Long Will a Vaccine Really Take?" *New York Times,* April 30, 2020, https://www.nytimes.com/interactive/2020/04/30/opinion/coronavirus-COVID-vaccine.html.

2. Dave Roos, "How a New Vaccine Was Developed in Record Time in the 1960s," *History.com*, October 29, 2021, https://www.history.com/news/mumps-vaccine-world-war-ii.

3. Natalie Colarossi, "How Long It Took to Develop 12 Other Vaccines in History," *Business Insider,* July 18, 2020, https://www.businessinsider.com/how-long-it-took-to-develop-other-vaccines-in-history-2020-7.

4. Patrick Boyle, "Here's Why We Can't Rush a COVID-19 Vaccine," *AAMC News*, March 31, 2020, https://www.aamc.org/news-insights/here-s-why-we-can-t-rush-a-COVID-19-vaccine.

5. Operation Warp Speed can't take entire credit for inventing COVID-19 vaccines: researchers published the SARS-CoV-2 coronavirus's genetic sequence on January 11, 2020, and dozens of developers moved quickly to vaccine candidates and clinical trials. Moderna began a Phase 1 trial for its mRNA-1273 vaccine in February 2020, nearly three months before OWS launched. See Tung Thanh Le et al., "The COVID-19 Vaccine Development Landscape," *Nature,* April 9, 2020, https://www.nature.com/articles/d41573-020-00073-5.

6. Stephanie Baker and Cynthia Koons, "Inside Operation Warp Speed's $18 Billion Sprint for a Vaccine," *Bloomberg Businessweek*, October 29, 2020, https://www.bloomberg.com/news/features/2020-10-29/inside-operation-warp-speed-s-18-billion-sprint-for-a-vaccine.

7. David Adler, "Inside Operation Warp Speed: A New Model for Industrial Policy," *American Affairs*, Summer 2021, https://americanaffairsjournal.org/2021/05/inside-operation-warp-speed-a-new-model-for-industrial-policy/.

8. US Department of Defense, "This Week in Operation Warp Speed—Nov. 20, 2020," November 20, 2020, https://www.defense.gov/News/Releases/Release/Article/2423778/this-week-in-operation-warp-speed-nov-20-2020/.

9. Rachel Sandler, "Biden, Some Democrats Say Trump Administration Deserves Credit for Vaccine Rollout," *Forbes*, December 21, 2020, https://www.forbes.com/sites/rachelsandler /2020/12/21/biden-some-democrats-say-trump-administration-deserves-credit-for-vaccine -rollout/; and *Boston Herald* editorial staff, "Editorial: Thank You Donald Trump for 'Warp Speed,'" *Boston Herald*, May 16, 2021, https://www.bostonherald.com/2021/05/16/editorial-thank -you-trump-for-warp-speed/.

10. "The U.S. Paid Billions to Get Enough COVID Vaccines Last Fall: What Went Wrong?" NPR, August 25, 2021, https://www.npr.org/sections/health-shots/2021/08/25/1029715721/pfizer -vaccine-operation-warp-speed-delay.

11. Arthur Herman, "Why Operation Warp Speed Worked," *Wall Street Journal*, February 1, 2021, https://www.wsj.com/articles/why-operation-warp-speed-worked-11612222129.

12. David Shulkin, "What Health Care Can Learn from Operation Warp Speed," *NEJM Catalyst*, January 21, 2021, https://catalyst.nejm.org/doi/full/10.1056/CAT.21.0001.

13. "'Other Transaction Authority' in the Federal Government," *The Pulse*, September 26, 2019, https://thepulsegovcon.com/article/2019-9-26-a-guide-to-other-transaction-authority-in -the-federal-government/.

14. Linda Auerbach Allderdice and Jameson B. Rice, "A Snapshot Look at COVID-19 Vaccine Distribution Logistics," *Holland & Knight Transportation Blog*, January 19, 2021. For two views of the rollout, see M. J. Lee, "Biden Inheriting Nonexistent Coronavirus Vaccine Distribution Plan and Must 'Start from Scratch,' Sources Say," *CNN*, January 21, 2021, https://www.cnn.com/2021 /01/21/politics/biden-COVID-vaccination-trump/index.html; and Austin Landis, "Biden Officials Say Trump Had No Plan for Vaccines: A Look Back Says Differently," *Spectrum News*, March 19, 2021, https://spectrumlocalnews.com/nys/central-ny/news/2021/03/19/officials-say-trump-had -no-plan-for-vaccines-a-look-back-says-differently, https://www.hklaw.com/en/insights /publications/2021/01/a-snapshot-look-at-COVID19-vaccine-distribution-logistics.

15. Federal Motor Carrier Safety Administration, "Expansion and Extension of the Modified Emergency Declaration No. 2020-002 under 49 CFR § 390.25," December 1, 2020, https://www.fmcsa.dot.gov/emergency/expansion-and-extension-modified-emergency -declaration-no-2020-002-under-49-cfr-ss-39025; and Federal Aviation Administration, "Transportation of COVID-19 Vaccines Requiring Large Quantities of Dry Ice," December 10, 2020, https://www.faa.gov/other_visit/aviation_industry/airline_operators/airline_safety/safo /all_safos/media/2020/SAFO20017.pdf.

16. Adler, "Inside Operation Warp Speed."

17. Rym Momtaz, "Macron Admires US 'Warp Speed' Vaccine Drive," *Politico*, January 29, 2021, https://www.politico.eu/article/emmanuel-macron-admires-us-warp-speed-coronavirus -vaccine/.

18. David Adler, "Inside Operation Warp Speed: A New Model for Industrial Policy."

19. George A. Akerlof, "The Market for 'Lemons': Quality Uncertainty and the Market Mechanism," *Quarterly Journal of Economics* 84, no. 3 (August 1970): 488–500, https://viterbi -web.usc.edu/~shaddin/cs590fa13/papers/AkerlofMarketforLemons.pdf; Michael Spence, "Job Market Signaling," *Quarterly Journal of Economics* 87, no. 3 (August 1973): 355–374, https:// viterbi-web.usc.edu/~shaddin/cs590fa13/papers/jobmarketsignaling.pdf; and Richard Arnott and Joseph Stiglitz, *Equilibrium in Competitive Insurance Markets with Moral Hazard,* National Bureau of Economic Research, 1991, https://www.nber.org/papers/w3588.

20. Robert Cyran, "Booster Jabs Are Easy Money for Pfizer and Moderna," *Reuters,* August 13, 2021, https://www.reuters.com/breakingviews/booster-jabs-are-easy-money-pfizer -moderna-2021-08-13/.

21. See E. S. Savas, *Privatization: The Key to Effective Government* (Chatham, NJ: Chatham House, 1987); and Stuart Butler, *Privatizing Federal Spending: A Strategy to Eliminate the Deficit* (New York: Universe Books, 1985).

22. Harvard Kennedy School Government Performance Lab, "Rhode Island Department of Children, Youth, and Families Performance Improvement," https://govlab.hks.harvard.edu /rhode-island-department-children-youth-and-families-performance-improvement.

23. "Trouble Is Brewing at the Rhode Island Department of Children, Youth, & Families (DCYF)," *Free Telegraph*, August 28, 2017, https://freetelegraph.com/trouble-brewing-rhode-island-department-children-youth-families-dcyf/.

24. Harvard Kennedy School Government Performance Lab, *Child Welfare Management and Delivery Solutions*, 2020, 18, https://govlab.hks.harvard.edu/files/govlabs/files/child_welfare_management_and_delivery_solutions_hks_gpl.pdf.

25. McDonald had some experience in the field; she served as deputy chief of staff and chief of staff for the Executive Office of Health and Human Services under Donald Carcieri, a previous Rhode Island governor. She is now a colleague at Deloitte with Eggers.

26. Since 2011, most Rhode Island family preservation and placement services for children and families had been contracted, delivered, and paid for through two networks of care, each managed by a lead agency that subcontracted with eight to fourteen direct care providers.

27. Harvard Kennedy School, "Rhode Island."

28. Interview with Jeffrey Liebman, October 1, 2021.

29. Interview with Jamia McDonald, January 18, 2022.

30. Interview with Jeffrey Liebman.

31. Interview with Margaret MacDuff, chief executive officer of Family Service of Rhode Island, November 1, 2021.

32. Harvard Kennedy School, "Rhode Island."

33. Interview with Jamia McDonald.

34. Interview with Margaret MacDuff.

35. Interview with Jamia McDonald.

36. Interview with Jeffrey Liebman.

37. William Eggers et al., "Linked-up Government: Building Connections for Greater Impact," *Deloitte Insights*, March 24, 2022, https://www2.deloitte.com/us/en/insights/industry/public-sector/government-trends/2022/joined-up-connected-government.html.

38. Harvard Kennedy School Government Performance Lab, "Results-Driven Contracting: An Overview," 2016, https://hwpi.harvard.edu/files/govlabs/files/results_driven_contracting_overview.pdf.

39. Interview with Jason Saul, executive director of the University of Chicago Center for Impact Sciences, November 4, 2021.

40. See Welsh Government, "Social Services: The National Outcomes Framework for People Who Need Care and Support and Carers Who Need Support," February 2019, https://gov.wales/sites/default/files/publications/2019-05/the-national-outcomes-framework-for-people-who-need-care-and-support-and-carers-who-need-support.pdf.

41. Scottish Government, "Transforming Social Care: Scotland's Progress Towards Implementing Self-Directed Support, 2011–2018," August 27, 2018, https://www.gov.scot/publications/transforming-social-care-scotlands-progress-towards-implementing-self-directed-support/pages/3/.

Chapter 7

1. US Centers for Disease Control and Prevention, "CDC's COVID-19 Data Improvement," October 29, 2021, https://www.cdc.gov/coronavirus/2019-ncov/science/data-improvements.html.

2. Yasmeen Abutaleb and Lena H. Sun, "How CDC Data Problems Put the U.S. Behind on the Delta Variant," *Washington Post*, August 19, 2021, https://www.washingtonpost.com/health/2021/08/18/cdc-data-delay-delta-variant/.

3. Kyle Swenson, "Millions Track the Pandemic on Johns Hopkins's Dashboard: Those Who Built It Say Some Miss the Real Story," *Washington Post*, June 29, 2020, https://www.washingtonpost.com/local/johns-hopkins-tracker/2020/06/29/daea7eea-a03f-11ea-9590-1858a893bd59_story.html.

4. Johns Hopkins University, "Coronavirus Resource Center," https://coronavirus.jhu.edu/.

5. Swenson, "Millions Track the Pandemic."

6. Lisa Cornish, Sara Jerving, and Jenny Lei Ravelo, "Data around COVID-19 Is a Mess and Here's Why That Matters," *Devex News*, May 11, 2020, https://www.devex.com/news/data-around-COVID-19-is-a-mess-and-here-s-why-that-matters-97077.

7. SEARCH Homeless Services, "Houston Leads the Nation in Reducing Homelessness," June 18, 2019, https://www.searchhomeless.org/houston-leads-the-nation-in-reducing-homelessness/.

8. Michael Kimmelman, "How Houston Moved 25,000 People from the Streets into Homes of Their Own," *New York Times*, updated June 24, 2022, https://www.nytimes.com/2022/06/14/headway/houston-homeless-people.html?referringSource=articleShare.

9. Audrey Jensen et al., "Two Cities Tried to Fix Homelessness, Only One Has Yet Succeeded," *Houston Chronicle*, December 28, 2020, https://www.houstonchronicle.com/news/houston-texas/houston/article/Two-cities-tried-to-fix-homelessness-only-one-15825633.php.

10. Henry Gass, "Houston, We Have a Solution: How the City Curbed Homelessness," *Christian Science Monitor*, November 18, 2019, https://www.csmonitor.com/USA/Society/2019/1118/Houston-we-have-a-solution-How-the-city-curbed-homelessness.

11. SEARCH Homeless Services, "Houston Leads the Nation in Reducing Homelessness."

12. City of Houston, "About Houston," https://www.houstontx.gov/abouthouston/houstonfacts.html.

13. Coalition for the Homeless of Houston/Harris County, "The Way Home Partner Portal," https://www.homelesshouston.org/hmis-v2.

14. Gass, "Houston, We Have a Solution."

15. Aubrey Vonck, "Unpacking HMIS," Coalition for the Homeless of Houston/Harris County, June 22, 2021, https://www.homelesshouston.org/unpacking-hmis; and Gass, "Houston, We Have a Solution."

16. US Department of Housing and Urban Development, "Homeless Management Information System," https://www.hudexchange.info/programs/hmis/; Coalition for the Homeless of Houston/Harris County, "The Way Home Partner Portal"; and Vonck, "Unpacking HMIS."

17. Jensen et al., "Two Cities Tried to Fix Homelessness"; Kimmelman, "How Houston Moved 25,000 People."

18. The Way Home, *The Way Home's Community Plan to End Homelessness: 2021–2026 Update*, 2021, https://irp-cdn.multiscreensite.com/2d521d2c/files/uploaded/FINAL%20TWH%20Community%20Plan.pdf; and Gass, "Houston, We Have a Solution."

19. Coalition for the Homeless of Houston/Harris County, "Unpacking HMIS."

20. Ernie Manouse, "Houston's Homeless Situation—Working on a Solution," *Houston Public Media*, October 8, 2018, https://www.houstonpublicmedia.org/articles/news/in-depth/2018/10/08/307243/houstons-homeless-situation-working-on-a-solution/.

21. SEARCH Homeless Services, "Michael Collier," https://www.searchhomeless.org/about/success-stories/michael-collier/.

22. Susan Wolf-Fordham, "Integrating Government Silos: Local Emergency Management and Public Health Department Collaboration for Emergency Planning and Response," *American Review of Public Administration*, July 24, 2020, https://doi.org/10.1177/0275074020943706.

23. Data Across Sectors for Health, "Linking Housing and Health Data to Improve Residents' Well-Being," October 6, 2016, https://dashconnect.org/2016/10/06/linking-housing-and-health-data-to-improve-residents-well-being/.

24. All In: Data for Community Health, "About Us," https://www.allindata.org/about-us/.

25. Data Across Sectors for Health, "Linking Housing and Health Data to Improve Residents' Well-Being."

26. As described in Eva H. Allen, Haley Samuel-Jakubos, and Timothy A. Waidmann, "Data Sharing in Cross-Sector Collaborations: Insights from Integrated Data Systems," Urban Institute, July 2021, https://www.urban.org/sites/default/files/publication/104548/data-sharing-in-cross-sector-collaborations_0.pdf.

27. Lauren Bonneau, "City Government of Buenos Aires Better Serves Its Citizens," *insiderPROFILES*, July 2013, https://www2.deloitte.com/content/dam/Deloitte/global /Documents/Technology/gx-cons-tech-sap-city-government-buenos-aires.pdf.

28. Deloitte, *Smart City/Smart Nation: Client Stories in Action*, "Buenos Aires Uses Technology for More Responsive Service Delivery," 2018, https://www2.deloitte.com/content /dam/Deloitte/global/Documents/Public-Sector/gx-gps-smart-cities-client-stories.pdf.

29. Bonneau, "City Government of Buenos Aires Better Serves Its Citizens."

30. David Betts et al., "The Future of the Public's Health," *Deloitte Insights*, November 29, 2021, https://www2.deloitte.com/us/en/insights/industry/health-care/the-future-of-public -health.html.

31. Interview with Ronald E. Brown, September 3, 2021.

32. Moira Inkelas and Patricia Bowie, "The Magnolia Community Initiative," *Community Investments*, Spring 2014, https://www.frbsf.org/community-development/publications /community-investments/2014/march/magnolia-community-initiative-measurement -improving-community-well-being/.

33. National Institutes of Health, National Human Genome Research Institute, "The Human Genome Project," 2020, https://www.genome.gov/human-genome-project.

34. National Institutes of Health, National Human Genome Research Institute, "Sequencing Consortium Announces 'Working Draft' of Human Genome," June 2000, https://www.genome .gov/10001457/2000-release-working-draft-of-human-genome-sequence.

35. SPARC, "From Ideas to Industries: Human Genome Project," https://sparcopen.org /impact-story/human-genome-project/.

36. Kendall Powell, "The Broken Promise That Undermines Human Genome Research," University of California Santa Cruz Genomics Institute, February 10, 2021, https://genomics .ucsc.edu/2021/02/10/the-broken-promise-that-undermines-human-genome-research/.

37. Jonathan Max Gitlin, "Calculating the Economic Impact of the Human Genome Project," National Human Genome Research Institute, June 12, 2013, https://www.genome.gov /27544383/calculating-the-economic-impact-of-the-human-genome-project.

38. Kelsie Nabben, "Hacking the Pandemic: How Taiwan's Digital Democracy Holds COVID-19 at Bay," *GCN*, September 11, 2020, https://gcn.com/2020/09/hacking-the-pandemic -how-taiwans-digital-democracy-holds-COVID-19-at-bay/314994/.

39. Echo Huang, "Taiwan's New Digital Minister Audrey Tang Is a Transgender Software Programmer Who Wants to Make Government More Open," *Quartz*, September 23, 2016, https://qz.com/767298/taiwans-new-digital-minister-is-a-transgender-software-programmer -who-wants-to-make-government-more-open/.

40. Centre for International Governance Innovation, "Audrey Tang," https://www .cigionline.org/people/audrey-tang/.

41. Audrey Tang, "How Digital Innovation Can Fight Pandemics and Strengthen Democracy," Presentation at TED2020, https://www.ted.com/talks/audrey_tang_how_digital_innovation _can_fight_pandemics_and_strengthen_democracy/transcript?language=en#t-807388.

42. Andrew Leonard, "How Taiwan's Unlikely Digital Minister Hacked the Pandemic," *Wired*, July 23, 2020, https://www.wired.com/story/how-taiwans-unlikely-digital-minister -hacked-the-pandemic/.

43. William D. Eggers et al., "Government as a Cognitive System," *Deloitte Insights*, March 4, 2021, https://www2.deloitte.com/us/en/insights/industry/public-sector/government -trends/2021/government-as-a-cognitive-system.html.

44. Nabben, "Hacking the Pandemic COVID."

45. Emma Cockerell, "Audrey Tang: Taiwan's Digital Minister on Harnessing Technology for Social Good," University of Southern California US-China Institute, March 11, 2021, https://china.usc.edu/audrey-tang-taiwans-digital-minister-harnessing-technology-social -good.

46. Arwa Mahdawi, "Humour Over Rumour? The World Can Learn a Lot from Taiwan's Approach to Fake News," *Guardian*, February 17, 2021, https://www.theguardian.com /commentisfree/2021/feb/17/humour-over-rumour-taiwan-fake-news.

47. Doden Aiko, "Taiwan: Boosting Social Innovation through IT," *NHK World-Japan News*, August 11, 2020, https://www3.nhk.or.jp/nhkworld/en/news/backstories/1239/.

48. Carnegie Council for Ethics in International Affairs, "Taiwan's Digital Response to COVID-19, with Audrey Tang," March 31, 2020, https://www.carnegiecouncil.org/studio /multimedia/20200331-taiwan-digital-response-COVID-19-audrey-tang.

49. Carnegie Council. "Taiwan's Digital Response to COVID-19."

50. E. Tammy-Kim, "Audrey Tang on Her 'Conservative-Anarchist' Vision for Taiwan's Future," *Rest of World*, September 29, 2020, https://restofworld.org/2020/audrey-tang-the -conservative-anarchist/.

51. Todd Konersmann et al., "Innovating R&D with the Cloud: Business Transformation Could Require Cloud-enabled Data, Ecosystems, and Services," *Deloitte Insights*, December 2, 2020, https://www2.deloitte.com/us/en/insights/topics/digital-transformation/cloud-enabled -research-and-development-innovation.html.

52. Interview with Siim Sikkut, chief information officer for Estonia, April 15, 2021.

53. Joe Mariani, "Leading to Chaos: A Conversation with General Stanley McChrystal," *Deloitte Review*, July 25, 2016, https://www2.deloitte.com/us/en/insights/deloitte-review/issue-19 /general-stanley-mcchrystal-interview-innovation-in-leadership.html.

54. Interview with Dale McFee, Chief of Edmonton Police, December 14, 2021.

55. GovLab, Data Collaboratives, "What Are Data Collaboratives," https://datacol laboratives.org/.

56. Juergen Klenk et al., "Fluid Government Data Dynamics," *Deloitte Insights*, March 4, 2021, https://www2.deloitte.com/uk/en/insights/industry/public-sector/government-trends /2021/fluid-government-data-dynamics.html.

57. Tang, "How Digital Innovation Can Fight Pandemics and Strengthen Democracy."

58. Klenk et al., "Fluid Government Data Dynamics."

59. National Center for Advancing Translational Sciences, "Announcement: Access to the COVID-19 Data Analytics Platform is Open," March 11, 2022, https://ncats.nih.gov/news /releases/2020/access-to-N3C-COVID-19-data-analytics-platform-now-open.

Chapter 8

1. CalFire, "Top 20 Largest California Wildfires," https://www.fire.ca.gov/media/4jandlhh /top20_acres.pdf

2. Alexander Ulmer, "Private Firefighters Fuel Tensions While Saving California Vineyards and Mansions," *Reuters* (May 14, 2021), https://www.reuters.com/world/us/private -firefighters-fuel-tensions-while-saving-california-vineyards-mansions-2021-05-14/

3. Philip Rucker, "Sen. DeMint of S.C. Is Voice of Opposition to Health-Care Reform," *Washington Post*, July 28, 2009, https://www.washingtonpost.com/wp-dyn/content/article/2009 /07/27/AR2009072703066.html?hpid=topnews&sid=ST2009072703107.

4. US Centers for Medicare and Medicaid Services, "CMS Fast Facts," 2022, https://www .cms.gov/Research-Statistics-Data-and-Systems/Statistics-Trends-and-Reports/CMS-Fast -Facts.

5. Craft.co, "The University of Texas at Austin," https://craft.co/the-university-of-texas -austin. Figure is an estimate for June 2022.

6. US Government Accountability Office, "Medicare Program and Improper Payments," https://www.gao.gov/highrisk/medicare-program-improper-payments.

7. Jody Freeman, "Extending Public Law Norms through Privatization," *Harvard Law Review* 116 (March 2003): 1285–1352, https://www.jstor.org/stable/1342728.

8. As described in Philip K. Howard, *The Rule of Nobody: Saving America from Dead Laws and Broken Government* (New York: W.W. Norton, 2014).

9. Paul C. Light, "The True Size of Government Is Nearing a Record High," *Brookings Institution FixGov Blog*, October 7, 2020, https://www.brookings.edu/blog/fixgov/2020/10/07/the -true-size-of-government-is-nearing-a-record-high/.

10. Office of Personnel Management, *FedScope*.

11. Justin Rohrlich, "The US Government Shutdown Cost Booz Allen Hamilton $20 Million in Revenue," *Yahoo News,* February 4, 2019, https://www.yahoo.com/now/us-government -shutdown-cost-booz-213808644.html.

12. John Palatiello, "With Automatic Spending Cuts Looming, the Federal Government Should Use Contracting," *Reason,* January 18, 2012, https://reason.org/commentary /sequestration-spending-cuts-contrac/.

13. Kate M. Manuel, "Definitions of 'Inherently Governmental Function' in Federal Procurement Law and Guidance," Congressional Research Service, December 23, 2014, Summary, https://sgp.fas.org/crs/misc/R42325.pdf.

14. Manuel, "Definitions of 'Inherently Governmental Function,'" 3.

15. US Government Accountability Office, *DHS Service Contracts: Increased Oversight Needed to Reduce the Risk Associated with Contractors Performing Certain Functions,* May 7, 2020, 8, https://www.gao.gov/assets/gao-20-417.pdf.

16. See, for instance, Donald F. Kettl, *Sharing Power: Public Governance and Private Markets* (Washington, DC: Brookings Institution, 1993).

17. Kaiser Health News, "Billions Spent by Medicare on Unnecessary Procedures," May 13, 2014, https://khn.org/morning-breakout/overtreatment-medicare/.

18. Heather Lyu et al., "Overtreatment in the United States," *PLOS One,* September 6, 2017, https://journals.plos.org/plosone/article?id=10.1371/journal.pone.0181970.

19. Statement of Seto J. Bagdoyan, US Government Accountability Office, Testimony Before the Subcommittee on Oversight, Committee on Ways and Means, US House of Representatives, "Medicare: Actions Needed to Better Manage Fraud Risks," July 17, 2018, 5, https://www.gao.gov /assets/gao-18-660t.pdf.

20. Office of Inspector General, US Department of Health and Human Services, "Medicare Fraud Strike Force," https://oig.hhs.gov/fraud/strike-force/.

21. US Government Accountability Office, "Medicare Program and Improper Payments," https://www.gao.gov/highrisk/medicare-program-improper-payments.

22. Find Law, "Is There a Time Limit to File a Lawsuit? What Are Statutes of Limitations?," Updated October 19, 2021, https://www.findlaw.com/litigation/filing-a-lawsuit/is-there-a-time -limit-to-file-a-lawsuit-what-are-statutes-of.html.

23. John Koskinen, "Responding to the Year 2000 Challenge: Lessons for Today," *IBM Center for the Business of Government Blog,* March 25, 2020, https://www.businessofgovernment .org/blog/responding-year-2000-challenge-lessons-today.

24. William D. Eggers, *Delivering on Digital: The Innovators and Technologies That Are Transforming Government* (Westlake, TX: Deloitte University Press, 2016).

25. Interview with Jenn Gustetic, Director of Early Stage Innovations and Partnerships at NASA, November 8, 2021.

26. Matt Ryan and others, "Using Collective Intelligence to Solve Public Problems," *Nesta,* October 2020, https://media.nesta.org.uk/documents/Using_Collective_intelligence_to_Solve _Public_Problems.pdf.

27. Interview with David Warm, September 30, 2021.

Chapter 9

1. Scott Pelley, "60 Minutes Remembers 9.11: The FDNY," *CBS News,* September 12, 2021, https://www.cbsnews.com/news/september-11-fdny-world-trade-center-60-minutes-2021-09-12/.

2. This case study is based on our interviews and Arlington County, "After-Action Report on the Response to the September 11 Terrorist Attack on the Pentagon," *National Policing Institute,* 2002, http://www.policefoundation.org/wp-content/uploads/2018/07/pentagon afteractionreport.pdf.

3. National Transportation Safety Board, "Aircraft Accident Report," January 13, 1982, 5, https://www.ntsb.gov/investigations/AccidentReports/Reports/AAR8208.pdf; and Ashley

Halsey III, "30 Years after Air Florida Crash, Skies Safer Than Ever," *Washington Post*, January 12, 2012, https://www.washingtonpost.com/local/30-years-after-air-florida-crash-skies-safer-than-ever/2012/01/05/gIQAW0GwtP_story.html.

4. Fred Hiatt and Howie Kurtz, "Emergency Services Reacted Quickly to Jetliner's Crash," *Washington Post*, January 15, 1982, https://www.washingtonpost.com/archive/politics/1982/01/15/emergency-services-reacted-quickly-to-jetliners-crash/d7697e6b-22a5-4895-a5d8-18fe0ff9d2fd/.

5. Arlington County, "After-Action Report on the Response to the September 11 Terrorist Attack on the Pentagon," *National Policing Institute*, 2002, A74, http://www.policefoundation.org/wp-content/uploads/2018/07/pentagonafteractionreport.pdf.

6. Arlington County, "After-Action Report," C-58.

7. Arlington County, "After-Action Report," 10.

8. Janice K. Popp et al., *Inter-Organizational Networks: A Review of the Literature to Inform Practice* (Washington, DC: IBM Center for the Business of Government, 2014), 7, https://www.businessofgovernment.org/sites/default/files/Inter-Organizational%20Networks.pdf; see also Jesse D. Lecy, Ines A. Mergel, and Hans Peter Schmitz, "Networks in Public Administration: Current Scholarship in Review," *Public Management Review* 16 (2014): 643–665, https://www.tandfonline.com/doi/abs/10.1080/14719037.2012.743577; and Patrick Kenis and Jorg Raab, "Back to the Future: Using Organization Design Theory for Effective Organizational Networks," *Perspectives on Public Management and Governance* 3, no. 2 (June 2020): 109–123, https://academic.oup.com/ppmg/article/3/2/109/5728879.

9. Robyn Keast et al., "Network Structures: Working Differently and Changing Expectations," *Public Administration Review* 64, no. 3 (May-June 2004): 365, https://onlinelibrary.wiley.com/doi/abs/10.1111/j.1540-6210.2004.00380.x.

10. Popp et al., *Inter-Organizational Networks*, 47–48.

11. Annie Correal, "Hockey Brawl Is Old Story of Policemen vs. Firemen," *New York Times*, April 8, 2014, https://www.nytimes.com/2014/04/08/nyregion/hockey-brawl-is-old-story-of-policemen-vs-firemen.html.

12. National Commission on Terrorist Attacks Upon the United States, "The 9/11 Commission Report, 2002," ch. 9, https://govinfo.library.unt.edu/911/report/911Report_Ch9.htm.

13. Interview with Regan Brewer, president at Jane Addams Resource Corporation, December 2021.

14. Data provided by JARC, December 14, 2021.

15. Interview with Mary Keller, EARN Maryland's program administrator, November 22, 2021.

16. Information provided by Maryland Department of Labor in February 2020.

17. Maryland Department of Labor, "EARN Maryland Annual Report Reveals Extremely High Return on Investment," February 28, 2018, https://www.dllr.state.md.us/whatsnews/earnannrep.shtml.

18. Information provided by Maryland Department of Labor in February 2020.

19. See Vernon Bogdanor, ed., *Joined-Up Government* (New York: Oxford University Press, 2005), https://academic.oup.com/british-academy-scholarship-online/book/28493.

20. David Osborne and Ted Gaebler, *Reinventing Government: How the Entrepreneurial Spirit Is Transforming the Public Sector* (Reading, MA: Addison-Wesley, 1992).

21. US General Accounting Office, "Executive Guide: Effectively Implementing the Government Performance and Results Act," June 1996, 1, https://www.gao.gov/assets/ggd-96-118.pdf.

22. US General Accounting Office, "Results-Oriented Government: GPRA Has Established a Solid Foundation for Achieving Greater Results," March 2004, Highlights page, https://www.gao.gov/assets/gao-04-38.pdf.

23. John Kamensky, "Cross-Agency Priority Goals: Do They Matter?" *Viewpoints*, Fall 2017, 65–68, https://www.businessofgovernment.org/sites/default/files/Viewpoints%20John%20Kamensky.pdf.

24. US Government Accountability Office, "Managing for Results: OMB Improved Implementation of Cross-Agency Priority Goals, but Could Be More Transparent about Measuring Progress," May 20, 2016, https://www.gao.gov/assets/gao-16-509.pdf.

25. Shaun Donovan et al., "Strengthening Employee Engagement and Organizational Performance," US Office of Management and Budget, December 23, 2014, https://www.fai.gov /sites/default/files/2014-12-23-OMB-Memo-Employee-Engagement.pdf.

26. Federal Permitting Improvement Steering Council, "FPISC Annual Report to Congress 2020," accessed April 19, 2022, https://www.permits.performance.gov/sites/permits.dot.gov/files /2021-01/FY2020%20Annual%20Report%20to%20Congress%20Fact%20Sheet.pdf.

27. US Government Accountability Office, "Federal Buying Power: OMB Can Further Advance Category Management Initiative by Focusing on Requirements, Data, and Training, GAO-21-40," November 2020, https://www.gao.gov/assets/gao-21-40.pdf.

28. Communication from Dustin Brown, deputy assistant director for management, US Office of Management and Budget, January 21, 2022.

29. US Government Accountability Office, "Government Performance Management: Key Considerations for Implementing Cross-Agency Priority Goals and Progress Addressing GAO Recommendations," September 2021, 1, https://www.gao.gov/assets/720/716998.pdf.

30. Kirsten Errick, "The Presidential Innovation Fellows Program Turned 10, What's Next?" GovernmentExecutive.com, October 12, 2022, https://www.govexec.com/workforce/2022/10 /presidential-innovation-fellows-program-turned-10-whats-next/378243/.

31. Elwood M. Hopkins and James M. Ferris, "Philanthropy & the City: What Does an Inclusive and Equitable Recovery Look Like?" The Center on Philanthropy and Public Policy, Sol Price School of Public Policy, University of Southern California, February 2022, https://cppp .usc.edu/local-problem-solving-for-a-more-equitable-recovery/.

32. Interview with Michael A. Nutter, former mayor of Philadelphia, January 6, 2022.

33. Interview with Joshua Marcuse, head of federal strategy at Google, November 8, 2021.

34. Interview with David B. Smith, CEO of X Sector Labs and former president of the Presidio Institute, November 9, 2021.

35. Interview with Kelly M. Schulz, former secretary of the Maryland Department of Commerce, November 30, 2021.

36. Interview with Mary Keller, EARN Maryland's program administrator, November 22, 2021.

Chapter 10

1. Bloomberg's company, Bloomberg LP, employs about 20,000 people in 120 countries. See Margot Adler, "Assessing Bloomberg's Legacy Is a Complex Task," NPR, December 30, 2013.

2. New York Times, "Text of Bloomberg's Inaugural Address," January 1, 2002, https://www .nytimes.com/2002/01/01/nyregion/text-of-bloombergs-inaugural-address.html.

3. Elizabeth Greenspan, "Mayor Bloomberg's Legacy," The New Yorker, September 18, 2013, https://www.newyorker.com/business/currency/mayor-bloombergs-legacy.

4. Lindsay K. Campbell, "Constructing New York City's Urban Forest: The Politics and Governance of the MillionTreesNYC Campaign," in Urban Forests, Trees, and Green Space: A Political Ecology Perspective, edited by L. Anders Sandberg et al., 249, https://www.fs.fed.us/nrs /pubs/jrnl/2014/nrs_2014_campbell-l_002.pdf.

5. Freedman Consulting, "The Collaborative City: How Partnerships Between Public and Private Sectors Can Achieve Common Goals," November 21, 2013, https://issuu.com/nycmayors fund/docs/ppp_report_-_final_web_version_11_2.

6. Campbell, "Constructing New York City's Urban Forest."

7. NYC Parks, "MillionTreesNYC," https://www.nycgovparks.org/trees/milliontreesnyc.

8. MillionTreesNYC, "NYC's Urban Forest: Benefits of NYC's Urban Forest, https://www .milliontreesnyc.org/.

9. See for instance Anemona Hartocollis, "Most 8th Graders in New York City Fail State Tests," New York Times, November 6, 1999, https://www.nytimes.com/1999/11/06/nyregion/most -8th-graders-in-new-york-city-fail-state-tests.html; John Sullivan et al., "Careless Contractors, Crumbling Schools," New York Times, July 26, 1999, https://www.nytimes.com/1999/07/26

/nyregion/careless-contractors-crumbling-schools.html; Diane Ravitch, "New York School Reform: A 'Long-Haul' Affair," *New York Times*, January 16, 1974, https://www.nytimes.com /1974/01/16/archives/new-york-school-reform-a-longhaul-affair-origins-of-citys-schools.html; Howard Kurtz, "New York's School System: An Intractable Mess," *Washington Post*, January 2, 1988, https://www.washingtonpost.com/archive/politics/1988/01/02/new-yorks-school-system -an-intractable-mess/bd6390ce-bf47-475d-81c4-4ba1ae46c7b8/; and James Traub, "What No School Can Do," *New York Times Magazine*, January 16, 2000, https://www.nytimes.com/2000 /01/16/magazine/what-no-school-can-do.html.

10. John Heilemann, "The Chancellor's Midterm Exam," *New York*, October 21, 2005, https://nymag.com/nymetro/urban/education/features/14869/.

11. Richard Whitmire, "A 'Founders' Excerpt: How Joel Klein Found His Disruptive Force—and Reshaped NYC Education," *The 74*, November 22, 2016, https://www.the74million.org/article/a -founders-excerpt-how-joel-klein-found-his-disruptive-force-and-reshaped-nyc-education/.

12. Catherine Gewertz, "N.Y.C. Mayor Gains Control over Schools," *Education Week*, June 19, 2002, https://www.edweek.org/leadership/n-y-c-mayor-gains-control-over-schools/2002/06.

13. Note that many observers were appalled by the very idea of public-private partnership with regard to public education. See for instance Joanne Barkan, "Got Dough? How Billionaires Rule Our Schools," *Dissent*, Winter 2011, https://www.dissentmagazine.org/article/got-dough -how-billionaires-rule-our-schools.

14. David M. Herszenhorn, "New York City's Big Donors Find New Cause: Public Schools," *New York Times*, December 30, 2005, https://www.nytimes.com/2005/12/30/nyregion/new-york -citys-big-donors-find-new-cause-public-schools.html.

15. Fund for Public Schools, "The Fund for Public Schools Announces This Year's Shop for Public Schools," *Cision PRWeb*, September 15, 2009, http://www.prweb.com/releases/2009/09 /prweb2881944.htm.

16. "'I've gotten calls from people I actually thought were dead,' said Toby Emmerich, head of New Line Cinema, from the podium, explaining that this was 'definitely the most sought-after ticket' in New York tonight (and that it was in fact a benefit for the Fund for Public Schools)." Meredith Bryan, "Sex Party Turns into Estrogen-Fueled Rock Concert as S.J.P. Blows Giant Air-Kiss at N.Y.C.," *The Observer*, May 28, 2008, https://observer.com/2008/05/isexi-party -turns-into-estrogenfueled-rock-concert-as-sjp-blows-giant-airkiss-at-nyc/.

17. Megan Sheekey, "Building Blocks to Effective Public-Private Collaboration," Mike Bloomberg.com, September 7, 2017, https://www.mikebloomberg.com/news/building-blocks -effective-public-private-collaboration/.

18. Sheekey, "Building Blocks."

19. New York City Global Partners, "Best Practice: Public-Private Investment Fund for Public School Reform," March 29, 2010, 4, https://www1.nyc.gov/assets/globalpartners /downloads/pdf/NYC_Education_FPS.pdf.

20. Ideally, too, leaders should construct programs to survive—if successful—beyond their tenure. A few years after Bloomberg left office, some observers lamented the lapsing of education reform efforts. See Eliza Shapiro, "How New York Stopped Being the Nation's Education Reform Capital," *Politico*, August 7, 2017, https://www.politico.com/states/new-york/albany/story/2017 /08/07/how-new-york-stopped-being-the-nations-education-reform-capital-113548; and Robert Pondiscio, "Education Reform in New York? Fuhgeddaboudit," Thomas B. Fordham Institute, April 5, 2017, https://fordhaminstitute.org/national/commentary/education-reform-new-york -fuhgeddaboudit.

21. Note that Bloomberg's education program as well as his management style were highly controversial throughout his tenure; see Peter Meyer, "New York City's Education Battles," *Education Next*, 2009, https://www.educationnext.org/new-york-citys-education-battles/. And while many praised him—see Paul T. Hill, "Bloomberg's Education Plan Is Working: Don't Ditch It," *Atlantic*, October 22, 2013, https://www.theatlantic.com/education/archive/2013/10 /bloombergs-education-plan-is-working-dont-ditch-it/280704/—it's worth mentioning that even programs widely deemed successful drew vocal criticism, especially in hindsight, as

Bloomberg launched his short-lived 2020 presidential campaign. For instance, see Jake Jacobs, "How Bloomberg Trashed Public Education in New York," *The Progressive*, February 24, 2020, https://progressive.org/public-schools-advocate/bloombergtrashedpubliced/.

22. "After 12 Years of Bloomberg, Data Reigns in the Schools," *WNYC*, July 11, 2013, https://www.wnyc.org/story/303900-bloombergs-schools-legacy-use-data/.

23. Horst W. J. Rittel and M. M. Webber, "Dilemmas in a General Theory of Planning," *Policy Sciences* 4 (1973): 155–169, https://link.springer.com/article/10.1007/BF01405730.

24. White House, "Remarks by the President on the BRAIN Initiative and American Innovation," April 2, 2013, https://obamawhitehouse.archives.gov/the-press-office/2013/04/02/remarks-president-brain-initiative-and-american-innovation.

25. David Kaldewey, "The Grand Challenges Discourse: Transforming Identity Work in Science and Science Policy," *Minerva* 56, September 4, 2017, https://link.springer.com/article/10.1007/s11024-017-9332-2; and Stefan Kuhlmann, "Next-Generation Innovation Policy and Grand Challenges," *Science and Public Policy* 45, August 2018, https://www.researchgate.net/publication/328677092_Next-Generation_Innovation_Policy_and_Grand_Challenges.

26. Grand Challenges for Social Work, "History," https://grandchallengesforsocialwork.org/about/history/; and Simons Foundation, "Hilbert's Problems: 23 and Math," May 6, 2020, https://www.simonsfoundation.org/2020/05/06/hilberts-problems-23-and-math/.

27. National Human Genome Research Institute, "What Is the Human Genome Project?" https://www.genome.gov/human-genome-project/What; and Bill Frist, "NIH Director Dr. Francis Collins: Connecting the Dots from the Human Genome Project to the COVID-19 Vaccine," *Forbes*, January 20, 2021, https://www.forbes.com/sites/billfrist/2021/01/20/nih-director-dr-francis-collins-connecting-the-dots-from-the-human-genome-project-to-the-COVID-19-vaccine/?sh=2a927e727543.

28. BRAIN Initiative, "Food and Drug Administration & the BRAIN Initiative," https://www.braininitiative.org/alliance/food-and-drug-administration/; Frist, "NIH Director Dr. Francis Collins"; Defense Advanced Research Projects Agency, "DARPA and the BRAIN Initiative," https://www.darpa.mil/program/our-research/darpa-and-the-brain-initiative; and BRAIN Initiative, "National Science Foundation & the BRAIN Initiative," https://www.braininitiative.org/alliance/national-science-foundation/.

29. See KAVLI Foundation, "The BRAIN Initiative: At the Frontiers of Neuroscience," October 12, 2016, https://kavlifoundation.org/news/brain-initiative-three-years; White House Office of Science and Technology Policy, "Obama Administration Proposes Over $434 Million in Funding for the Brain Initiative," March 2016, https://obamawhitehouse.archives.gov/sites/whitehouse.gov/files/documents/BRAIN%20Initiative%20FY17%20Fact%20Sheet.pdf; and National Institute of Neurological Disorders and Stroke, "NIH Greatly Expands Investment in BRAIN Initiative," November 2, 2018, https://www.ninds.nih.gov/News-Events/News-and-Press-Releases/Press-Releases/NIH-greatly-expands-investment-BRAIN-Initiative.

30. Nick Paul Taylor, "Google Joins Brain Initiative to Help with Petabyte-Scale Data Sets," *Fierce Biotech*, October 6, 2014, https://www.fiercebiotech.com/data-management/google-joins-brain-initiative-to-help-petabyte-scale-data-sets.

31. BRAIN Initiative Alliance, "IEEE Brain Joins the BIA: Bolstering Technological Expertise in Neuroscience and Health Applications of Engineering," April 10, 2019, https://www.braininitiative.org/2019/04/10/ieee-brain-joins-the-bia-bolstering-technological-expertise-in-neuroscience-and-health-applications-of-engineering/; and KAVLI Foundation, "The BRAIN Initiative."

32. National Institutes of Health, "The BRAIN Initiative," November 2021, https://braininitiative.nih.gov/sites/default/files/pdfs/brain_technical_one_pager_11012021_508c.pdf; and Gianluca Quaglio et al., "The International Brain Initiative: Enabling Collaborative Science," *Lancet* 20, no. 12 (December 1, 2021), https://www.thelancet.com/journals/laneur/article/PIIS1474-4422(21)00389-6/fulltext.

33. Ganesh Mani, "Artificial Intelligence's Grand Challenges: Past, Present, and Future," *AI Magazine*, Spring 2021, https://www.andrew.cmu.edu/user/ganeshm/GrandChallengesAIMagazineSpring2021.pdf.

34. Grand Challenges, "About Grand Challenges Initiatives," https://grandchallenges.org/about.

35. Grand Challenges, "Grand Challenges in Global Health Announced," January 23, 2003, https://gcgh.grandchallenges.org/article/grand-challenges-global-health-announced; and Kaldewey, "The Grand Challenges Discourse."

36. C. D. Mote Jr. et al., "The Power of an Idea: The International Impacts of the Grand Challenges for Engineering," *Engineering* 2, 2016, https://uppm.poliupg.ac.id/wp-content/uploads/2016/08/1-s2.0-S2095809916301308-main.pdf.

37. Rajshree Agarwal, Seojin Kim, and Mahka Moeen, "Leveraging Private Enterprise: Incubation of New Industries to Address the Public Sector's Mission-Oriented Grand Challenges," *SSRN*, March 18, 2021, https://papers.ssrn.com/sol3/papers.cfm?abstract_id=3769182.

38. Vanessa Peña and Chelsea A. Stokes, "Use of Grand Challenges in the Federal Government," Institute for Defense Analyses, June 2019, A-1, https://www.ida.org/-/media/feature/publications/u/us/use-of-grand-challenges-in-the-federal-government/d10699final.ashx.

39. US Department of Energy, "The SunShot Initiative: Making Solar Energy Affordable for All Americans," June 2016, https://www.energy.gov/sites/prod/files/2016/06/f32/SunShot-factsheet-6-10_final-508.pdf.

40. Agarwal et al., "Leveraging Private Enterprise"; and Cancer Grand Challenges, "The Power of Discovery: 7 Teams Leading the Way," November 16, 2020, https://cancergrandchallenges.org/news/power-discovery-7-teams-leading-way.

41. National Cancer Institute, "Cancer Grand Challenges," 2021, https://www.cancer.gov/grants-training/grants-funding/cancer-grand-challenges.

42. Daniel P. Gross and Bhaven N. Sampat, "Crisis Innovation Policy from World War II to COVID-19," National Bureau of Economic Research, June 2021, https://www.nber.org/papers/w28915.

43. National Institutes of Health, "Accelerating COVID-19 Therapeutic Interventions and Vaccines (ACTIV)," https://www.ida.org/-/media/feature/publications/u/us/use-of-grand-challenges-in-the-federal-government/d10699final.ashx.

44. Joshua Newman and Brian W. Head, "Wicked Tendencies in Policy Problems: Rethinking the Distinction Between Social and Technical Problems," *Policy and Society* 36, no. 3 (August 14, 2017), https://www.tandfonline.com/doi/full/10.1080/14494035.2017.1361635. See also Franz Wohlgezogen et al., "The Wicked Problem of Climate Change and Interdisciplinary Research: Tracking Management Scholarship's Contribution," *Journal of Management and Organization* 26, no. 6 (2020): 1048–1072, https://www.proquest.com/openview/3fefdbf32463780e2a6cd1a2aeb6f259/1?pq-origsite=gscholar&cbl=38879; and Frank P. Incropera, *Climate Change: A Wicked Problem: Complexity and Uncertainty at the Intersection of Science, Economics, Politics, and Human Behavior* (Cambridge: Cambridge University Press, 2015).

45. United Nations, "Secretary-General's Statement on the IPCC Working Group 1 Report on the Physical Science Basis of the Sixth Assessment," August 9, 2021, https://www.un.org/sg/en/content/secretary-generals-statement-the-ipcc-working-group-1-report-the-physical-science-basis-of-the-sixth-assessment.

46. Michael Raynor and Derek Pankratz, "A New Business Paradigm to Address Climate Change," *Deloitte Insights,* October 16, 2020, https://www2.deloitte.com/us/en/insights/topics/strategy/corporate-climate-change-sustainability.html.

47. Scott Corwin and Derek Pankratz, "Leading in a Low-Carbon Future: A 'System of Systems' Approach to Addressing Climate Change," *Deloitte Insights*, May 24, 2021, https://www2.deloitte.com/us/en/insights/topics/strategy/low-carbon-future.html.

48. Interview with Simona Petrova-Vassileva, secretary of the United Nations Chief Executives Board, November 2021.

49. Bruce Chew, Tiffany Fishman, and Richard Longstaff, "Climate-Forward Government: Seven Lessons for Effective Climate Action," *Deloitte Insights*, July 30, 2021, https://www2.deloitte.com/us/en/insights/industry/public-sector/government-policy-climate-change-innovation.html.

50. See, for instance, William D. Eggers and Anna Muoio, "Wicked Opportunities," Deloitte University Press, 2015, https://www2.deloitte.com/content/dam/Deloitte/za/Documents/strategy/za_Wicked_Opportunities_3.pdf.

51. Interview with Jennifer Park, Results for America, April 13, 2022.

52. Nicole Ogrysko, "Hybrid Work Brings New Professional Development Possibilities to NASA," *Federal News Network*, December 17, 2021, https://federalnewsnetwork.com/federal-insights/2021/12/hybrid-work-brings-new-professional-development-possibilities-to-nasa/.

53. "Building Blocks to Effective Public-Private Collaboration," Mike Bloomberg.com, September 7, 2017, https://www.mikebloomberg.com/news/building-blocks-effective-public-private-collaboration/.

54. Interview with Joshua Marcuse, head of Federal Strategy for Google, November 8, 2021.

55. Anna Muoio et al., "Shifting a System: The Reimagine Learning Network and How to Tackle Persistent Problems," *Deloitte Insights*, 2019, 10, https://www2.deloitte.com/content/dam/insights/us/articles/5139_shifting-a-system/DI_Reimagining-learning.pdf.

56. Deloitte, "Aligned Action: Organizing for System Change," https://www2.deloitte.com/us/en/pages/monitor-institute/solutions/aligned-action-for-wicked-problems.html.

57. Corwin and Pankratz, "Leading in a Low-Carbon Future."

58. Kevin Bingham, Terri Cooper, and Lindsay Hough, "Fighting the Opioid Crisis," *Deloitte Insights*, August 15, 2016, https://www2.deloitte.com/us/en/insights/industry/public-sector/fighting-opioid-crisis-heroin-abuse-ecosystem-approach.html.

Conclusion

1. "However Justified, More Government Intervention Risks Being Counterproductive," *The Economist*, January 15, 2022, https://www.economist.com/special-report/2022/01/10/however-justified-more-government-intervention-risks-being-counterproductive.

2. Kaitlan Collins Interviews Robert Califf, *CNN New Day*, May 16, 2022, https://www.cnn.com/videos/business/2022/05/16/fda-commissioner-robert-carliff-baby-formula-supply-shortage-newday-vpx.cnn.

3. Eric Garton, "Employee Burnout Is a Problem with the Company, Not the Person," *Harvard Business Review*, April 6, 2017, https://hbr.org/2017/04/employee-burnout-is-a-problem-with-the-company-not-the-person.

4. Tom Rath, *Strengthsfinder 2.0* (Washington, DC: Gallup Press, 2007).

5. Interview with Joellen Jarrett, February 17, 2022.

6. National Academy of Public Administration, *No Time to Wait: Building a Public Service for the Twenty-First Century*, Parts 1 (July 2017) and 2 (September 2018), https://napawash.org/academy-studies/no-time-to-wait-part-2-building-a-public-service-for-the-21st-century.

Index

Figures are indicated by *f*; tables are indicated by *t*

Acknowledgments

While our names may be on the cover, in reality, many talented individuals contributed to this book's research, writing, editing, and design.

Glynis Rodrigues and Aishwarya Rai of the Deloitte Center for Government Insights were the book's lead researchers. Involved in the project from the very beginning, they contributed significantly to many aspects of the manuscript, from unearthing myriad research gems to tracking reviewer feedback. We have little doubt that their prodigious talent will help them build a successful career ahead. Thank you also to Meenakshi Venkateswaran for creating the compelling visuals you see in each chapter.

Many of Bill's Deloitte Center for Government Insights colleagues also played a critical role in helping to shape the book. Dave Noone, John O'Leary, Joe Mariani, Adam Routh, Bruce Chew, Tiffany Fishman, Alison Muckle, Amrita Datar, Sushumna Agarwal, Mahesh Kelkar, and Pankaj Kishnani provided helpful feedback on various aspects of the manuscript. Akash Keyal and Kannan Thirumalai lent research assistance to shaping the bridgebuilder boxes.

Bill would also like to thank many other Deloitte colleagues for their detailed feedback on book chapters and case studies, including Tiffany Plowman, Joshua Knight, Jesse Goldhammer, Kevin Brault, Jamia McDonald, Sam Korta, Mark Bussow, Davin O'Regan, Caroline Faught, Randy Turkel, Bob Sapio, Lauren Savoy, Margaret Anderson, Wade Horn, Derek Pankratz, Josh Sawislak, Anna Holland, John Mennel, Shira Beery, Kwasi Mitchell, Stasha Stantifort, Paul Macmillan, Steve Watkins, Lucy Melvin, Forest Richardson, Jacqueline Winters, Jackie Gainer, Gabriel Kaspers, Max Meyers, Kenneth Wojdon, Juergen Klenk, Steven Watkins, Mariam Mansury, Chris Eshman, Vishal Kapur, Adita Karkera, and Mark Urbancyk. A special thanks to leaders Mike Canning and Rod Sides for their strong support of the book's development.

We would also like to thank the dozens of leading bridgebuilders, inside and outside government, who lent us their time and expertise and imparted myriad tips and strategies for successful cross-sector collaboration, including Anne-Marie Slaughter, Paul Polman, Zack Schwartz, Simona Petrova-Vassileva, Barbara Morton, Chief Dale McFee, Charles Boldin, Jenn Gustetic, David Warm, Michael Nutter, Kelly M. Schulz, Andrew Deutz, Mark Tercek, Amanda Daflos, David Smith, Jeffrey Liebman, Tom Allin, Deborah Wince Smith, Dustin Brown, Margaret McDuff, Jason Saul, Jamie Van Leeuwen, John Kamensky, Ed DeSeve, Jennifer Park, Eli Allen, Aleem Ali, Josh Marcuse, Regan Brewer Johnson, Thad Allen, Daniel Chenok, and James M. Ferris.

Two talented individuals, Matthew Budman and Christopher Benz, were also vital to the book's development, helping to develop several of the case studies and modules. Bruce Wright has lent his deft touch to editing nearly all of Bill's books over the past two decades. Once again, Bruce did an amazing job editing earlier drafts of this one. Ramani Moses, one of Deloitte's in-house editors, offered excellent suggestions throughout the process.

We would also like to express our gratitude to the Harvard Business Review Press team. This is the third book Bill has done with HBR Press, and the first for Don. We couldn't have asked for a more professional and engaged team. Our editor, Jeff Kehoe, has long been incredibly passionate about government reform and the important role that effective government plays in our lives. He believed in the book's concept—and in us—from the beginning, guided the project through the publishing process, and provided candid feedback to improve the manuscript. We would also like to thank the rest of the team at HBR Press, including Jennifer Waring and Erin Davis for their copyediting and production support; Stephani Franks, who did a masterful job designing the cover; and Julie Devoll, who led the marketing. We feel grateful to have had such professionals behind us from the world's premier management publishing house.

Mark Fortier of Fortier Public Relations has led the promotion for each of Bill's previous HBR Press books and once again did a masterful job with this one. We were also pleased to work with Kenneth Gilbert of Target Marketing and his talented team to promote the book through various channels and help build a bridgebuilder movement.

We also couldn't have finished this project without tremendous support from friends and family. Brooke provided inspiration and a deep reservoir of understanding and encouragement to Bill throughout the process. For Don, Sue was both muse and friend, and she supplied the ongoing encouragement that has been her unfailing trademark for many, many years.

About the Authors

WILLIAM D. EGGERS is the executive director of Deloitte's Center for Government Insights, where he is responsible for the firm's public-sector thought leadership. He also serves as a fellow at the National Academy of Public Administration; a governance futures council member at the World Economic Forum; an advisory board member at What Works Cities; and chairs the Leadership Council for New America.

He is the author of numerous books, including *Delivering on Digital* (2016); *The Solution Revolution* (2013), named to ten best-book-of-the-year lists; the *Washington Post* bestseller *If We Can Put a Man on the Moon* (2009); *The Public Innovator's Playbook* (2009); and *Governing by Network* (2004), winner of the Louis Brownlow book award, which recognizes outstanding contributions in the field of public administration. Eggers coined the term *Government 2.0* in a book by the same name. His books have won numerous other national best-book awards.

His commentary has appeared in dozens of major media outlets, including the *New York Times, Wall Street Journal, The Guardian*, and the *Washington Post*. He can be reached at weggers@deloitte.com or on Twitter @wdeggers.

DONALD F. KETTL is professor emeritus and former dean at the University of Maryland School of Public Policy. Until his retirement, he was the Sid Richardson Professor at the Lyndon B. Johnson School of Public Affairs at the University of Texas at Austin. He is also a senior adviser at the Volcker Alliance, a nonresident senior fellow at the Brookings Institution, and a fellow of the National Academy of Public Administration.

Kettl is the author or editor of twenty-five books, including *The Divided States of America* (2020); *Can Governments Earn Our Trust?* (2017); *Little Bites of Big Data for Public Policy* (2017); *The Politics of the Administrative Process* (8th edition, 2020); *Escaping Jurassic Government: Restoring America's Lost Commitment to Competence* (2016); *System under Stress: The Challenge to 21st Century American Democracy* (2013) *System Under Stress: Homeland Security and American Politics* (2004); *The Next Government of the United States: Why Our Institutions Fail Us and How to Fix Them* (2008); and *The Global Public Management Revolution* (2005).

He has received three lifetime achievement awards, and three of his books have received national best-book awards. Kettl holds a PhD in political science from Yale University. He consults broadly for government organizations at all levels around the world and has appeared frequently in national and international media. He is also a shareholder of the Green Bay Packers.